# AI Agents
# at Work

Scott Burk
Kinshuk Dutta
Harman Kaur

Technics Publications
SEDONA, ARIZONA

# TECHNICS PUBLICATIONS

115 Linda Vista, Sedona, AZ 86336 USA
https://www.TechnicsPub.com

Edited by Steve Hoberman
Cover design by Lorena Molinari

First Printing 2025

| ISBN, print ed. | 9798898160524 |
| ISBN, Kindle ed. | 9798898160531 |
| ISBN, PDF ed. | 9798898160548 |

**Scott's dedication:**

*To my wife Jackie, thank you for all your support and the greatest adventure of my life. You are simply the best.*

**Kinshuk's dedication:**

*To my parents, Krishna Dutta and Lal Mohan Dutta, who taught me that wisdom precedes knowledge.*
*To my wife, Noirita, and daughter, Rachael, you remind me that even in an age of autonomous intelligence, purpose is still measured in love, not logic.*

**Harman's dedication:**

*To my parents, Upkar Kaur and Balbir Singh, I am forever grateful for your strength and unwavering support. To my brother, Anmol Singh, for laughing with me through life.*

# Contents

# Figures

# Tables

# Introduction

The age of agentic AI has arrived. Not as a distant promise, but as a present-day operational reality. *AI Agents at Work* explores this transformation with clarity, rigor, and enterprise relevance. Across industries and infrastructures, autonomous agents are reshaping workflows, augmenting decision-making, and redefining what it means to scale intelligence. This book provides a strategic and technical blueprint for organizations that are ready to move beyond automation and embrace autonomy. While traditional AI systems have delivered incremental gains, agentic architectures offer exponential potential. They reason, coordinate, adapt, and act, often in real time and across distributed environments. Each chapter equips leaders, architects, and practitioners with the frameworks, case studies, and governance models needed to deploy agentic systems responsibly and effectively:

- **Chapter 1: Introduction to AI Agents**. Sets the stage by defining agentic AI and positioning it as the fourth paradigm after rule-based systems, machine learning, and deep learning. It introduces the five-layer agentic architecture and outlines the enterprise case for autonomy, including ROI benchmarks and vertical-specific case studies.
- **Chapter 2: Understanding Agent Systems**. Explores agent taxonomy, design patterns (single versus multi-agent), and reasoning architectures. It introduces deployment frameworks and culminates in a healthcare case study from ClearPath Health, showcasing reactive, deliberative, and generative agents in action.
- **Chapter 3: Solving Enterprise Challenges with Multi-Agent Systems**. Focuses on business workflows and infrastructure readiness. It compares cloud versus on-prem deployment, highlights compliance considerations, and introduces modern frameworks like LangGraph, CrewAI, and AutoGen. A manufacturing case study illustrates coordinated agent orchestration.
- **Chapter 4: Advanced Architectures and Data Integration**. Dives into federated versus centralized MAS architectures, microservices, and integration patterns. It presents cost allocation models and resilience strategies, followed by nine enterprise case studies, ranging from JPMorgan to Siemens Energy, that quantify the agentic impact.
- **Chapter 5: LLMs and Conversational Agent Platforms**. Examines how large language models (LLMs) power conversational agents. It covers architectural components, graph-based

workflows, and integration strategies. Case studies from Pfizer, HSBC, and Mayo Clinic demonstrate LLM-driven agentic transformation.

- **Chapter 6: Agentic Workflow Orchestration**. Unpacks orchestration layers, DAG execution models, and hybrid architectures. It addresses failure management and resilience, with a detailed case study from Alight and Automation Anywhere on scaling claims processing.

- **Chapter 7: Agent Memory and State Persistence**. Introduces the three tiers of agent memory and explores durability, idempotency, and the RAG continuum. A Petrobras case study illustrates the role of memory in tax compliance, followed by strategic guidance on governance and cost efficiency.

- **Chapter 8: Governance and Performance Management**. Defines Master Agent Management (MAM), AgentOps, and FinOps strategies. It presents governance metrics, Service Level Objectives (SLOs), and dashboards for managing cost, resilience, and quality across agentic systems.

- **Chapter 9: Ethics, Privacy, and Explainability**. Builds an ethical framework for agentic AI, covering data sovereignty, federated learning, and explainability techniques. It includes case studies from Microsoft and ServiceNow, and introduces audit pipelines and compliance loops.

- **Chapter 10: Coordination in AI-Powered Organizations**. Details messaging protocols, event streaming, and semantic interoperability. It introduces integration platforms and governance layers, accompanied by a vignette on financial risk monitoring to illustrate real-time coordination.

- **Chapter 11: Operationalizing Agentic AI**. Focuses on monitoring, visualization, and decision delivery. It highlights real-time dashboards, BI integration, and dynamic claims processing use cases, offering implementation guidance for CTOs.

- **Chapter 12: Avoiding Pitfalls and Looking Ahead**. Concludes with emerging trends, ethical safeguards, and future business impacts. It includes a supply chain optimization case study and offers strategic foresight into agent-generated insights and enterprise transformation.

- **Chapter 13: The Agents Evolved While We Were Writing**. Chronicles the rapid rise of enterprise agent platforms during the book's development, spotlighting Microsoft 365 Copilot Agents and Glean's Agent Builder. Compares their architectures using an IT Helpdesk scenario and highlights the shift from chatbots to workflow-capable agents. Concludes with guidance for enterprises navigating this fast-moving frontier.

Whether you're a CTO, architect, data scientist, or strategist, *AI Agents at Work* is your field guide to operationalizing autonomy: ethically, scalable, and with measurable impact. Let's dive in.

# Chapter 1

# Introduction to AI Agents

The landscape of enterprise technology is undergoing a profound transformation, driven by the convergence of advanced artificial intelligence (AI), new regulatory frameworks, and shifting business imperatives. At the heart of this transformation lies the emergence of AI agents: autonomous, collaborative, and context-aware systems that promise to redefine how organizations operate at scale.

This chapter focuses exclusively on enterprise agentic systems, distinct from consumer-facing AI assistants and chatbots. Enterprise agents are engineered for complex, mission-critical environments where reliability, compliance, and scalability are paramount. Their role spans operational optimization, workflow orchestration, decision support, and direct interaction with both human and digital ecosystems.

The timing for enterprise AI agents is not coincidental. Multiple forces are converging to make their adoption not just viable but necessary. Among them are:

- **Cost Pressures**: Enterprises face relentless demands to reduce operational expenses while maintaining service quality.
- **Regulatory Demands**: Compliance with evolving frameworks (GDPR, SOX, EU AI Act) requires systems capable of adaptive governance and auditable decision-making.
- **Talent Shortages**: The scarcity of specialized talent, particularly in data science and process engineering, is accelerating the shift toward intelligent automation.

- **Competitive Pressures**: The rapid pace of digital innovation means laggards risk losing market share to more agile, AI-enabled competitors.

## Global Adoption Stats (2023–2025)

- Over 60% of Fortune 500 companies are piloting or deploying agentic AI systems in some form.
- The Compound Annual Growth Rate (CAGR) for agentic AI platforms is projected at 25%–45% through 2028.
- The global market for agentic AI is forecasted to reach $52.6 billion by 2030.

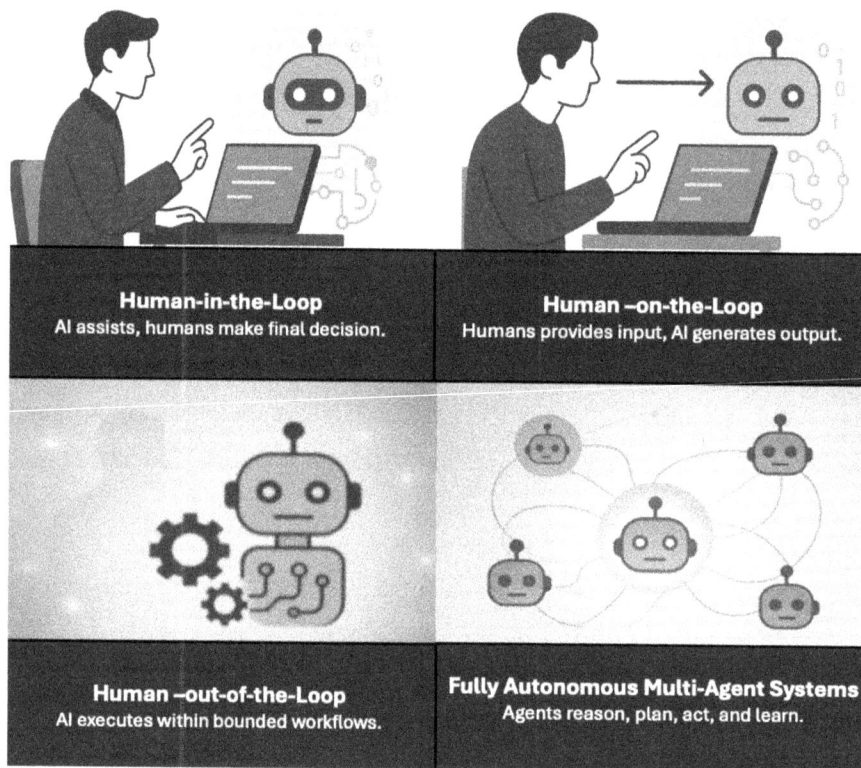

Figure 1: Rise of Enterprise Agents.

To contextualize the rise of enterprise agents, it is useful to consider the evolution of human-machine interaction:

1. **Human-in-the-loop**: Humans direct and oversee every step of the process, with automation serving as a tool.

2. **Human-on-the-loop**: Automation handles routine tasks, but humans supervise and can intervene as needed.

3. **Human-out-of-the-loop**: Systems operate independently within predefined parameters, with little or no human supervision.

4. **Agents as Collaborators**: Adaptive, orchestrated, and goal-driven agents work alongside humans, other agents, and systems to make complex decisions in dynamic environments.

---

## 1.1 From Automation to Autonomy: Why Agentic Architecture Matters

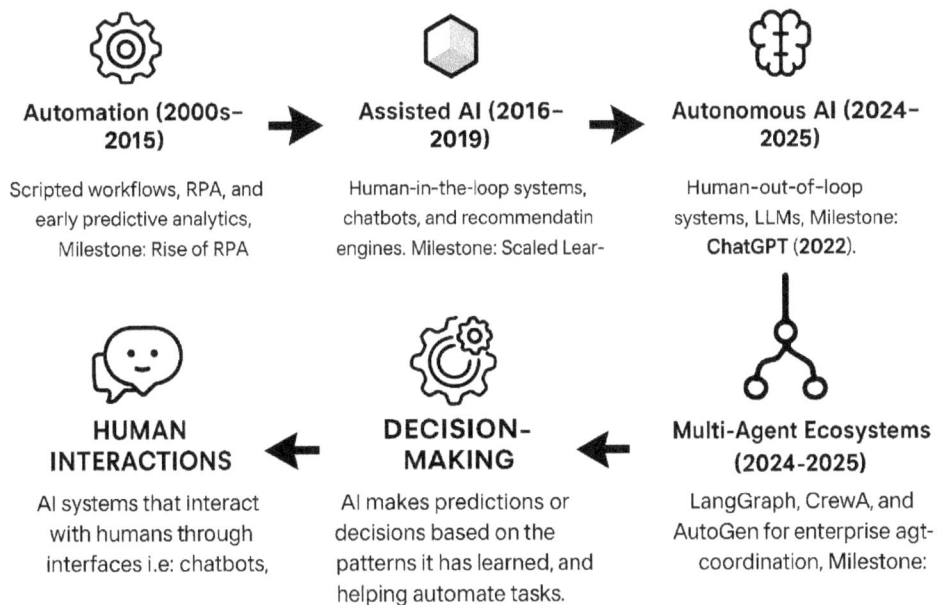

**Automation (2000s–2015)**
Scripted workflows, RPA, and early predictive analytics, Milestone: Rise of RPA

**Assisted AI (2016–2019)**
Human-in-the-loop systems, chatbots, and recommendatin engines. Milestone: Scaled Lear-

**Autonomous AI (2024–2025)**
Human-out-of-loop systems, LLMs, Milestone: **ChatGPT (2022)**.

**HUMAN INTERACTIONS**
AI systems that interact with humans through interfaces i.e: chatbots,

**DECISION-MAKING**
AI makes predictions or decisions based on the patterns it has learned, and helping automate tasks.

**Multi-Agent Ecosystems (2024-2025)**
LangGraph, CrewA, and AutoGen for enterprise agt-coordination, Milestone:

Figure 2: Evolution of AI: From Automation to Multi-Agent Ecosystems.

The history of enterprise automation is rich with incremental advances, from rule-based scripts to Robotic Process Automation (RPA) and machine learning. Yet traditional approaches remain fundamentally limited:

- **Brittle Automation**: Static rules break when confronted with real-world variability, requiring constant human oversight and maintenance.
- **Siloed Workflows**: Legacy systems and point solutions rarely communicate, leading to inefficiencies and missed opportunities for holistic optimization.
- **Limited Adaptability**: Most automation cannot learn or adapt beyond its explicit programming.

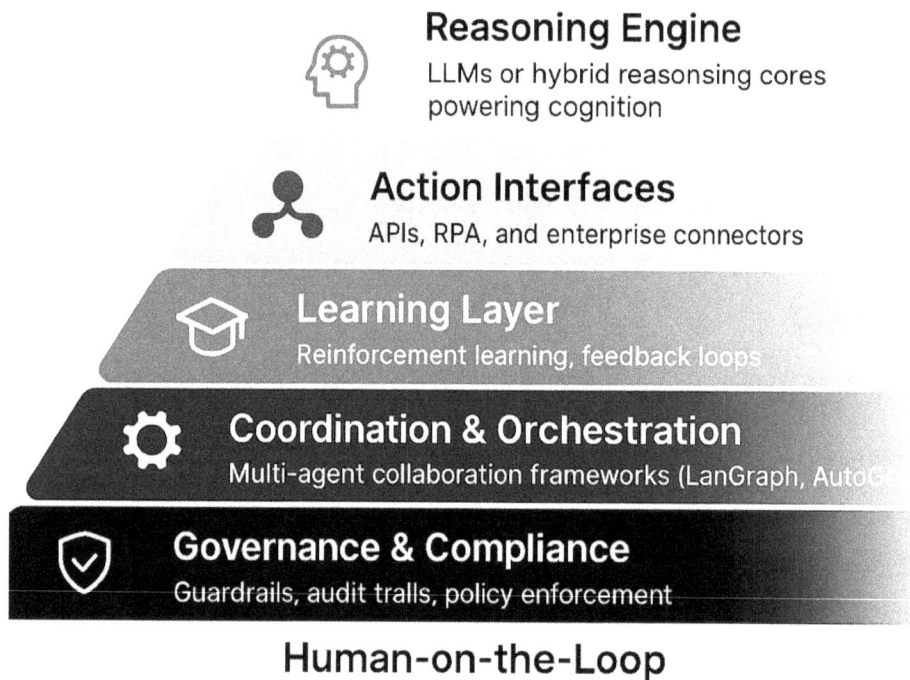

## Reasoning Engine
LLMs or hybrid reasonsing cores powering cognition

## Action Interfaces
APIs, RPA, and enterprise connectors

## Learning Layer
Reinforcement learning, feedback loops

## Coordination & Orchestration
Multi-agent collaboration frameworks (LanGraph, AutoG

## Governance & Compliance
Guardrails, audit tralls, policy enforcement

## Human-on-the-Loop

Figure 3: The Five-Layer Agentic Architecture Stack.

At its core, agentic architecture is a layered stack that separates concerns and enables adaptability:

- **Reasoning Engine**: The "brain" of the agent, responsible for planning, goal decomposition, and decision-making.
- **Action Interfaces**: Connectors to enterprise systems, APIs, and workflows, enabling agents to execute tasks in the real world.
- **Learning Module**: Mechanisms for continuous improvement, feedback assimilation, and self-optimization.

- **Orchestration Layer**: Coordination of multiple agents, task allocation, and prioritization to ensure efficient operation at scale.
- **Governance Layer**: Policy enforcement, compliance checks, audit trails, and trust management.

This architecture appears in contemporary frameworks such as LangGraph (dependency-aware reasoning and orchestration), CrewAI (collaborative agent teams), and AutoGen (generative agent stacks).

The most frequently cited motivations for enterprise adoption of agentic systems include:

- **Productivity Gains**: 66% of enterprises report significant increases in output per employee.
- **Cost Savings**: 57% achieve measurable reductions in operational expenses within the first year of deployment.
- **Faster Decision-Making**: 55% accelerate time-to-decision for critical business processes.
- **Improved Customer Experience (CX)**: 54% enhanced satisfaction via personalized, responsive, and error-free interactions.

## 1.2 Enterprise Blueprint: Readiness and ROI

No two organizations are identical in their journey toward agent adoption. Readiness assessment and ROI modeling are critical to ensuring successful outcomes. Here are five readiness questions:

1. Do we have the data infrastructure to support agentic reasoning and learning?
2. Are our workflows sufficiently standardized to benefit from orchestration, or do they require adaptation?
3. How mature is our governance (compliance, risk management, and auditability)?
4. Do we have the cultural buy-in and change management resources needed for agentic transformation?
5. Is there a clear business case (productivity, cost, CX, and compliance) driving the initiative?

## Agents versus RPA versus Large Language Model (LLM) Apps

- **RPA**: Best for deterministic, repetitive tasks with minimal need for context or adaptation.
- **LLM Apps**: Ideal for language understanding, summarization, and generative tasks where context is bounded and outputs are non-critical.
- **Agents**: Designed for adaptive, multi-step workflows requiring real-time reasoning, coordination, and interaction with multiple systems and stakeholders.

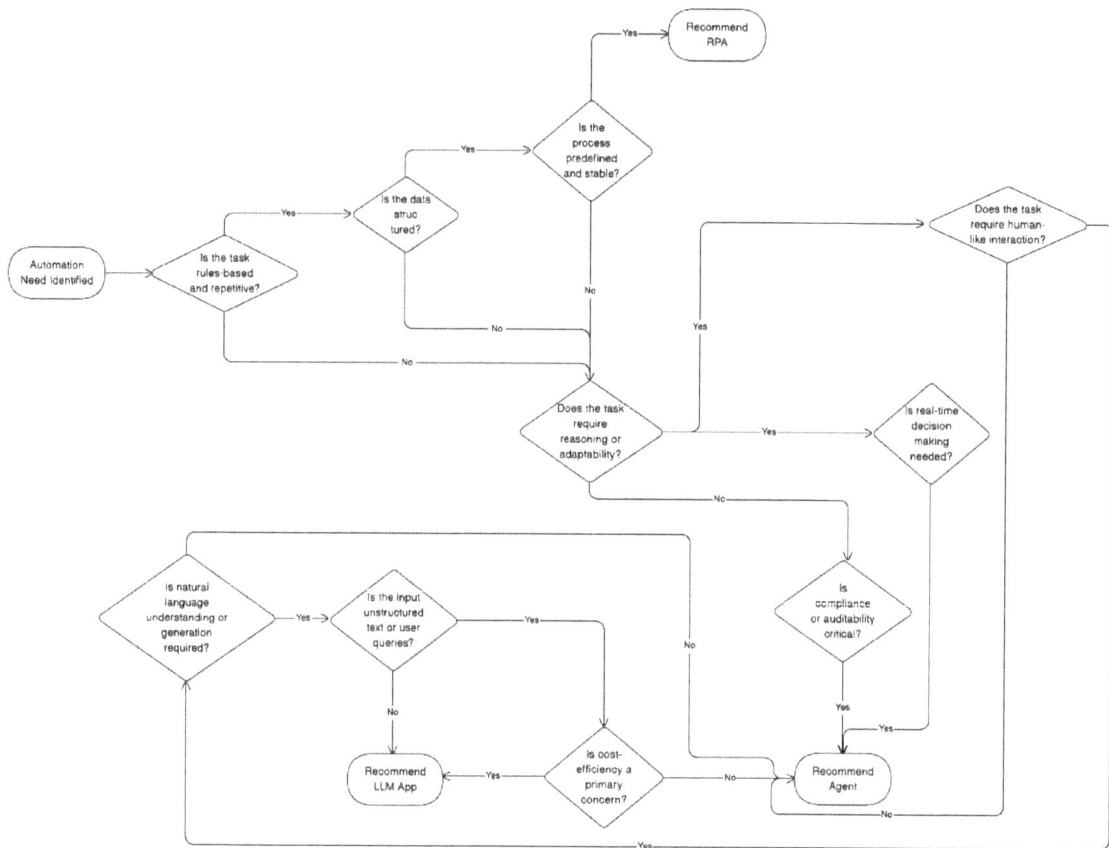

Figure 4: Decision Tree for Selecting AI Approaches.

## ROI Benchmarks from Industry Leaders

- McKinsey reports that agentic systems yield 20–40% time savings and 30–50% reduction in process backlogs.

- In the Korean financial sector, AI agents have delivered 80% faster document processing and improved compliance rates.
- ServiceNow's deployment of agents in case management cut resolution times by 52%.

## 1.3 When Agents Excel Beyond Traditional AI

A direct comparison highlights the transformative impact of agentic systems:

- **Traditional AI**: Static, siloed, designed for single-task execution; limited in adaptation and orchestration.
- **Agents**: Adaptive, cross-domain, capable of orchestrating complex workflows and learning continuously from outcomes and feedback.

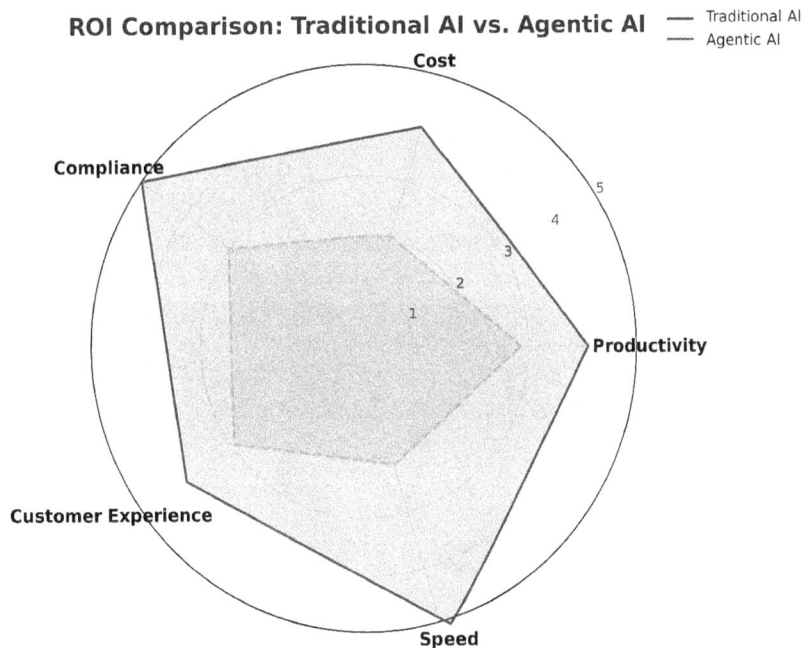

Figure 5: ROI Comparison of Traditional AI Versus Agentic AI.

These benchmarks illustrate why agentic AI is more than an incremental improvement over traditional automation. As shown in the spider chart, agentic systems deliver balanced gains across productivity, compliance, customer experience, speed, and cost efficiency. This holistic uplift ensures organizations not only accelerate processes but also enhance governance, reduce risks, and improve customer satisfaction, delivering a multidimensional ROI that traditional AI approaches cannot match.

The rise of multi-agent systems marks a critical evolution, enabling collaborative problem-solving, dynamic task allocation, and peer-to-peer communication. This leap is evident in platforms such as LangGraph and CrewAI, which support dependency-aware workflows and collaborative agent teams.

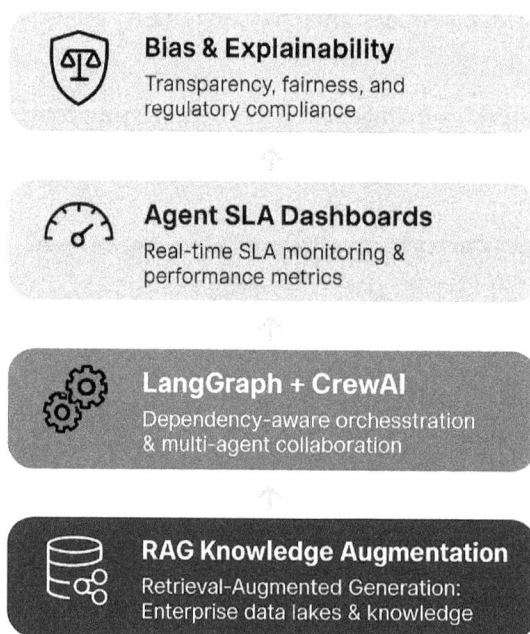

**Bias & Explainability**
Transparency, fairness, and regulatory compliance

**Agent SLA Dashboards**
Real-time SLA monitoring & performance metrics

**LangGraph + CrewAI**
Dependency-aware orchesstration & multi-agent collaboration

**RAG Knowledge Augmentation**
Retrieval-Augmented Generation: Enterprise data lakes & knowledge

Figure 6: Multi-Agent Orchestration Architecture.

Emerging Advancements (2023–2025) include:

- **LangGraph**: Dependency-aware orchestration for complex enterprise tasks.
- **CrewAI**: Multi-agent collaboration and specialization.
- **Retrieval-Augmented Generation (RAG)**: On-demand augmentation of agent knowledge with retrieval from enterprise data lakes and knowledge graphs.

- **Agent SLA Management**: Real-time dashboards for monitoring service level adherence and performance metrics.
- **Bias/Explainability Frameworks**: Tools to ensure transparency, fairness, and regulatory compliance in agentic systems.

## 1.4 Case Studies Across Verticals

To ground these concepts in practice, consider the following enterprise deployments, each delivering quantifiable outcomes:

- **Finance (ERP/FinRobot):** A multinational financial institution reported significant efficiency gains by deploying autonomous agents within its enterprise resource planning (ERP) environment. By automating invoice processing workflows, the organization achieved 40% faster cycle times and a 94% reduction in manual data entry errors, redeploying staff to higher-value tasks. Similar findings were observed in Deloitte's *Global RPA Survey*, which documented reductions of over 50% in invoice handling times and improved compliance accuracy after the introduction of intelligent automation in accounts payable processes (Deloitte, 2022).

- **Healthcare (Patient Triage):** Hospitals are increasingly leveraging AI triage systems to reduce waiting times and improve care outcomes. In a systematic review of emergency department deployments, AI-based triage reduced processing delays by **25–37%** and improved overall triage accuracy (Cureus, 2024). A U.K. National Health Service (NHS) pilot showed that machine-learning-enabled triage reduced average patient wait times by 30%, while increasing patient satisfaction through more consistent clinical prioritization (NHS Digital, 2023). These results validate the growing consensus that AI triage agents, when integrated with clinical workflows, can enhance throughput without sacrificing safety.

- **Retail (Inventory Optimization):** Retailers face persistent challenges in balancing inventory levels. Agent-based forecasting and replenishment systems have shown measurable improvements. For example, H&M's global adoption of AI-driven inventory optimization reduced stockouts below 2% and cut overstocking waste by nearly 18%, while driving a reported 30% increase in profitability (McKinsey, 2023) (Gibion, 2024). A 2024 MIT Sloan study further confirmed that agentic AI in inventory planning can reduce excess inventory by 15–30% while increasing forecast accuracy by up to 40%, highlighting both cost savings and sustainability benefits (MIT Sloan, 2024).

- **Cybersecurity (Incident Response):** Security operations centers (SOCs) are adopting autonomous agents for alert triage and incident response. A global logistics firm reported a 60% reduction in mean-time-to-detect (MTTD) after deploying agentic AI systems that correlated threat signals and initiated first-response actions (SuperAGI, 2025). IBM's *Cost of a Data Breach Report* found that organizations with AI-driven security automation contained breaches 108 days faster on average and saved $3.05M per incident compared to peers without such capabilities (IBM, 2023). These findings underscore how autonomous threat triage agents can shift SOCs from reactive to proactive defense.

- **Supply Chain (Logistics Optimization):** Dynamic rescheduling agents have transformed logistics optimization by adapting to disruptions in real time. A European logistics provider documented a 25% reduction in transport delays after implementing multi-agent systems that recalculated routes based on traffic, weather, and port congestion data (LITSLINK, 2024). Business Insider reports that companies like Amazon and Veho are similarly deploying AI routing agents to improve last-mile delivery, yielding double-digit gains in delivery accuracy and customer satisfaction (Business Insider, 2025). These outcomes illustrate the resilience benefits of embedding agentic AI into supply chain orchestration.

## 1.5 Governance, Risks, and Inaction

The potential value of agentic AI is staggering, yet realization at scale remains elusive. Capgemini estimates that $450B in economic value could be unlocked by 2028, but less than 2% of organizations have achieved production-scale deployments.

## Governance Gaps

- Compliance failures due to opaque agent decision-making, especially under evolving regulations like the EU AI Act.
- Erosion of stakeholder trust, often due to insufficient transparency or explainability.
- Security vulnerabilities, created by autonomous actions in interconnected systems.

Failure to invest in agentic transformation carries existential risks. 95% of generative AI pilots fail to deliver ROI, largely due to inadequate architecture, governance, or readiness. Laggards face long-term competitiveness erosion as peers automate and optimize at scale.

Figure 7: Agent Governance Loop.

1. **Monitoring**: Continuous observation of agent actions and performance.
2. **Audit**: Maintenance of detailed logs for retrospective analysis and accountability.
3. **Compliance**: Real-time checks against regulatory requirements and organizational policies.
4. **Risk Management**: Proactive identification and mitigation of operational, ethical, and financial risks.
5. **Optimization**: Iterative refinement based on performance data, stakeholder feedback, and environmental changes.

## 1.6 Key Takeaways

- While the ROI is substantial and demonstrable, organizations must assess their readiness, address risk, and build for scale for AI agents to fully capture the benefits.
- Agentic systems are not just the next step in automation, but a transformation in how enterprises operate and compete.
- Architecture and governance are foundational; shortcuts here imperil long-term value realization.
- Value is real, measurable, and proven across industry verticals and geographies.
- Agentic AI is enterprise-ready and already delivering value; it is no longer future speculation.
- Governance, especially for compliance and trust, is non-negotiable.
- Multi-agent orchestration unlocks new levels of value and agility, far surpassing traditional automation and standalone LLM apps.
- ROI is proven in finance, healthcare, retail, cybersecurity, and supply chain contexts, with quantifiable outcomes.
- Inaction comes with mounting risks to competitiveness, resilience, and regulatory compliance.

## 1.7 Discussion Questions / Exercises

1. How would you re-architect a workflow in your enterprise using multi-agent orchestration?
2. What governance safeguards would you need for regulatory compliance in agentic systems?
3. Which of your current RPA or automation workflows could benefit most from an autonomous agent upgrade, and why?
4. How would you measure agent ROI in your organization? What metrics and benchmarks would you use?

# CHAPTER 2

# Understanding Agent Systems

In this chapter, we cover the foundational understanding of agent systems. Agent classification helps distinguish between different types of autonomous systems, from simple reactive agents to sophisticated reasoning agents. We provide frameworks for understanding when and how to deploy different agent architectures within an enterprise context.

## 2.1 Introduction: Why Agent Systems Matter

In the evolving landscape of artificial intelligence with the shift from static models to dynamic, autonomous agents marks a profound transformation. Agentic AI refers to systems that not only process information but also reason, plan, and act independently, often in coordination with other agents or human stakeholders. These agents are designed to pursue goals, adapt to changing environments, and make decisions with minimal human intervention. In an enterprise context, this shift unlocks new possibilities for automation, scalability, and strategic agility. Figure 8 illustrates some characteristics of Agentic AI.

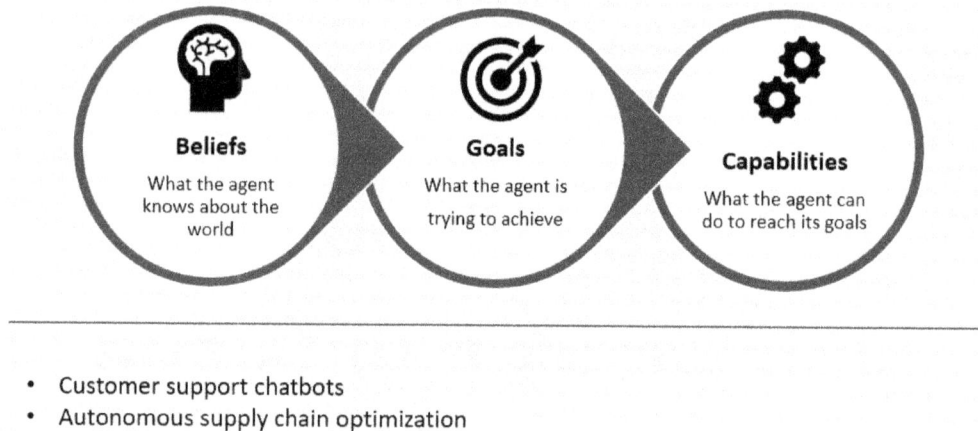

- Customer support chatbots
- Autonomous supply chain optimization

Figure 8: What is Agentic AI?

These characteristics are beliefs, goals, and capabilities. These are consistent with human decision-making and action. Example applications of agents include customer support chatbots and automated supply chain optimization.

Unlike traditional AI systems that operate within narrow, pre-defined boundaries, agentic systems are goal-driven and context-aware. They can navigate complex workflows, interact with other systems, and even collaborate with humans in real time. This evolution from simple automation to intelligent autonomy is not just a technical upgrade; it's a reimagining of how businesses operate, compete, and deliver value.

To understand and deploy agentic AI effectively, organizations must grasp the taxonomy of agent systems, ranging from reactive agents that respond to stimuli to deliberative agents that plan actions to generative agents that create new content or strategies. They must also understand the architectural patterns that govern agent behavior, including single-agent and multi-agent designs, and the reasoning frameworks that power autonomous decision-making.

This chapter provides a foundational understanding of agent systems. We begin by classifying agents based on their capabilities and roles. We then explore design patterns that shape how agents are deployed individually or in coordinated teams. Finally, we examine the reasoning architectures that enable agents to think, adapt, and act in enterprise environments. By the end of this chapter, readers will have a clear framework for evaluating, designing, and deploying agentic AI systems that align with business goals and operational realities.

## 2.2 Agent Taxonomy: Types of Autonomous Systems

Understanding agentic AI begins with knowing what kinds of agents exist. Not all agents are built the same. Some are simple responders, while others are capable of reasoning, learning, and even creating. This section introduces a practical taxonomy that distinguishes among these types, providing a framework for matching agent capabilities to enterprise needs.

At the most basic level, we have **reactive agents**. These agents don't plan or learn. They simply respond to inputs based on predefined rules. They're fast, reliable, and ideal for tasks like monitoring systems or triggering alerts. Think of a temperature sensor that activates a cooling system when it gets too hot. It doesn't ask why. It just acts.

A step up in complexity brings us to **deliberative agents**. These agents build internal models of the world and use them to plan actions. They're capable of strategic thinking and can evaluate future outcomes before making decisions. In a logistics context, a deliberative agent might analyze traffic patterns and delivery schedules to choose the most efficient route. It's not just reacting, it's reasoning.

Then there are **utility-based agents**, which make decisions by weighing options and selecting the one that delivers the best result. These agents are especially useful in business environments where trade-offs are constant. For example, an AI system might choose the best supplier based on cost, speed, and reliability. It's not just about following rules; it's about optimizing.

**Learning agents** take things further. These systems improve over time by analyzing feedback and adjusting their behavior. They're adaptive, evolving with each interaction. A customer service chatbot that gets better at answering questions by learning from past conversations is a classic example. These agents don't just perform, they grow.

Finally, we have **generative agents,** which are the most advanced in this taxonomy. Powered by large language models and other generative technologies, these agents can create new content, ideas, or strategies. They're capable of reasoning, planning, and collaborating with humans or other agents. In marketing, a generative agent might draft campaign emails, generate product descriptions, or even propose new messaging strategies based on customer data.

Each of these agent types plays a distinct role in enterprise systems. Reactive agents are great for monitoring and control. Deliberative and utility-based agents shine in planning and decision-making. Learning agents bring adaptability, and generative agents unlock creativity and scale.

As organizations begin to adopt agentic AI, this taxonomy becomes more than a classification; it becomes a strategic tool. It helps leaders decide which agents to deploy, where to deploy them, and how to design systems that are not just functional, but intelligent and future-ready.

Figure 9 summarizes the key characteristics of each agent classification with an example.

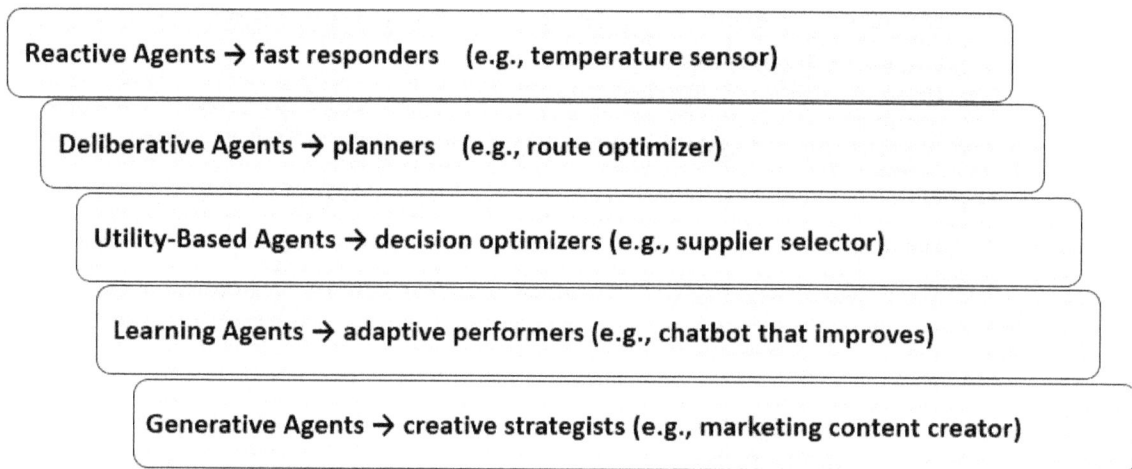

Reactive Agents → fast responders   (e.g., temperature sensor)

Deliberative Agents → planners   (e.g., route optimizer)

Utility-Based Agents → decision optimizers (e.g., supplier selector)

Learning Agents → adaptive performers (e.g., chatbot that improves)

Generative Agents → creative strategists (e.g., marketing content creator)

Figure 9: Agent Taxonomy: Types of Autonomous Systems.

This taxonomy illustrates the progression from simple to sophisticated agent types, each defined by its level of autonomy and reasoning capability. At the base are reactive agents that are fast, rule-based responders ideal for monitoring and control. As complexity increases, we encounter deliberative agents that plan, utility-based agents that optimize, and learning agents that adapt. At the top are generative agents, which not only reason and learn but also create. They draft content, propose strategies, and collaborate with humans or other agents. This hierarchy isn't just academic; it's strategic. It helps leaders match agent types to enterprise needs, ensuring systems are not only functional but also intelligent, scalable, and future-ready.

Now that we've classified agents by capability, let's explore how they're deployed, either solo or in coordinated teams.

## 2.3 Single-Agent Versus Multi-Agent Design Patterns

Now that we've explored the different types of agents, it's time to look at how they're organized. In enterprise systems, agents don't just exist in isolation; they're part of a larger design. And that design usually follows one of two patterns: single-agent or multi-agent.

A single-agent system is exactly what it sounds like: one agent doing all the work. It might be responsible for gathering data, making decisions, and executing tasks from start to finish. These systems are straightforward and often easier to manage. For example, a single agent might handle all HR inquiries in a company, pulling data from databases, generating responses, and logging interactions. It's efficient for focused tasks, especially when the scope is narrow and well-defined.

But as the task's complexity grows, so does the need for specialization. That's where multi-agent systems come in. Instead of having one agent try to do everything, you have a team, each agent with its own role, skill set, and domain expertise. One agent might handle data retrieval, another might focus on analysis, and a third might be responsible for generating reports or triggering actions. These agents communicate with one another, share content, and coordinate their efforts to complete more complex workflows.

Think of it like comparing a solo entrepreneur to a full business team. The solo operator might be able to handle everything, including marketing, sales, and operations, but only up to a point. A coordinated team, on the other hand, can scale, adapt, and tackle more ambitious goals.

Of course, multi-agent systems come with their own challenges. They require careful orchestration, clear communication protocols, and robust infrastructure to keep everything running smoothly. But the payoff is significant: greater flexibility, better performance, and the ability to handle enterprise-scale problems with precision.

*Choosing between single-agent and multi-agent design isn't just a technical decision; it's strategic.*

It depends on the complexity of the task, the need for specialization, and the organization's readiness to support coordinated systems. Many enterprises start with single-agent deployments and evolve toward multi-agent orchestration as their needs grow and their confidence in agentic AI deepens.

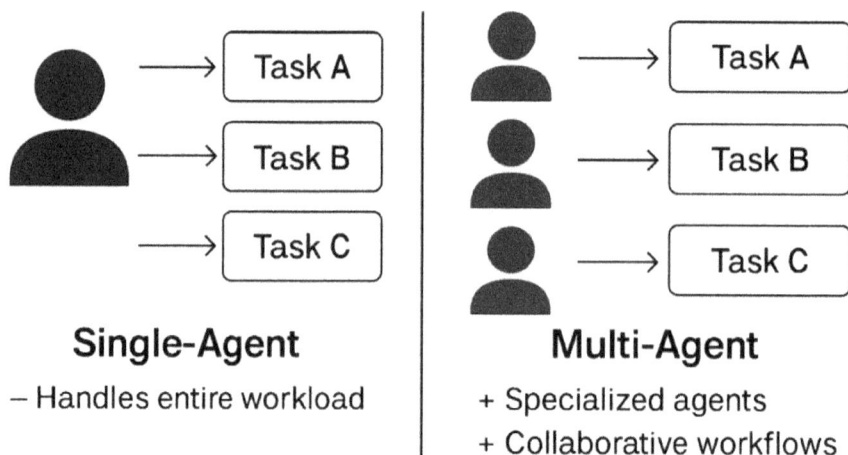

Figure 10: Single-Agent Versus Multi-Agent Design.

Figure 10 illustrates the structural choices behind agent systems, whether they operate independently or as part of a coordinated ensemble. A single-agent design is like a solo entrepreneur: focused, fast, and self-contained. It's ideal for narrow tasks like monitoring or responding to specific queries. Multi-agent systems, on the other hand, resemble a well-run team.

*Each agent has a role. Some gather data, others reason, and some act; together, they tackle complex workflows.*

These design patterns aren't just technical choices. They shape how agents interact, scale, and deliver value. In enterprise settings, multi-agent orchestration is increasingly common, especially when tasks require collaboration, fallback logic, or human oversight.

In the next section, we'll explore how agents actually think, diving into the reasoning architectures that power autonomous decision-making and give these systems their intelligence. Whether working solo or in coordinated teams, agents require more than structure; they need the ability to reason. That's where architecture comes in.

## 2.4 Reasoning Architectures That Power Autonomous Decision-Making

If agent taxonomy tells us what kinds of agents exist, reasoning architecture explains how they operate beneath the surface. It's the mental machinery: logic, memory, and decision-making systems that allow agents to move beyond simple reactions and into thoughtful, autonomous behavior.

In traditional automation, systems follow fixed rules: "If X happens, do Y." But agentic AI is different. These agents can evaluate situations, weigh options, and choose actions based on goals, context, and even past experience. That's where reasoning architecture comes in.

One of the most well-known models is the **Belief-Desire-Intention (BDI)** framework. It's inspired by how humans think. An agent using BDI starts with beliefs like what it knows about the world. Then it considers its desires: what it wants to achieve. Finally, it forms intentions: what it plans to do next. This structure allows agents to act purposefully, even in dynamic environments. For example, a supply chain agent might believe that inventory is low, desire to restock efficiently, and intend to place an order with the fastest supplier.

Another approach is **chain-of-thought reasoning**, which is especially common in language-based agents. Instead of jumping straight to an answer, the agent walks through its logic step by step, like showing its work in a math problem. This makes the agent's decisions more transparent and often more accurate, especially when solving complex or ambiguous tasks.

Some agents rely on **utility-based reasoning**, where they evaluate different actions based on expected outcomes. They choose the option that maximizes a certain value like speed, cost savings, customer satisfaction, or some combination. These agents are especially useful in business environments where trade-offs are constant, and decisions need to be optimized.

There are also **learning-based architectures**, where agents improve over time by analyzing feedback and adjusting their behavior. These systems don't just reason, they evolve. They might use reinforcement learning, supervised training, or even human feedback to refine their decision-making. Over time, they become more effective, more accurate, and more aligned with enterprise goals.

Each of these reasoning styles has its strengths. BDI is great for goal-driven planning. Chain-of-thought helps with transparency and logic. Utility-based reasoning is ideal for optimization. And learning architectures bring adaptability and long-term improvement.

Choosing the right reasoning architecture depends on the task, the environment, and the required level of autonomy. In enterprise systems, it's common to mix and match using BDI for strategic planning, utility-based reasoning for operational decisions, and learning agents for customer-facing roles.

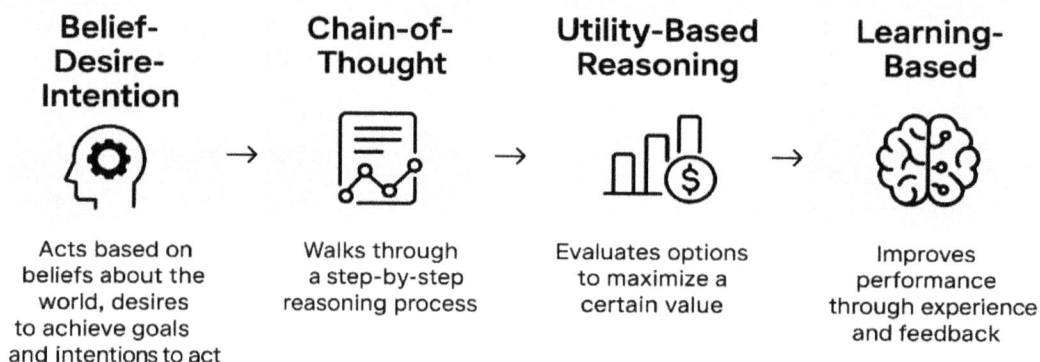

Figure 11: Reasoning Architectures.

Each reasoning architecture shown in Figure 11 supports a different kind of autonomy. BDI agents excel at goal-driven planning, making them ideal for strategic tasks like supply chain coordination or policy enforcement. Chain-of-thought agents shine in complex, ambiguous scenarios, especially those involving language, logic, or multi-step reasoning. Utility-based agents are built for optimization, perfect for environments where trade-offs must be weighed, such as pricing, routing, or resource allocation. Learning-based agents bring adaptability, improving over time through feedback and experience.

In practice, enterprise systems often blend these styles, using BDI for long-term planning, utility-based reasoning for operational decisions, and learning agents for customer-facing roles that demand continuous improvement.

*As agentic AI continues to mature, reasoning architecture will be one of the key differentiators between systems that simply automate and those that truly think.*

In the next section, we'll explore how to deploy these agents effectively, matching architecture to task, and building systems that are not just intelligent, but enterprise-ready.

Once agents can think, the next challenge is putting them to work.

## 2.5 Frameworks for Deployment

Once you've identified the right type of agent and the reasoning architecture that fits your business need, the next question is: how do you deploy it? In enterprise environments, deployment isn't just about turning on a model; it's about integrating agents into workflows, systems, and governance structures that ensure they perform reliably and responsibly.

At its core, deploying agentic AI means matching the right agent architecture to the right task. A reactive agent might be perfect for monitoring a server's temperature, while a generative agent could transform how your marketing team creates content. But beyond the agent itself, you need a framework that supports its operation. That is, one that includes infrastructure, communication protocols, memory systems, and oversight.

For simpler tasks, deployment might involve a single-agent system embedded in a cloud-based workflow. These agents can be lightweight, fast, and easy to manage. But as complexity grows, so does the need for orchestration. Multi-agent systems require coordination tools, such as platforms, that enable agents to share information, delegate tasks, and respond to changing conditions in real time.

This is where modern orchestration frameworks come into play. Tools like LangGraph, CrewAI, and AutoGen are designed to help developers build agent pipelines that are modular, scalable, and secure. They provide the backbone for agent communication, task routing, and memory management, which are essential for enterprise-grade deployments.

But technology alone isn't enough. Deployment also requires thoughtful design around governance and oversight. Agents must be monitored for accuracy, compliance, and performance. They need access controls, audit trails, and fallback mechanisms in case something goes wrong. In regulated industries, this isn't optional; it is foundational.

Ultimately, deploying agentic AI is a strategic decision. It's not just about what the agent can do; it is about how it fits into the broader system.

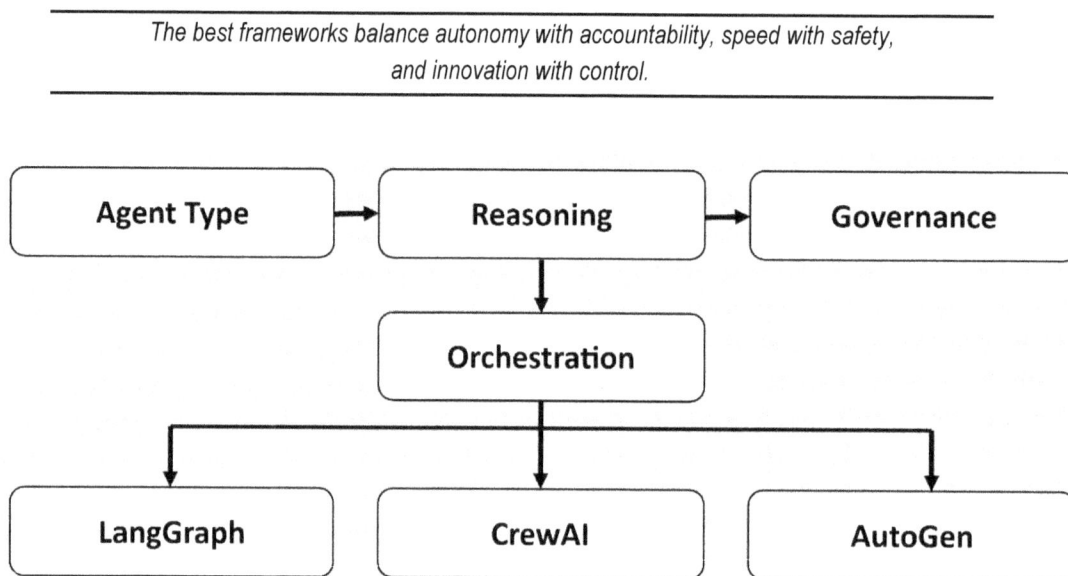

*The best frameworks balance autonomy with accountability, speed with safety, and innovation with control.*

Agent Type → Reasoning → Governance

Reasoning → Orchestration

Orchestration → LangGraph, CrewAI, AutoGen

Figure 12: Frameworks for Deployment.

In the next chapter, we'll explore how these frameworks scale, how they move from foundational deployment to full orchestration across enterprise workflows. But for now, the key takeaway is this: successful deployment starts with alignment. Align the agent's capabilities with the task, the architecture with the environment, and the governance with the risk. That's how agentic AI becomes not just powerful but practical.

Deployment is the bridge between design and impact. With the right framework in place, organizations can begin to scale agentic systems across workflows, unlocking new levels of autonomy and performance.

## 2.6 Building the Foundation for Agentic Transformation

Agentic AI isn't just a new tool; it's a new way of thinking about how work gets done. In this chapter, we've laid the groundwork for understanding agent systems: what they are, how they're classified, how they're organized, and how they reason. These foundational concepts aren't academic; they're practical. They shape how enterprises design, deploy, and scale intelligent systems that can act autonomously and with purpose.

We started by exploring the spectrum of agent types from reactive responders to generative collaborators. Then we looked at how agents are structured, whether working solo or as part of a coordinated team. We examined the reasoning architectures that give agents their intelligence, and finally, we walked through deployment frameworks that turn theory into enterprise reality.

Together, these elements form the backbone of agentic transformation. They help organizations move beyond static automation and into dynamic, adaptive systems that can learn, plan, and act. And while the technology is powerful, it's the architecture (the thoughtful design of agents, workflows, and governance) that determines whether agentic AI delivers real business value.

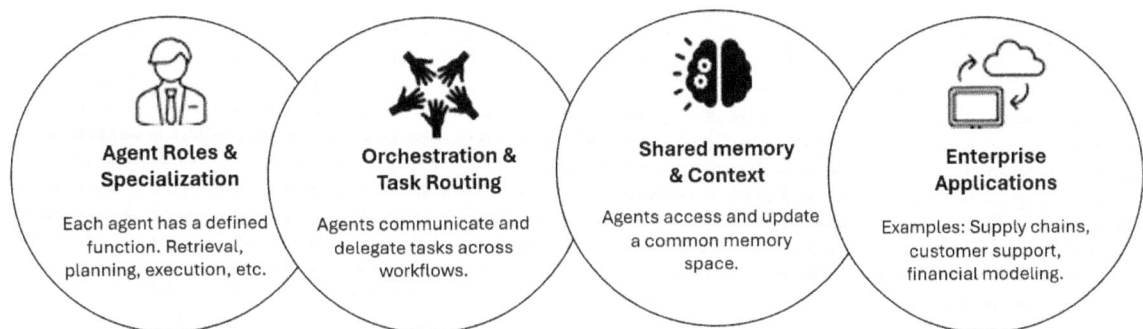

**Agent Roles & Specialization**

Each agent has a defined function. Retrieval, planning, execution, etc.

**Orchestration & Task Routing**

Agents communicate and delegate tasks across workflows.

**Shared memory & Context**

Agents access and update a common memory space.

**Enterprise Applications**

Examples: Supply chains, customer support, financial modeling.

Figure 13: Orchestrating the Agentic Ensemble.

As Figure 13 illustrates, there are four key components to the agentic ensemble: the agent roles and specification, the individual agent tasks and communication, the shared memory of the agents, and the applicable enterprise application. Together, these components can deliver or fail to deliver business success.

## 2.7 Case Study: Optimizing Patient Flow with Agent Systems at ClearPath Health

ClearPath Health is a mid-sized hospital network in the Midwest, and, like many healthcare systems, it was struggling with patient flow. ER wait times were creeping up, discharges were often delayed, and bed turnover wasn't keeping pace with demand. Leadership knew they needed a smarter, more adaptive approach, but not just another dashboard or static rules engine. They wanted agents.

So, they started small.

### 2.7.1 Starting with Simplicity: Reactive Agents

The first agent deployed was a reactive one: simple, fast, and focused. It monitored ER wait times in real time and triggered alerts when thresholds were breached. No reasoning, no planning. Just stimulus and response. But even that small step made a difference. Staff no longer had to guess when the ER was overwhelmed. They had a signal.

### 2.7.2 Thinking Ahead: Deliberative Agents Join the Team

Next came a deliberative agent they called the Discharge Planner. This one was more sophisticated. It didn't just react; it reasoned. It pulled in vitals, lab results, physician notes, and even downstream bed availability to assess whether a patient was ready to be discharged. It used a BDI architecture: Beliefs about the patient's condition, Desires to optimize bed usage, and Intentions to recommend safe discharges. It wasn't perfect, but it was thoughtful and it saved time.

### 2.7.3 Planning the Future: Generative Agents Take the Lead

Then came the Flow Strategist, a generative agent designed to simulate different bed allocation scenarios. It didn't just make decisions; it imagined possibilities. Using chain-of-thought prompting and utility-based reasoning, it explored staffing shifts and patient transfers, and even predicted bottlenecks before they occurred. It was the first agent that felt collaborative. It didn't replace staff; it partnered with them.

## 2.7.4 Orchestrating the System

To tie it all together, ClearPath used LangGraph to orchestrate the agents. The workflow looked something like this:

1. The ER Sentinel detects a surge.
2. It triggers the Discharge Planner to evaluate early discharges.
3. The Flow Strategist simulates bed reallocation.
4. A proposed plan is sent to a human supervisor for final approval.

Each agent had scoped permissions, fallback protocols, and audit trails. If the Discharge Planner couldn't reach a confidence threshold, the system defaulted to manual review. Every decision was logged, timestamped, traceable, and compliant.

## 2.7.5 Results That Mattered

Within three months, ER wait times dropped by 18%. Bed turnover improved by 12%. Staff reported less friction and more clarity. And perhaps most importantly, the agents didn't just automate, they augmented. They became part of the team.

## 2.8 Key Takeaways

- Agent systems represent a foundational shift from static automation to dynamic, goal-driven autonomy.
- Taxonomy matters: reactive, deliberative, utility-based, learning, and generative agents each serve distinct enterprise roles.

- Multi-agent design patterns enable scalability, specialization, and collaborative workflows far beyond single-agent capabilities.
- Reasoning architectures: BDI, chain-of-thought, utility-based, and learning-based define how agents think, adapt, and act.
- Deployment frameworks like LangGraph, CrewAI, and AutoGen support modular, orchestrated agent systems with governance and oversight.
- Successful agentic transformation requires alignment between agent type, reasoning style, deployment architecture, and enterprise goals.
- Architecture is not optional. It's the backbone of intelligent autonomy and the key to enterprise-grade performance.

## 2.9 Discussion Questions / Exercises

1. Which agent types (reactive, deliberative, generative, etc.) are most applicable to your current enterprise workflows, and why?
2. How would you structure a multi-agent system to handle a complex business process like order fulfillment or claims processing?
3. What reasoning architecture (BDI, utility-based, learning) would best support decision-making in your organization's customer service or logistics operations?
4. Evaluate your current deployment infrastructure. What orchestration tools or governance mechanisms would be required to support agentic AI?
5. How would you measure the effectiveness of agent reasoning in a live enterprise setting? What metrics or feedback loops would you implement?

In the chapters ahead, we'll build on this foundation. We'll explore how multi-agent systems solve complex enterprise challenges, how orchestration frameworks enable coordination at scale, and how governance ensures agents behave reliably and ethically. But it all starts here with a clear understanding of what agents are, how they think, and how they fit into the enterprise ecosystem. With taxonomy, architecture, and deployment now in place, the foundation is set. In the next chapter, we'll explore how multi-agent systems collaborate, coordinate, and scale. Transforming enterprise operations from the inside out.

# CHAPTER 3

# Solving Enterprise Challenges with Multi-Agent Systems

## 3.1 Agent Technology for Business Workflows

Modern enterprises are built on complexity. From supply chains to customer service, internal operations often span dozens of systems, departments, and decision layers. Traditional automation tools, while powerful, often struggle to adapt to this dynamic landscape. They're rigid, rule-bound, and often siloed.

---

*Multi-agent systems offer a new path forward.*

---

In this chapter, we explore how coordinated agents, each with specialized roles and capabilities, can work together to solve real business problems. These systems don't just automate tasks; they collaborate, delegate, and adapt in ways that mirror human teams. When designed well, they can streamline workflows, reduce operational friction, and unlock new levels of responsiveness across the enterprise.

We begin by examining the infrastructure required to support agent orchestration, including the platforms and architectural patterns that enable scalable coordination. We then compare cloud-based and on-premises deployment models, with a focus on security, compliance, and performance trade-offs.

Next, we tackle the technical challenges of agent communication. How agents share context, resolve conflicts, and maintain continuity across workflows. Finally, we introduce modern orchestration frameworks like LangGraph, CrewAI, and AutoGen, which are rapidly changing how organizations build and manage agentic systems.

Finally, we lay the groundwork for agent governance and quality assurance, concepts that will echo throughout the book.

> *Reliability isn't optional in enterprise settings, it's the difference between innovation and disruption.*

## 3.2 A Modern Tale: When Automation isn't Enough

At a global logistics firm, the operations team faced a familiar challenge: coordinating shipments across dozens of warehouses, each running on different systems, with varying levels of automation. A delay in one region triggered a cascade of manual interventions like emails, spreadsheets, and late-night calls, to reroute inventory and update delivery estimates.

They had automation tools. They had dashboards. But what they lacked was coordination.

Enter multi-agent systems.

Instead of relying on static workflows, the company deployed a network of intelligent agents. Each was responsible for monitoring a region, negotiating delivery windows, and escalating issues when thresholds were breached. These agents didn't just execute tasks; they collaborated. One agent flagged a delay, another rerouted inventory, and a third updated customer-facing systems. All without human intervention.

The result? Fewer bottlenecks, faster response times, and a system that could adapt in real time.

## 3.3 Infrastructure and Platforms Necessary to Support Agent Orchestration

Building enterprise-grade multi-agent systems requires more than just intelligent agents. It demands a resilient, scalable infrastructure that can support coordination, communication, and continuity across complex workflows. Without the right foundation, even the most capable agents will struggle to deliver consistent value.

Here are the core architectural components that enable agent orchestration at scale, with a focus on modularity, interoperability, and enterprise integration:

- **Microservices Architecture**: Agentic systems thrive in modular environments. A microservices architecture allows each agent or agent function to operate as an independent service. This design promotes specialization, fault isolation, and easier scaling. Agents can be updated, replaced, or reconfigured without disrupting the broader system, making it easier to evolve capabilities over time. For enterprises, this modularity also supports integration with existing services, enabling agents to interact with legacy systems, APIs, and business logic without requiring wholesale platform changes.

- **Containerization and Kubernetes**: To deploy agents reliably across environments, containerization is essential. Tools like Docker encapsulate agents with their dependencies, ensuring consistency across development, testing, and production. Kubernetes adds orchestration, automatically managing agent lifecycles, scaling workloads, and handling failures. In multi-agent systems, Kubernetes can also be used to group agents into logical clusters, dynamically assign resources, and enforce policies for availability and performance. This is especially valuable in hybrid cloud environments where agents may span multiple regions or data centers.

- **Message Brokers (Kafka, RabbitMQ)**: Coordination between agents depends on robust communication. Message brokers like Apache Kafka and RabbitMQ enable asynchronous, event-driven messaging, allowing agents to publish and subscribe to events without direct coupling. This decoupled architecture supports scalability and resilience. Agents can react to changes in real time, queue tasks for later execution, and maintain loose coordination across distributed systems. Message brokers also provide durability and replay capabilities, which are critical for auditability and fault recovery.

- **State Management**: Agents need memory not just for short-term context but also for long-term learning and continuity. State management solutions such as Redis, PostgreSQL, and vector databases (FAISS and Pinecone) enable agents to store and retrieve structured and unstructured data. Persistent state enables agents to track progress, recall prior decisions, and personalize interactions. In enterprise settings, this memory layer can be integrated with existing data lakes or knowledge graphs, allowing agents to operate with richer context and domain awareness.

- **Security and Identity**: As agents assume greater responsibility, ensuring the security of their actions becomes paramount. Role-based access control (RBAC) ensures that agents operate within defined boundaries, while API gateways enforce authentication, rate limiting, and traffic inspection. Audit trails are equally important. Enterprises must be able to trace agent decisions, monitor interactions, and validate compliance with internal policies and external regulations. This is especially critical in sectors like finance, healthcare, and government, where agent actions may have legal or operational consequences.

Agent orchestration platforms must integrate seamlessly with existing enterprise systems, such as ERP, CRM, and data warehouses. But integration should not introduce fragility. Systems must be loosely coupled, resilient to change, and able to handle partial failures gracefully.

The best orchestration platforms act as connective tissue linking agents to enterprise data and workflows without becoming a bottleneck. They support observability, governance, and extensibility, allowing organizations to scale agentic capabilities without compromising stability.

Enterprise-grade agent orchestration demands a robust, modular infrastructure that enables intelligent agents to operate reliably, scale efficiently, and integrate seamlessly across complex workflows. Key architectural components include microservices for modularity and fault isolation, containerization and Kubernetes for consistent deployment and dynamic resource management, and message brokers like Kafka and RabbitMQ for asynchronous, decoupled communication. State management systems such as Redis and vector databases provide agents with memory and continuity, while security frameworks like RBAC and API gateways ensure safe and auditable operations. Crucially, orchestration platforms must connect agents to existing enterprise systems like ERP, CRM, and data lakes, without introducing fragility, supporting resilience, governance, and extensibility across hybrid environments. These concepts appear in Figure 14.

Figure 14: Infrastructure and Platforms Necessary to Support Agent Orchestration.

Figure 14 illustrates the layered architecture required to support enterprise-grade multi-agent systems. Each component plays a distinct role in enabling agents to operate with precision, resilience, and continuity. Microservices Architecture promotes modularity and fault isolation, allowing agents to function as independent services that integrate seamlessly with existing enterprise systems. Containerization and Kubernetes ensure consistent deployment across environments, with Kubernetes managing agent lifecycles, scaling, and availability, especially vital in hybrid or distributed setups. Message Brokers (Kafka, RabbitMQ) facilitate asynchronous, event-driven communication between agents, enabling loose coupling, real-time coordination, and fault-tolerant workflows. State Management provides agents with persistent memory through tools such as Redis, PostgreSQL, and vector databases, which are critical for learning, personalization, and long-term context. Security and Identity enforces boundaries through RBAC, API gateways, and audit trails, ensuring agents operate safely and in compliance with enterprise policies. Enterprise Insight highlights the importance of integration without fragility. Agents must connect to ERP, CRM, and data platforms without introducing systemic risk or bottlenecks. Together, these layers form the backbone of scalable agent orchestration, aligning technical capabilities with enterprise priorities around agility, governance, and trust.

Now, let's explore the trade-offs and strategic considerations that come with choosing the right deployment environment for multi-agent systems.

## 3.4 Cloud and On-Premises Solutions for Agent Deployment

Deploying multi-agent systems is not solely a technical exercise. It is a strategic decision that reflects an organization's priorities around agility, control, compliance, and scalability. The deployment environment directly influences how agents interact with enterprise systems, how data is managed, and how governance is enforced. Here are the advantages and limitations of cloud-native, on-premises, and hybrid deployment models, providing guidance for selecting the most appropriate approach based on operational and regulatory constraints:

- **Cloud Advantages are Speed, Scale, and Seamless Integration**: Cloud-native environments offer significant advantages for organizations seeking rapid development and scalable execution. Elastic compute resources allow agent workloads to expand or contract based on demand, while managed services reduce the operational burden of infrastructure maintenance. Cloud platforms also provide seamless integration with large language model APIs and orchestration frameworks, enabling faster iteration and experimentation. For enterprises focused on innovation, time-to-market, and dynamic scaling, cloud deployment is often the preferred model. However, reliance on third-party infrastructure raises concerns about data residency, vendor lock-in, and shared security responsibility.

- **On-Premises Advantages are Control, Compliance, and Customization**: Organizations operating in highly regulated sectors such as healthcare, finance, and defense often require tighter control over data and infrastructure. On-premises deployment provides full autonomy over system configuration, access controls, and compliance enforcement. It also mitigates risks associated with external dependencies and allows for tailored optimization of agent performance. While on-premises solutions offer enhanced security and data sovereignty, they typically involve higher upfront costs, longer implementation timelines, and increased internal resource requirements.

- **Hybrid Models Bridge the Best of Both Worlds**: Hybrid models combine the strengths of cloud and on-premises environments, enabling agents to operate across distributed infrastructures while maintaining compliance and performance. Sensitive data and critical operations can remain on-premises, while cloud-based agents handle less regulated tasks or provide burst capacity during peak demand. Federated agent architectures, secure tunneling, and edge computing technologies support this model, allowing agents to collaborate across boundaries with clearly defined data governance protocols. Hybrid deployment requires careful orchestration but offers a balanced approach for enterprises with diverse operational needs.

## 3.4.1 Compliance Considerations: More Than a Checkbox

The deployment strategy has direct implications for regulatory compliance. Frameworks such as HIPAA, GDPR, and FedRAMP impose specific requirements on data handling, access control, and auditability. Cloud providers may offer certifications and compliance tooling, but these do not always align with the nuanced demands of enterprise use cases, particularly when agents are autonomous or interacting with sensitive information.

On-premises deployments offer greater control but place full responsibility on the organization to implement and maintain compliant systems. Regardless of the model chosen, compliance must be embedded into the deployment architecture from the outset.

## 3.4.2 Enterprise Insight: Choosing What Fits

Selecting a deployment model requires a structured evaluation of organizational priorities, including risk tolerance, latency sensitivity, data classification, and operational maturity. A decision matrix, mapping these factors against deployment options, can support informed, strategic choices.

Ultimately, agent deployment is not just about infrastructure. It is about aligning technological capabilities with enterprise values, regulatory obligations, and long-term objectives. The following figure can help determine the correct deployment option:

| Factor | Cloud Deployment | On-Premises Deployment | Hybrid Deployment |
|---|---|---|---|
| Scalability | Elastic scaling; ideal for dynamic workloads | Limited by internal infrastructure | Scalable cloud components with controlled local capacity |
| Speed to Deploy | Rapid provisioning and iteration; minimal setup | Slower setup; requires internal coordination | Moderate speed; depends on integration complexity |
| Security Control | Shared responsibility with provider; strong defaults | Full control over security protocols and data access | Split control; sensitive data stays local, cloud handles less critical tasks |
| Compliance Readiness | Certifications available (e.g., SOC 2, HIPAA, FedRAMP), but may not cover all use cases | Tailored compliance; direct control over audit and governance | Flexible compliance; requires clear boundaries and documentation |
| Cost Structure | Pay-as-you-go; variable costs based on usage | Fixed costs; capital expenditure for hardware and maintenance | Mixed model; requires careful budgeting across environments |
| Vendor Lock-In Risk | Higher risk; dependent on provider APIs and pricing | Lower risk; more autonomy over tech stack | Moderate risk; mitigated by modular design and open standards |
| Latency Sensitivity | May introduce latency for real-time or edge use cases | Low latency; ideal for time-critical operations | Tuned latency; local agents handle real-time tasks, cloud agents handle async tasks |
| Integration Complexity | Easier with cloud-native tools and APIs | Requires custom connectors and middleware | Complex but flexible; needs orchestration across environments |

Table 1: Deployment Decision Matrix.

Table 1 presents a strategic deployment decision matrix designed to help enterprises evaluate the most suitable environment for hosting multi-agent systems. It compares cloud, on-premises, and hybrid models across eight critical factors: scalability, deployment speed, security controls, compliance readiness, cost structure, vendor lock-in risk, latency sensitivity, and integration complexity. Cloud deployments offer rapid provisioning, elastic scaling, and seamless integration with modern AI services, but come with trade-offs in control and vendor dependency.

On-premises solutions provide full autonomy, enhanced security, and tailored compliance, making them ideal for regulated industries, though they require greater internal investment and slower rollout. Hybrid models aim to balance flexibility and control, allowing sensitive operations to remain local while leveraging cloud resources for scalability and non-critical tasks. By mapping organizational priorities against these dimensions, the matrix supports informed, context-aware decisions that align technical architecture with business strategy and regulatory obligations.

No deployment model is perfect, but each one reflects a set of priorities. Cloud favors agility and experimentation. On-premises prioritizes control and compliance. Hybrid models offer flexibility but demand thoughtful architecture and governance.

This matrix isn't just a checklist; it's a conversation starter for aligning technical decisions with business strategy.

Deployment decisions reflect organizational priorities around agility, governance, and risk management. Selecting the appropriate model requires a structured evaluation of factors such as latency sensitivity, data classification, and regulatory posture. As enterprises scale their agentic capabilities, deployment architecture becomes a foundational pillar of trust, performance, and long-term viability. Figure 15 provides a quick reference graphic for deployment.

With infrastructure and deployment strategies in place, the next challenge lies in enabling agents to work together effectively. Multi-agent systems are inherently collaborative, but without robust coordination mechanisms, they risk fragmentation, redundancy, and failure. In the following section, we explore the technologies and design patterns that support agent-to-agent communication, task delegation, conflict resolution, and temporal synchronization. These capabilities are essential for transforming individual agents into cohesive, intelligent networks capable of executing complex enterprise workflows.

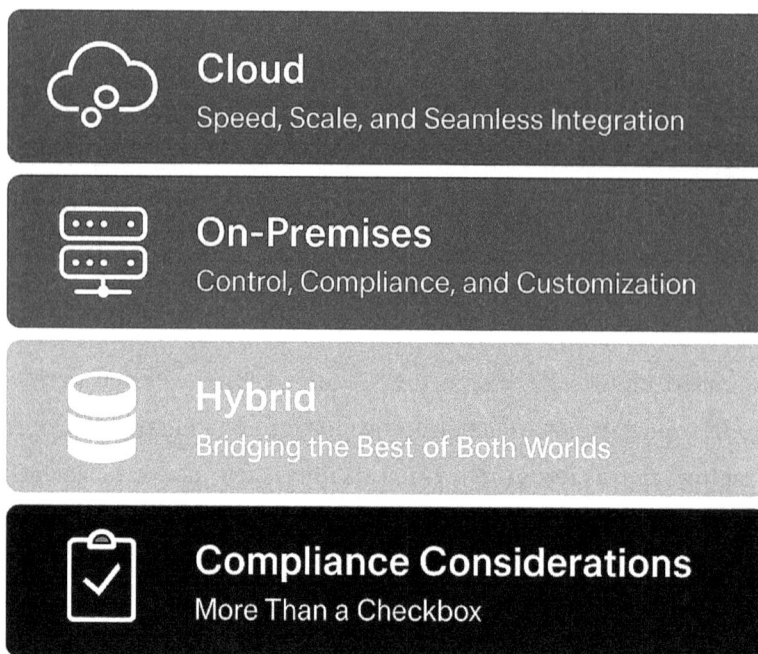

Figure 15: Deployment Option Reference.

## 3.5 Leveraging Modern Frameworks like LangGraph, CrewAI, and AutoGen

Building multi-agent systems used to mean stitching together custom logic, brittle APIs, and a lot of trial and error. Today, that landscape is changing fast. A new wave of orchestration frameworks is making it easier than ever to design, deploy, and manage coordinated agent teams with real-world utility.

Let's explore these three frameworks:

- **LangGraph**: LangGraph introduces a graph-based approach to agent orchestration. Instead of linear workflows, you define nodes (agents or functions) and edges (transitions based on conditions or outcomes). This allows for flexible, stateful coordination; agents can loop, branch, or retry based on context. For enterprise teams, LangGraph shines when workflows are complex and dynamic. Whether it's a multi-step approval process or a recursive data enrichment loop, LangGraph makes it easier to model logic that adapts in real time. LangGraph integrates well with vector databases and memory layers, making it ideal for agents that need persistent context across sessions.

- **CrewAI**: CrewAI takes a team-based approach to agent orchestration. You define roles (e.g., researcher, analyst, reviewer), assign tasks, and let agents collaborate based on their personas and capabilities. It's like staffing a virtual department, each agent knows its job and how to interact with others. This framework is especially useful for workflows that mirror human collaboration. Think of use cases like content creation, market analysis, or customer support, where agents need to pass work back and forth with clarity and purpose. CrewAI supports dynamic task assignment and human-in-the-loop checkpoints, making it a strong fit for regulated industries or high-stakes decision-making.

- **AutoGen**: AutoGen focuses on modularity and feedback loops. It allows you to chain agents together, define interaction protocols, and incorporate human oversight where needed. Agents can critique each other's outputs, refine responses, and escalate tasks all within a structured framework. AutoGen is particularly valuable for iterative workflows such as code generation, document drafting, or data validation, where quality improves through cycles of review and refinement. AutoGen supports LLM chaining and external tool integration, making it a flexible choice for organizations already working with OpenAI, Azure AI, or custom models.

Each framework brings something unique to the table. LangGraph offers precision and control. CrewAI brings structure and collaboration. AutoGen delivers adaptability and refinement. The best choice depends on your workflow complexity, team structure, and integration needs.

Here's a quick comparison to help guide that decision:

| Framework | Strengths | Best For | Enterprise Fit |
| --- | --- | --- | --- |
| LangGraph | Graph-based logic, stateful workflows | Complex, branching processes | High control, persistent memory |
| CrewAI | Role-based teams, persona modeling | Collaborative, human-like workflows | Regulated industries, human-in-the-loop |
| AutoGen | Modular chaining, feedback loops | Iterative tasks, refinement cycles | Flexible integration, LLM-heavy workflows |

Table 2: Modern Framework Reference Guide.

Table 2 compares LangGraph, CrewAI, and AutoGen. The core strengths, ideal use cases, and enterprise alignment for each of these leading agent orchestration frameworks are shown. Each framework offers a distinct approach: LangGraph excels in complex, stateful logic; CrewAI enables structured collaboration through role-based agents; and AutoGen supports iterative refinement with modular chaining and flexible integration.

---

*These frameworks aren't just tools. They're accelerators.*
*They help enterprises move faster, build smarter, and deploy agentic systems*
*that are both powerful and practical.*

---

With a clear understanding of how modern frameworks like LangGraph, CrewAI, and AutoGen enable structured, adaptive agent orchestration, the next step is seeing these tools in action. The following study illustrates how coordinated agents deployed using these frameworks can transform manufacturing operations, driving efficiency, resilience, and real-time decision-making across complex industrial workflows.

## 3.6 Case Study: Coordinated Agents in Manufacturing Operations

A global manufacturing company was struggling with production delays across its facilities. Each plant operated semi-independently, using different systems to manage inventory, maintenance schedules, and supplier communications. When a critical part ran low in one location, it often triggered a chain reaction: halted production, emergency procurement, and missed delivery deadlines.

The company had automation tools, but they weren't talking to each other. What they needed was coordination.

They deployed a multi-agent system built on a hybrid infrastructure: cloud-based agents handled supplier negotiations and global inventory tracking. In contrast, on-prem agents managed plant-level operations and compliance-sensitive data. Using LangGraph, they modeled workflows as dynamic graphs, enabling agents to escalate issues, reroute tasks, and retry failed actions in response to real-time conditions.

CrewAI was used to structure agent roles: one agent monitored inventory thresholds, another handled supplier outreach, and a third coordinated logistics. AutoGen added feedback loops, enabling agents to refine procurement strategies based on historical performance and supplier responsiveness.

The result? Production delays dropped by 40%. Inventory waste was reduced. And for the first time, the company had a system that could adapt, not just automate.

## 3.7 Key Takeaways

- Multi-agent systems offer a strategic upgrade from static automation, enabling coordination, adaptability, and real-time responsiveness across enterprise workflows.
- Infrastructure matters: microservices, containerization, message brokers, and persistent state management form the backbone of scalable agent orchestration.
- Deployment architecture: cloud, on-premises, or hybrid must align with enterprise priorities around agility, compliance, and control.
- Governance and security are non-negotiable: role-based access, audit trails, and integration boundaries ensure safe and compliant agent operations.
- Modern orchestration frameworks like LangGraph, CrewAI, and AutoGen accelerate agent deployment, each offering distinct strengths for workflow modeling, collaboration, and iterative refinement.
- Case studies demonstrate measurable impact: coordinated agents reduce delays, optimize inventory, and improve operational resilience in manufacturing and logistics.
- Successful agentic deployment requires more than smart agents. It demands thoughtful architecture, strategic alignment, and robust coordination mechanisms.

## 3.8 Discussion Questions / Exercises

1. Which enterprise workflows in your organization suffer from coordination bottlenecks, and how might multi-agent systems address them?

2. How would you architect a multi-agent system using microservices, message brokers, and persistent memory to support a dynamic business process?

3. What deployment model (cloud, on-premises, hybrid) best fits your organization's regulatory posture and operational needs? Why?

4. Compare LangGraph, CrewAI, and AutoGen. Which orchestration framework would you choose for a collaborative, regulated workflow like financial reporting or healthcare triage?

5. What governance safeguards exist, such as access control? Auditability? Fallback logic? Would you implement measures to ensure safe and compliant agent behavior in a multi-agent system?

In the next chapter, we shift our focus to advanced agent architectures and data integration. We'll explore how agents interface with enterprise systems, APIs, and data pipelines to support large-scale coordination. We'll also examine integration patterns that enable agents to communicate securely, efficiently, and at scale with each other and external platforms.

# CHAPTER 4

# Advanced Agent Architectures and Data Integration

This chapter examines the architectural foundations and integration strategies that enable multi-agent systems (MAS) to operate at enterprise scale, coordinating diverse autonomous agents across systems, data pipelines, and governance domains. It spans technical design, integration, governance, and strategic deployment.

Gartner forecasts that by 2028, 15% of day-to-day business decisions will be automated by agents, according to TechRadar. A TechRadarPro executive survey confirms that 61% of business leaders are actively adopting AI agents but warns of the persistent danger of deployment silos.

Recent analyses from PwC, Accenture, and Deloitte underscore the accelerating adoption of multi-agent systems worldwide, with notable variation across industry sectors:

- **Finance**: According to Accenture's 2025 Digital Transformation Outlook, 42% of global banking and financial services firms have implemented or piloted multi-agent systems for applications such as fraud detection, algorithmic trading, and automated compliance. Deloitte's 2024 AI in Financial Services report notes that 63% of institutions expect to increase their investments in agent-based automation within two years.

- **Healthcare**: PwC's 2024 Global Health AI Survey reports that 35% of large healthcare providers and payers have adopted agentic AI to support personalized patient care, clinical workflow automation, and real-time data integration. Deloitte reports a 28% adoption rate among hospital networks in North America and Europe, with a focus on clinical decision support and predictive analytics.

- **Supply Chain and Logistics**: Accenture's Global Supply Chain Automation Study (2024) found that 47% of supply chain leaders have deployed multi-agent orchestration for tasks such as demand forecasting, inventory optimization, and vendor negotiations. PwC highlights that the Asia-Pacific region leads with a 51% adoption rate, driven by large-scale manufacturing and logistics operations.

According to the latest PwC Global AI Barometer, overall enterprise adoption of MAS is at 18% worldwide, expected to rise to 34% by the end of 2026, with finance, supply chain, and healthcare as the leading verticals. Deloitte's cross-industry survey finds that 67% of organizations planning to adopt MAS cite integration with legacy systems as a primary challenge, emphasizing the importance of robust data pipelines and architectural agility.

Accenture reports that only 10–15% of clients currently use multi-agent systems but expects that to exceed 30% within 18–24 months, according to the Wall Street Journal. PwC's new "agent OS" platform further exemplifies the shift toward orchestrated, interoperable agent ecosystems. TechRadar highlights a strategic roadmap for transitioning legacy systems and organizational knowledge to support multi-agent architectures. Meanwhile, security concerns are prompting enterprises to move away from Retrieval-Augmented Generation (RAG) architectures toward agent-based systems that query data in place and respect existing access controls. Some statistics:

- MAS is rapidly expanding in enterprise usage, with projected adoption aligned with decision automation (15% by 2028), according to TechRadar.
- Global adoption is highest in the finance (42%), supply chain (47%), and healthcare (35%) verticals, according to PwC, Accenture, and Deloitte.
- Orchestration platforms (e.g., agent OS) and multi-agent protocols are essential to overcoming silos and enabling interoperability, according to the Wall Street Journal and Business Insider.
- Secure, compliant integration (moving beyond RAG) is critical for scaling agent adoption safely, according to TechRadar.

With adoption accelerating across industries, understanding the technical foundations of multi-agent systems becomes essential.

## 4.1 Core Technical Depth

### 4.1.1 Definitions and Taxonomy

A multi-agent system (MAS) consists of autonomous AI agents each pursuing domain-specific subgoals coordinated to achieve overarching enterprise objectives.

| Agent Type | Core Behavior | Decision-Making | Strengths | Limitations | Typical Use Cases | Example Technologies |
|---|---|---|---|---|---|---|
| Reactive | Responds to environmental changes or events without internal planning | Rule-based, immediate action | Fast, simple, scalable | Lacks foresight, no strategic planning | Real-time monitoring, anomaly detection | Event-driven microservices, stream processors |
| Deliberative | Maintains an internal model and plans actions to achieve goals | Goal-driven, uses reasoning and prediction | Strategic, adaptable, capable of complex problem solving | Slower response, higher resource consumption | Supply chain optimization, workflow automation | Planning engines, knowledge graphs |
| Hybrid | Combines reactive responsiveness with deliberative planning | Balances immediate reaction and strategic reasoning | Adaptive, robust, context-aware | Complex design and implementation | Autonomous vehicles, advanced robotics | Integrated agent frameworks (e.g., AutoGen, CrewAI) |
| Multi-modal | Processes and synthesizes information across multiple data types or modalities | Integrates sensory input and reasoning across channels | Rich context under-standing, cross-domain intelligence | Requires sophisticated fusion and alignment techniques | Healthcare diagnostics, multimodal chatbots | Vision-Language models, multimodal transformers |

Table 3: Agents may be Reactive (Responding to Events), Deliberative (Planning), or Hybrids, Combining both Behaviors.

## 4.1.2 Federated Versus Centralized MAS Architectures

When designing Multi-Agent Systems (MAS) for compliance-heavy industries such as finance, healthcare, and government, the architectural approach profoundly influences operational agility, resilience, and regulatory alignment. Two dominant paradigms emerge: centralized and federated architectures.

Centralized MAS architectures consolidate agent control, coordination, and data within a core platform. This model offers tight governance, streamlined auditing, and unified security policies. For compliance-heavy environments, centralization simplifies regulatory reporting and ensures consistent enforcement of standards. However, centralized systems can become bottlenecks; scaling demands exponential resources, and a single point of failure presents risk to business continuity. Moreover, strict centralization may inhibit local innovation and adaptability, particularly in global organizations with varied regulatory jurisdictions.

**Federated MAS** architectures distribute agents and their data-handling capabilities across autonomous domains. Each node, potentially representing a division, region, or partner, maintains local compliance and operational logic while interoperating with the broader ecosystem. Federated models excel in environments that require data sovereignty and granular policy enforcement, as local agents can adapt swiftly to jurisdiction-specific requirements. This decentralization bolsters resilience; outages in a single node rarely affect the entire system. Yet, federated designs challenge governance, demanding sophisticated trust, synchronization, and oversight frameworks to prevent fragmentation or compliance gaps. Integration and audit processes grow complex as data typologies and agent behaviors diverge.

Pros for Centralized MAS in Compliance-Heavy Industries:
- Unified compliance enforcement and policy management
- Simplified data governance and auditing
- Streamlined incident response and reporting.

Cons:
- Increased risk of a single point of failure
- Potential latency and bottlenecks at scale
- Less adaptable to local or changing regulatory requirements.

Pros for Federated MAS in Compliance-Heavy Industries:

- Localized compliance and policy adaptation
- Enhanced resilience and system availability
- Improved data sovereignty for multinational operations.

Cons:

- Complex governance, monitoring, and audit trails
- Risk of inconsistent compliance standards between domains
- Higher integration costs and potential interoperability challenges.

## 4.1.3 Architectural Components

A robust enterprise MAS architecture typically includes:

- **Data Integration Layer**: ETL/ELT pipelines, API gateways, or streaming platforms (e.g., Kafka) to connect systems like ERP, CRM, IoT, and cloud storage.
- **Orchestration Layer**: Electronic "conductor" coordinating agents via DAGs or workflows, examples include LangGraph, CrewAI, and AutoGen.
- **Agent Layer**: Domain-specific agents (compliance, supply chain, security) interacting with systems or other agents.
- **Governance Layer**: Monitoring, SLA dashboards, audit logs, bias detection, and compliance infrastructure.

## 4.1.4 Microservices and Federated Architecture

Shifting MAS from a monolithic architecture to a microservices architecture improves scalability and maintainability by deploying each agent or orchestrator as an independent service. Federated architecture further supports autonomous cooperation across organizational domains with loose coupling and common messaging models. Standardized communication protocols are emerging:

- **MCP (Model Context Protocol)**: Framework for agents to invoke tools securely, supported by Microsoft and others as the "USB-C for AI".

- **ACP**, **A2A**, **ANP**: Progressive capabilities for REST messaging, peer-to-peer task outsourcing, and agent discovery via DID graphs.
- **BlockA2A**: A blockchain-based trust framework offering immutable auditability, smart contract–enforced access controls, and real-time defense against malicious agents.

## 4.1.5 Decision Model: Monolith Versus Microservices Versus Service Mesh

When architecting agent-based systems, choosing between a monolithic, microservices, or service mesh architecture requires careful evaluation of system needs, scale, and operational realities:

### Monolithic Architecture

- **Characteristics**: All functionality: UI, business logic, and data access reside in a single deployable unit. Internal calls are in process, and deployment is straightforward.
- **Advantages**: Simpler to develop, test, and deploy in early-stage or low-complexity environments. Fewer network boundaries reduce latency and debugging complexity.
- **Limitations**: As complexity grows, modularity suffers; a single fault can cascade. Scaling parts of the system independently is impossible, and updates require redeploying the entire application.
- **Recommended for**: Small teams, proof-of-concept projects, or systems with limited scalability and integration requirements.

### Microservices Architecture

- **Characteristics**: The application is split into independently deployable services, each encapsulating a specific business capability. Services interact via well-defined interfaces (REST, gRPC, messaging).
- **Advantages**: Enables independent scaling, polyglot development, and isolated deployments. Faults are contained. Teams can deliver features autonomously, supporting continuous delivery. Suits organizations seeking rapid change, modular scalability, and operational resilience.

- **Limitations**: Introduces distributed systems complexity, including network latency, data consistency, and increased operational overhead. Observability and security across service boundaries must be managed explicitly.
- **Recommended for**: Large, fast-evolving systems where modularity, resilience, and independent scaling are required.

## Service Mesh

- **Characteristics**: Sits atop microservices, providing a dedicated infrastructure layer for secure service-to-service communication, traffic management, observability, and policy enforcement (typically with a sidecar proxy like Envoy).
- **Advantages**: Offloads cross-cutting concerns (e.g., retries, timeouts, encryption, authentication) from business logic, enabling zero-trust security and fine-grained traffic policies. Centralizes telemetry for distributed tracing and monitoring.
- **Limitations**: Adds operational and cognitive overhead, as mesh components themselves must be deployed and maintained. Not suited for small-scale or low-change environments due to added complexity.
- **Recommended for**: Large-scale, security-sensitive, and highly dynamic microservices environments where advanced traffic management, policy enforcement, and unified observability are needed.

To choose the right model:

- Start with a monolith if rapid prototyping, simple deployment, or resource constraints dominate.
- Adopt microservices as teams or product domains grow and demands for scalability, modularity, or velocity increase.
- Introduce a service mesh when microservices proliferation creates challenges around security, reliability, or traffic control that cannot be efficiently solved in code or simple orchestration.
- Prioritize organizational maturity: A service mesh requires strong DevOps and platform engineering capability.

## 4.2 Integration Patterns

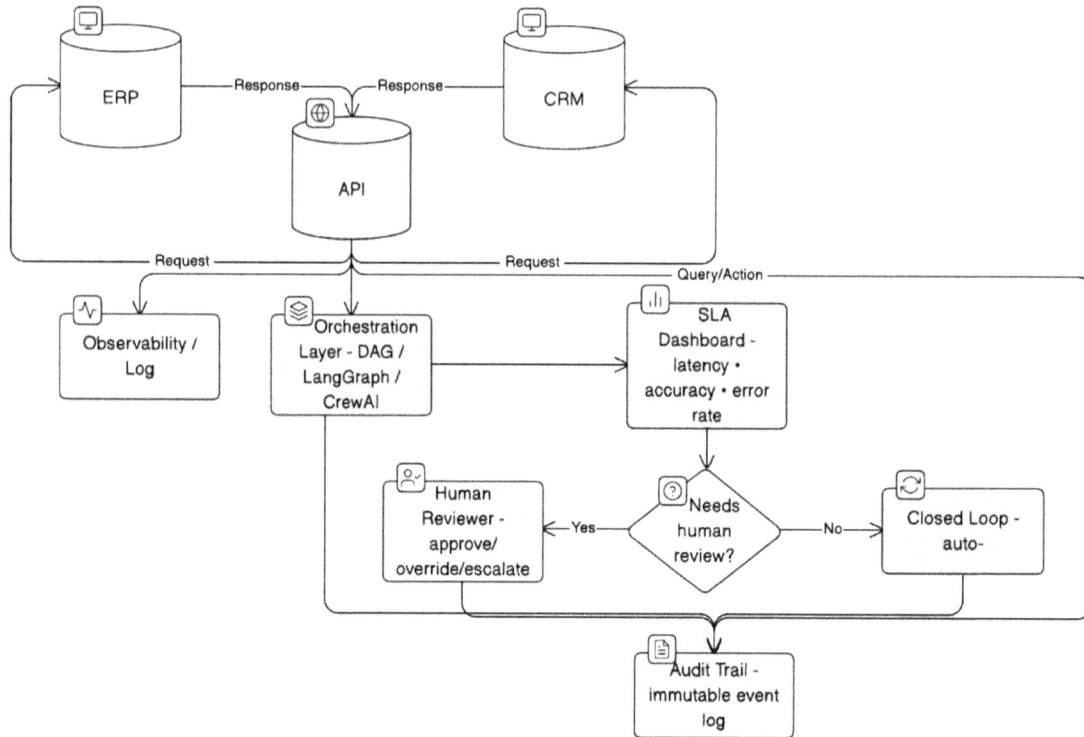

Figure 16: Agent-to-System Flow.

### Agent-to-System Integration

- **API-Driven**: Agents invoke REST or GraphQL APIs with proper authentication and authorization. Ensures controlled access to ERP, CRM, and other services.

- **Event-Driven**: Agents subscribe to topics via Kafka, AWS EventBridge, or message queues, reacting in real time to events such as orders, anomalies, or alerts.

- **Direct Data Connectors**: Agents with governed credentials query data sources directly (e.g., via SQL, APIs). Security and audit, enforced via a governance layer, are essential.

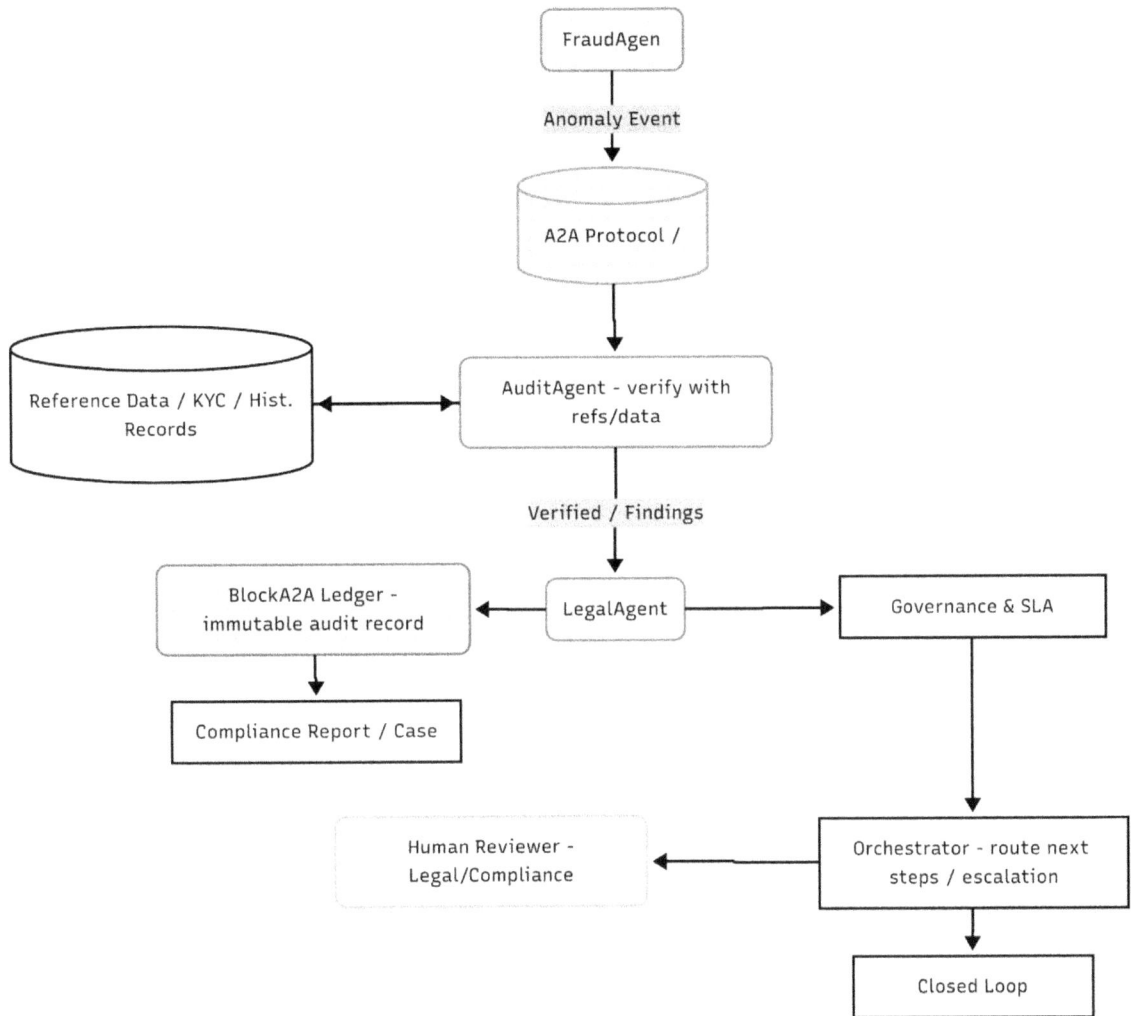

Figure 17: Agent-to-Agent Flow.

## Agent-to-Agent Integration

- **Messaging Queues**: Agents communicate via RabbitMQ, NATS, or similar queues supporting robust, decoupled coordination.

- **Blackboard Models**: A shared state or knowledge repository where agents post and read context for coordination.

- **Orchestrator-Based DAGs**: The master orchestrator assigns tasks, sequences agents, and manages task dependencies within a flow (e.g., LangGraph, CrewAI).

- **Protocol-Driven Messaging**: Using MCP, A2A, or ACP for standardized tool invocation, capability exchange, and peer communication.

| Protocol | Scope | Security | Adoption | Best Use Case | Limitations |
|---|---|---|---|---|---|
| MCP | Agent-to-tool invocation | Strong, standardized | Backed by Microsoft/Anthropic | Secure API/tool usage | Early-stage ecosystem |
| ACP | REST-based agent-to-agent messaging | Medium | Conceptual research | Low-latency APIs | Not widely deployed |
| A2A | Peer-to-peer outsourcing | Medium | Startups/enterprise pilots | Distributed MAS | Trust/identity gaps |
| ANP | Networked agent discovery | High | Research only | Dynamic MAS | Complex governance overhead |
| BlockA2A | Blockchain trust + zero-trust | Very High | Experimental, EU defense pilots | Critical infrastructure, finance | Latency, energy costs |

Table 4: Protocols.

## Hybrid Integration Patterns

**Service Meshes** (Istio, Linkerd) can be applied to manage communications securely across agent clusters, providing observability, security, and traffic control.

**Enterprise Diagram (Described)**

Picture an event streaming backbone:

- The Integration Layer publishes the following topics: "OrderCreated," "FraudAlert," and "ComplianceFlag."
- Agents subscribe to domains InventoryAgent, FraudAgent, or AuditAgent.
- Some agents "publish" new events ("RestockOrder," "InvestigationInitiated").
- An orchestrator routes tasks when a chain of agents must collaborate (e.g., FraudAgent → AuditAgent → ManagerNotificationAgent).

## 4.3 Workflow Resilience and Cost Allocation Models

In enterprise MAS deployments, resilience is as critical as raw performance. Unlike static automation, agents continuously interact, adapt, and sometimes fail. Without structured resilience strategies, enterprises risk silent failures, regulatory breaches, or cascading outages.

### Core Mechanisms

- **Escalation Protocols**: When an agent exceeds its decision boundary (e.g., a confidence score below a threshold or an SLA violation), the system automatically routes the task to a supervisory agent or a human-in-the-loop reviewer.
- **Performance Degradation Detection**: MAS should include observability hooks to monitor drift in accuracy, latency, or anomaly-detection rates. Example: A fraud-detection agent's spike in false negatives triggers automatic rollback to a prior stable model version.
- **Automated Remediation**: Integration with orchestration layers (e.g., LangGraph, CrewAI) enables DAG-based fallback plans. If one agent fails, alternate paths can be activated dynamically.
- **Workflow Version Control**: Borrowing principles from software DevOps, enterprises must manage *agent workflow versions* with rollback capabilities. This ensures that when an updated orchestration pipeline causes regressions, previous validated versions can be restored seamlessly.

### Illustrative Architecture

- The Monitoring Layer (sidecar services or a service mesh) continuously tracks SLA metrics.
- If an SLA breach occurs, the Orchestration Layer triggers the Escalation Agent.
- EscalationAgent either:
    o Routes to the HumanOperator node (human-in-the-loop), or
    o Rolls back workflow to the last "golden" configuration snapshot.
- Governance Layer logs the entire sequence for audit and compliance.

**Lesson**: Embedding resilience ensures MAS not only *scales* but also *sustains* under stress.

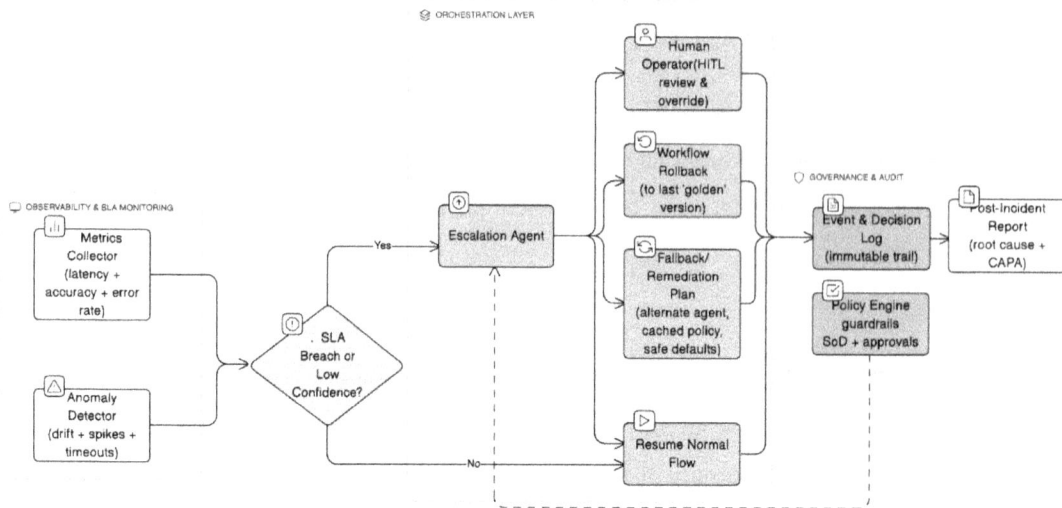

Figure 18: "Trust but Verify" MAS Resilience Loop.

## 4.3.1 Cost Allocation and Resource Attribution in MAS

Enterprises deploying large fleets of agents often face unexpected costs, including API calls, GPU inference spikes, streaming data subscriptions, and redundant agent interactions. Without attribution, costs spiral and ROI weakens.

### Key Models

### Agent-Level Cost Tracking

- Each agent logs compute, storage, and external service usage.
- Example: ComplianceAgent consumes 80% of the cloud API quota while InventoryAgent consumes 20%.
- Attribution enables proportional budgeting across departments.

### Shared Resource Pools

- MAS can adopt multi-tenant cloud models where agents share GPU clusters or API pools.
- Costs are allocated via weighted fair-share schedulers (similar to Kubernetes QoS classes).

## Workflow-Based Cost Attribution

- Costs are attributed to business workflows (e.g., "KYC onboarding process = $1.45/transaction").
- Supports FinOps-style dashboards, enabling leadership to measure agent ROI per workflow rather than just infrastructure line items.

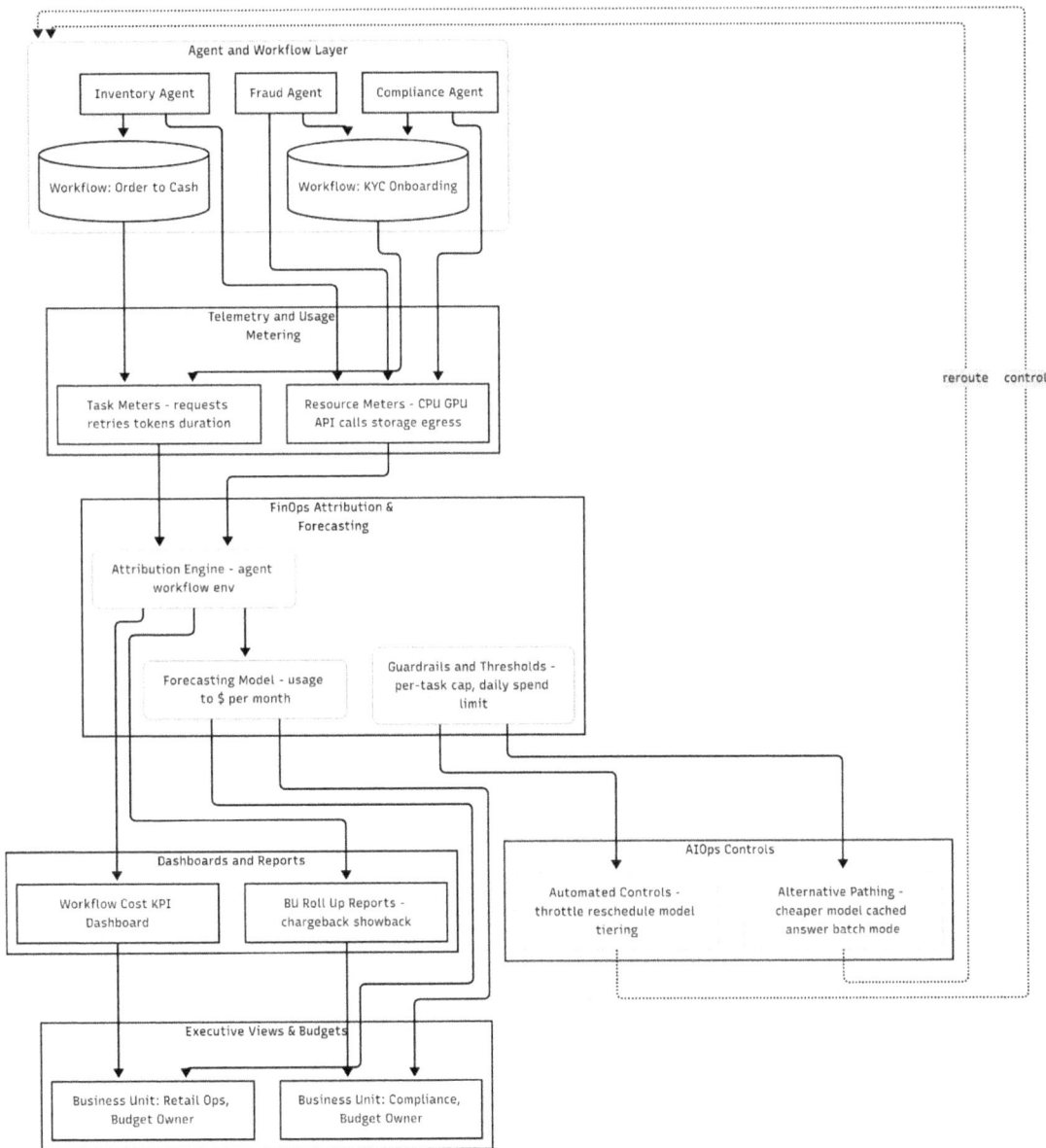

Figure 19: FinOps for Agents.

**Predictive Cost Modeling**

- Using historical MAS telemetry, enterprises can forecast the cost impact of scaling agent fleets.

- Example: Scaling from 100 → 500 agents increases monthly spend by 3.2x, not 5x, due to amortized resource reuse.

**Quantified Guidance**

- Target less than a 5% variance between forecasted and actual agent resource consumption.
- Introduce SLA clauses tied to cost ceilings, ensuring agents do not exceed per-task or per-decision budget allocations.
- Implement FinOps + AIOps convergence: automated systems that throttle, reschedule, or consolidate agents when costs breach thresholds.

---

## 4.4 Real-World Case Studies

### 4.4.1 JPMorgan – AML False Positives Reduced 95%

JPMorgan has invested over $12 billion annually in technology with significant emphasis on AI for compliance and risk. Its anti-money laundering (AML) workflows historically suffered from excessive false positives, leading to costly manual investigations.

| ① Deliver best-in-class products, platforms, and experiences | | ② Strengthen our development capabilities and infrastructure | | ③ Unlock the power of data | ④ Protect the Firm and our customers |
|---|---|---|---|---|---|
| Customer and client experiences | Product and platform development | Modernize technology | Drive software development excellence | Embed data and insights into everything | Proactively defend against cyber threats |

- Continued to release new products and experiences that delight our customers:
  - **Account validation:** custom-built engine that validates bank accounts to protect customers
  - **Cash optimization:** enable utilization of residual cash to generate alpha
  - **Connected Commerce:** ecosystem of products connected via reusable APIs
  - **Fusion:** cloud-native data management and reporting platform
  - **Versana:** reduce settlement times and improve liquidity management for syndicated loan market

- Improved **speed-to-market of product features** by 20% (in days)
- Continued **application modernization** through refactoring, SaaS replacement, and legacy decommissioning
- Enabled **multi-vendor public cloud** as target state infrastructure
- Completed ~60% of our **application migrations** to strategic data centers
- Optimized **data center footprint** to facilitate public cloud journey

- Ahead of our plan to deliver $1B business value
- +34% YoY growth in AI/ML use cases in production
- Accelerated large-language-model (LLM) enablement

- Matured ability to respond to new threats, including quantum safe encryption
- Delivered business value through cyber as a differentiator
- Maintained flat expense relative to volume increases

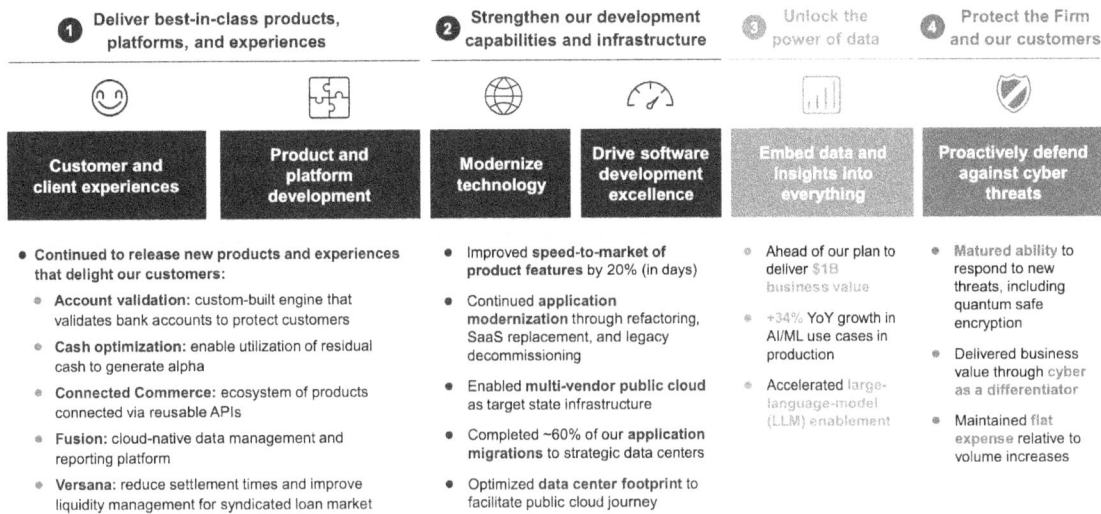

Figure 20: JPMorgan Firmwide Tech Strategy Underpinning Agent Systems (Investor Day 2023).

**CONTINUING TO ACCELERATE THE POWER OF OUR DATA AND AI/ML**

Building an industry-leading team

| | |
|---|---|
| **900+** data scientists | **600+** ML engineers |
| **200+** AI researchers | **Ranked #1** Evident AI Index[1] |

Expanding our technology platforms

- Improving capabilities, with embedded governance and Responsible AI

- Integrating ML Ops capability to support teams to develop models faster and measure performance

- Increased use cases leveraging firmwide model development and training platform by 2.2x YoY

Figure 21: Regulatory-Grade Data and Reporting Platform. Source: Investor Day 2023, Global Technology, Slide 2.

**Markets Regulatory
Reporting Platform**

Regulatory data warehouse
responsible for global regulatory
reporting for **Cash Equities,
Futures, and Options in 15+
countries**

Running on **public cloud**,
enabling **real-time** audit
trail calculation and report
generation

Increased ability to scale to
**2.5B trades per day on
public cloud** from 500mm
trades per day on-premise

Reduced monthly running
cost by **>50%**

Figure 22: Unlock the Power of Data with AI/ML. Business Impact and Platform Governance Data "AI-Ready" LLM Suite and Cloud Migration.

Figure 23 is a reconstructed schematic developed from publicly available descriptions of JPMorgan Chase's AI and data modernization strategy. It is not an official diagram released by the firm. The visualization is intended solely for explanatory purposes, illustrating how enterprise data platforms (JADE, OmniAI, LLM Suite) and governance layers interact to enable multi-agent systems and compliance-ready AI workflows.

JPMorgan Chase's multi-year effort to modernize its data ecosystem underpins its AI agent strategy. The firmwide JADE data mesh and cloud migration ensure data assets are discoverable, accurate, and governed. The LLM Suite, rolled out to more than 200,000 employees, provides secure access to generative AI and reasoning agents, all supported by an $18B technology budget and more than an exabyte of daily data flow across global business lines. Jamie Dimon, the CEO of JPMorgan Chase, said:

*"Getting the data in the form that it's usable is the hard part."*

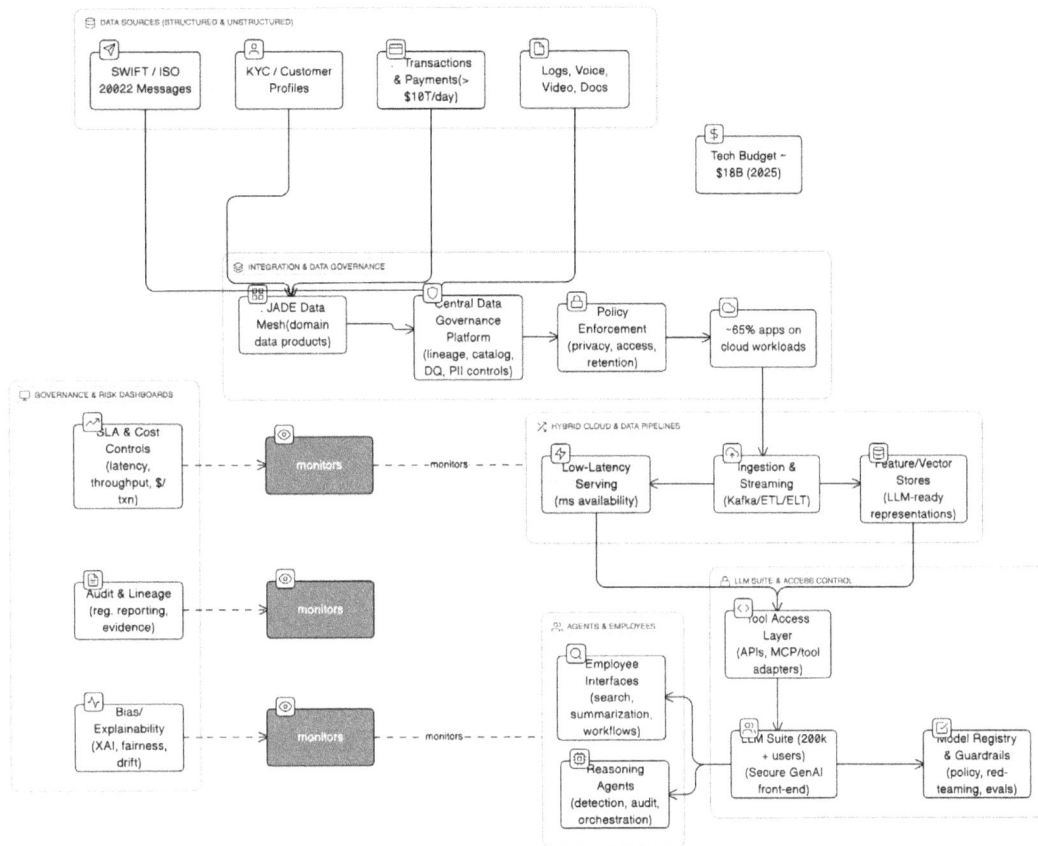

Figure 23: (Reconstructed): Data "AI-Ready" LLM Suite and Cloud Migration at JPMorgan Chase.

## Architecture Diagram (Described)

- **Data Sources**: Transactional databases, SWIFT messages, KYC systems.
- **Integration Layer**: API gateway connecting to regulatory and financial reporting systems.
- **Agent Layer**: DetectionAgent flags anomalies; AuditAgent validates against historical compliance records; EscalationAgent routes to human analysts.
- Governance Layer: Audit trail and SLA dashboard monitoring false positive ratios.

## Quantified Outcome

- 95% reduction in false positives.
- Investigators reallocated to high-value casework.

**Executive Quote**

"AI agents have transformed compliance, not by replacing investigators but by ensuring they focus on real risk rather than noise." JPMorgan Tech and Innovation Report.

**Lesson**: MAS can directly reduce compliance costs while enhancing regulatory responsiveness.

## 4.4.2 PwC – Agent OS Interoperability Platform

PwC launched its Agent OS in 2025 to orchestrate agent workflows across Microsoft, Anthropic, and Google Cloud ecosystems.

### Architecture Diagram (Described)

- **Data Sources**: Client ERP/CRM systems integrated via connectors.
- **Integration Layer**: Agent OS as middleware with secure APIs.
- **Agent Layer**: Specialized AuditAgent, AdvisoryAgent, TaxAgent.
- **Governance Layer**: Central SLA dashboard ensuring compliance across cloud vendors.

### Quantified Outcome

- Interoperability across three cloud ecosystems.
- 20–30% faster project turnaround in consulting engagements.

### Executive Quote

"Agent OS is our switchboard. It connects, orchestrates, and governs multi-agent workflows at scale." - PwC Global CTO.

**Lesson**: Middleware orchestration is vital when enterprises rely on multi-cloud agent ecosystems.

## 4.4.3 Accenture – Multi-Agent Marketing Orchestration

Accenture operates 50+ MAS today, with plans to scale to 100+. A flagship use case is marketing campaign orchestration, where multiple agents handle segmentation, personalization, and analytics.

### Architecture Diagram (Described)

- **Data Sources**: Customer data platforms, social media APIs.
- **Integration Layer**: Event bus routing customer events.
- **Agent Layer**: SegmentAgent, ContentAgent, AnalyticsAgent.
- **Governance Layer**: SLA metrics for campaign reach, cost, and personalization success.

### Quantified Outcome

- 25% faster campaign cycle times.
- 12% uplift in customer engagement.

### Executive Quote

"Our agents don't replace marketers, they give them leverage." Accenture Managing Director of Applied Intelligence.

**Lesson**: MAS thrives in customer-facing workflows with high data volume and personalization needs.

## 4.4.4 Mayo Clinic – Triage and Scheduling Integration with Epic EMR

Mayo Clinic piloted MAS for patient triage, scheduling, and care routing integrated with its Epic EMR system.

### Architecture Diagram (Described)

- **Data Sources**: Epic EMR, IoT vitals monitors, patient intake forms.
- **Integration Layer**: HL7/FHIR APIs for EMR interoperability.

- **Agent Layer**: TriageAgent prioritizes cases; SchedulingAgent books appointments; ComplianceAgent checks HIPAA rules.
- **Governance Layer**: Privacy dashboard with consent audit logs.

## Quantified Outcome

- 30% reduction in patient wait times.
- 18% increase in patient satisfaction scores.

## Executive Quote

"Our goal is faster, safer care, and agents are proving themselves as safe collaborators in that mission." Mayo Clinic CIO.

**Lesson**: Compliance-aware MAS integration is essential in healthcare.

## 4.4.5 Walmart – Supply Chain Optimization with SAP ERP + IoT

Walmart uses MAS to connect IoT sensors, SAP ERP, and forecasting systems for dynamic inventory management.

## Architecture Diagram (Described)

- **Data Sources**: IoT shelf sensors, SAP ERP, supplier APIs.
- **Integration Layer**: Kafka streams broadcasting "StockLow" and "OrderCreated" events.
- **Agent Layer**: InventoryAgent predicts demand; OrderAgent triggers replenishment; WasteAgent flags overstock.
- **Governance Layer**: Dashboard with KPIs for waste reduction and fulfillment SLAs.

## Quantified Outcome

- Stockouts were reduced to less than 2%.
- Waste due to overstock was reduced by 18%.

**Executive Quote**

"Agents ensure shelves are stocked and waste is minimized, all while reducing human intervention."
- Walmart Supply Chain VP.

**Lesson**: Event-driven MAS excel in real-time supply chain optimization.

## 4.4.6 Siemens Energy – Predictive Maintenance with IoT MAS

Siemens deployed MAS for predictive maintenance of turbines and industrial assets.

### Architecture Diagram (Described)

- **Data Sources**: IoT telemetry, vibration sensors, SCADA logs.
- **Integration Layer**: Real-time streaming with anomaly detection.
- **Agent Layer**: MaintenanceAgent predicts failures; SchedulerAgent allocates technicians; ProcurementAgent orders spare parts.
- **Governance Layer**: Cost dashboard tracking downtime savings.

### Quantified Outcome

- 12% reduction in maintenance costs.
- Downtime reduced by 20%.

### Executive Quote

"Agents are the difference between reacting to breakdowns and preventing them." - Siemens CTO.

**Lesson**: MAS brings measurable value in high-capital, IoT-driven industries.

## 4.4.7 DARPA OFFSET – Multi-Agent Swarms in Defense

DARPA's OFFSET program demonstrated agent swarms for tactical coordination in urban operations.

## Architecture Diagram (Described)

- **Data Sources**: Sensor arrays, UAV telemetry.
- **Integration Layer**: Federated communication protocols, edge computing nodes.
- **Agent Layer**: ReconAgent, LogisticsAgent, CommandAgent.
- **Governance Layer**: Human-in-the-loop override and mission dashboard.

## Quantified Outcome

- Swarms of 250+ agents coordinated with sub-second latency.

## Executive Quote

"OFFSET shows the power of MAS under real-world constraints." = DARPA Program Manager.

**Lesson**: Defense MAS highlights federated architectures with strict governance and edge integration.

## 4.4.8 Tanium / CrowdStrike – Endpoint Security MAS

Cybersecurity firms use MAS to triage threats in SOCs (Security Operations Centers).

## Architecture Diagram (Described)

- **Data Sources**: Endpoint telemetry, SIEM logs.
- **Integration Layer**: Event bus distributing alerts.
- **Agent Layer**: ThreatAgent detects anomalies; ResponseAgent isolates devices; ComplianceAgent logs for audit.
- **Governance Layer**: SLA metrics for mean-time-to-detect (MTTD) and mean-time-to-respond (MTTR).

## Quantified Outcome

- 60% faster MTTD and 40% faster MTTR.

## Executive Quote

"Agents cut through noise, ensuring analysts focus only on credible threats." - CrowdStrike CTO.

**Lesson**: MAS thrives in high-volume, real-time detection and response environments.

### 4.4.9 Maersk – Port Logistics MAS

Maersk integrated MAS to optimize container movements and port scheduling.

### Architecture Diagram (Described)

- **Data Sources**: Port IoT sensors, shipping manifests, customs systems.
- **Integration Layer**: Event-driven scheduling engine.
- **Agent Layer**: DockingAgent, CustomsAgent, LogisticsAgent.
- **Governance Layer**: Dashboard tracking vessel turnaround times.

### Quantified Outcome

- 15% faster port turnaround.
- Improved global logistics efficiency.

### Executive Quote

"MAS keeps global trade moving efficiently in a world of volatility." - Maersk CIO.

**Lesson**: Orchestration across customs, logistics, and shipping requires secure, event-driven MAS.

### 4.4.10 Bank of America – Compliance Reporting and Fraud Detection MAS

Bank of America employs MAS for compliance reporting and fraud detection.

### Architecture Diagram (Described)

- **Data Sources**: Transactions, AML/KYC databases.
- **Integration Layer**: API-driven integration with regulatory bodies.
- **Agent Layer**: ComplianceAgent automates reporting; FraudAgent flags suspicious activity.
- **Governance Layer**: Audit logs and compliance dashboard.

### Quantified Outcome

- 25% reduction in compliance reporting costs.
- Improved fraud detection accuracy.

### Executive Quote

"Autonomous agents ensure compliance without ballooning operational costs." - Bank of America CTO.

**Lesson**: MAS can be embedded in regulated environments when auditability and compliance are prioritized.

---

## 4.5 Cutting-Edge Advancements (2023–2025)

- **Agentic RAG**: Integrating RAG with agents to enable dynamic retrieval; though the trend, many enterprises are shifting away from RAG due to centralized security risks.

- **Voice Agents, DeepResearch Agents, Coding Agents, CUA**: Diverse agent types emerging that specialize in multimodal interaction, deep analytics, code generation, etc.

- **Protocols**:

    o **MCP** is gaining traction as a secure agent–tool integration standard across platforms such as Azure, GitHub Copilot, and Microsoft and Anthropic SDKs.

  - o **A2A**, **ACP**, and **ANP** are maturing according to research proposing phased adoption and interoperability standards.

  - o **BlockA2A** adds further layers of zero-trust identity, auditability, and a defense orchestrator for secure MAS deployments.

- **Security and Governance Trends**: A shift away from RAG toward direct runtime agent queries supports stronger compliance; governance emphasis in agentic system design is rising.

- **Networking and Cybersecurity**: Agentic AI is now actively used in adaptive network management and proactive cybersecurity, enhancing resilience and policy enforcement.

---

## 4.6 Strategic Enterprise Guidance

### 4.6.1 Decision Frameworks

#### Integration Mode Decision Tree

- High real-time responsiveness and event-driven workflows → **Event-driven integration.**
- Interaction with structured business logic and CRUD systems → **API-driven integration.**
- Hybrid environments or legacy systems → **Hybrid approach** with mesh infrastructure.

#### Deployment Models

- **Cloud-native**: For scalability, elasticity, and microservices features.
- **On-premises/hybrid**: For data sovereignty, low-latency, or regulatory constraints.
- **Federated**: Cross-department autonomy with federated data access and messaging models.

## *4.6.2 ROI Modeling and Maturity Assessment*

### Sample ROI Metrics

- Compliance audit savings: percent reduction in manual audits (e.g., 50%).
- Operational efficiency: latency reduction in agent response or decision-making.
- Error mitigation: reduction in false positives (e.g., 95%).
- Scale: agent deployment count and coverage expansion over time (e.g., Accenture's trajectory).

### Maturity Checklist

- **Data readiness**: Unified data fabric, no silos, and governance control.
- **Infrastructure readiness**: Microservices, mesh, and observability, protocol support (MCP/A2A).
- **Governance readiness**: Audit trails, SLA dashboards, bias detection, and compliance mapping.

### Governance, Compliance, and Risk Management

- Align agent operations to relevant regulations: GDPR, HIPAA, EU AI Act.
- Embed auditing: BlockA2A for immutable logging, traceability.
- Implement SLA dashboards for performance, security, drift, and bias.
- Prepare for drift and adversarial agents with real-time defense orchestration (e.g., DOE in BlockA2A).

---

## 4.7 Key Takeaways

- A layered architecture (data, integration, orchestrator, agents, governance) enables clear separation of concerns and scalability.
- Microservices and federated patterns support agility, autonomy, and domain flexibility.

- Adoption of MCP/A2A and secure frameworks like BlockA2A is essential for interoperable and trustworthy agent networks. Agent-to-system integrations should leverage existing enterprise APIs and event streams rather than bypass them.
- Agent-to-agent coordination requires structured interfaces: messaging, shared context, orchestrated flows, and open protocols.
- Hybrid architectures (e.g., service meshes) enhance security and stability across agent networks.
- Resilience mechanisms (escalation, rollback, and remediation) prevent MAS failures from going unnoticed and ensure enterprise continuity.
- Cost allocation frameworks (agent-level, workflow-level, and predictive) are essential for justifying MAS adoption and for sustaining enterprise budgets.
- Together, resilience + cost attribution move MAS from "experimental pilots" to "enterprise-grade infrastructure."
- MAS delivers measurable ROI across domains: compliance, error reduction, monitoring, and operational scale.
- Architectures vary from single-use pipelines to orchestrated multi-agent systems coordinating multiple workflows.
- Platforms like agent OS reflect the enterprise shift toward systematic orchestration infrastructures.
- The agentic AI landscape is rapidly evolving with new agent types, protocols (MCP, A2A), and architectures emerging.
- Security-conscious enterprises favor runtime, agent-based architectures over centralized RAG to maintain compliance.
- Agentic AI now underpins advanced applications like network management and cybersecurity automation.
- Enterprise MAS adoption is accelerating, but only those with orchestration and integration strategies will unlock value.
- A layered architecture with microservices, federated patterns, and interoperability protocols underpins scalable MAS.
- Structured API/event/hybrid patterns and orchestrator-mediated coordination are essential for robust agent ecosystems.

- Real-world deployments (Akira AI, JPMorgan, Accenture, PwC) deliver quantifiable benefits.
- New agent types, secure protocols (MCP, BlockA2A), and governance models are shaping MAS architecture paradigms.
- Enterprises need decision frameworks, ROI modeling, and embedded governance to safely deploy MAS at scale.

## 4.8 Discussion Questions / Exercises

- **Architectural Exercise**: Map your enterprise's data and system landscape. Which integration pattern (API, event, or direct connector) best enables agents across domains such as finance, operations, and IT?
- **Governance Challenge**: Design SLA metrics, audit trails, and a dashboard concept for your agent orchestration layer. How would you monitor drift, bias, or SLA violations?
- **Protocol Assessment**: Evaluate whether MCP, A2A, or security frameworks like BlockA2A would fit your environment. What are the trade-offs in complexity, governance, and interoperability?
- **Enterprise Readiness**: Assess your organization against the maturity checklist for data readiness, infrastructure, and governance. What are the top three gaps to address for MAS adoption?

As agent architectures grow more modular and data integration becomes increasingly seamless, the next leap in enterprise AI is driven by cognitive scale. Chapter 5 explores how Large Language Models (LLMs) are reshaping agentic systems, transforming them from orchestrated frameworks into intelligent, decision-making collaborators.

# CHAPTER 5

# LLMs and Conversational Agent Platforms

The integration of Large Language Models (LLMs) into enterprise systems marks a transformative shift in how organizations leverage AI for operational excellence, decision-making, and competitive advantage. LLMs, such as GPT-4o, Claude 3.5, and Llama 3, have evolved from conversational tools into the cognitive core of agentic systems, enabling autonomous reasoning, multi-step workflows, and seamless integration with enterprise ecosystems. Today, these models are no longer experimental curiosities but critical components driving automation across finance, healthcare, manufacturing, and beyond.

Deloitte's 2025 AI Enterprise Report highlights that organizations adopting LLM-powered agents achieve 25–40% improvements in operational efficiency, yet only 30% have scaled beyond pilots due to challenges in integration, governance, and data security. PwC's 2025 Global AI Survey notes that 65% of executives view LLM integration as essential for maintaining competitive advantage amid economic volatility and regulatory pressures, such as the EU AI Act and GDPR. TechRadar Pro (2025) emphasizes that the shift from standalone LLMs to orchestrated agent platforms is critical for realizing measurable ROI, moving from text generation to governed, actionable outcomes.

Adoption varies by sector, with key insights from recent analyses:

- **Finance**: Accenture's 2025 Banking AI Outlook reports 55% of global financial institutions have deployed LLMs for compliance, fraud detection, and customer onboarding, with 70% planning increased investments by 2027.

- **Healthcare**: PwC's 2025 Health AI Index indicates 45% adoption for clinical workflows, patient triage, and research acceleration, with North America leading at 52%.

- **Manufacturing**: Deloitte's 2025 Manufacturing AI Report notes 52% adoption for predictive maintenance and supply chain optimization, driven by IoT integration.

- **Cross-Industry**: PwC's Global AI Barometer shows overall LLM adoption at 28% in 2025, projected to reach 50% by 2027, with integration complexity and compliance cited as primary barriers.

The urgency to adopt LLM-powered agents stems from their ability to address enterprise pain points: cost reduction, regulatory compliance, and agility in dynamic markets. As TechRadar Pro (2025) notes, enterprises are moving away from Retrieval-Augmented Generation (RAG) toward agent-based architectures that query data in place, respect access controls, and enhance security.

As LLMs become central to enterprise strategy, the next step is to understand the technical architecture that enables agentic intelligence. Section 5.1 explores the core mechanics, the definitions, agent types, and deployment models that turn conversational AI into operational infrastructure.

# 5.1 Core Technical Depth

## 5.1.1 Definitions and Taxonomy

Large Language Models (LLMs) are transformer-based neural networks trained on vast datasets to generate human-like text, reason over complex inputs, and perform tasks like summarization, code generation, and decision-making. In enterprise agentic systems, LLMs serve as the reasoning engine, augmented by orchestration frameworks, external tools, and memory systems for context persistence. The taxonomy of LLM-powered agents aligns with Chapter 2's agent classifications, adapted for enterprise contexts:

| Agent Type | Core Ascendant | Decision-Making | Strengths | Limitations | Use Cases | Technologies |
|---|---|---|---|---|---|---|
| **Reactive** | Immediate response to input | Prompt-based | Fast, simple | Limited reasoning | Customer queries | Basic LLM inference |
| **Deliberative** | Multi-step planning and reasoning | Chain-of-thought | Strategic, explainable | Slower, resource-heavy | Workflow automation | LangGraph, CrewAI |
| **Hybrid** | Combines LLM reasoning with external tools | Utility-driven | Versatile, grounded | Integration complexity | Data-driven tasks | RAG, API connectors |
| **Multi-Modal** | Processes text, vision, or voice | Fusion-based | Contextual, rich | High compute needs | Diagnostics, chatbots | GPT-4o, Claude 3.5 |

Table 5: Core Definitions and Taxonomy.

Table 5 compares four types of LLM-powered agents: Reactive, Deliberative, Hybrid, and Multi-Modal, highlighting their decision-making styles, strengths, limitations, and enterprise use cases. This taxonomy provides a practical framework for selecting agent architectures aligned with operational needs and technical constraints.

## 5.1.2 Centralized versus Federated LLM Architectures

To evaluate deployment strategies for LLM-powered agents, enterprises must weigh the trade-offs between centralized and federated architectures. Especially in compliance-heavy environments where governance, scalability, and resilience are paramount. The following table contrasts the pros and cons of these architectures:

Table 6 illustrates the trade-offs between centralized and federated LLM architectures, particularly in compliance-heavy industries. Centralized models offer streamlined governance and simplified auditing but face scalability and adaptability challenges. Federated approaches enhance resilience and data sovereignty yet introduce complexity in synchronization and policy enforcement. This comparison helps guide architectural decisions based on regulatory demands, operational scale, and enterprise priorities.

| Architecture Type | Description | Pros | Cons |
| --- | --- | --- | --- |
| Centralized | LLM inference consolidated on platforms like Azure OpenAI or AWS Bedrock, with unified governance and auditing. | Unified compliance enforcement Simplified auditing and security Streamlined incident response | Scalability bottlenecks Single-point failure risks Limited adaptability to regional regulations |
| Federated | Agents distributed across domains (e.g., edge devices, regional nodes), enabling localized compliance and data sovereignty. | Localized compliance and policy adaptation Enhanced resilience and availability Improved data sovereignty for multinational operations | Complex governance and audit trails Risk of inconsistent standards across domains Higher integration costs |

Table 6: Centralized versus Federated LLM Architectures in Compliance-Heavy Enterprises.

## 5.1.3 Architectural Components

A robust enterprise LLM architecture comprises:

- **Reasoning Layer**: LLM inference with prompting strategies (e.g., chain-of-thought, few-shot learning).
- **Orchestration Layer:** Frameworks like LangGraph, CrewAI, or AutoGen for task decomposition and routing.
- **Integration Layer**: API gateways and event buses (e.g., Kafka, Azure Event Hub) for system connectivity.
- **Data Layer**: Knowledge bases, vector databases (e.g., Pinecone), and data warehouses for grounded responses.
- **Governance Layer**: Guardrails, SLA monitoring, and audit logs for compliance and performance.

Figure 24 illustrates the flow of data through an enterprise LLM system, from user or system triggers to reasoning, orchestration, integration, data access, and governance. It highlights key components like prompt builders, guardrails, API gateways, vector databases, and observability hooks, ensuring secure, scalable, and compliant operations.

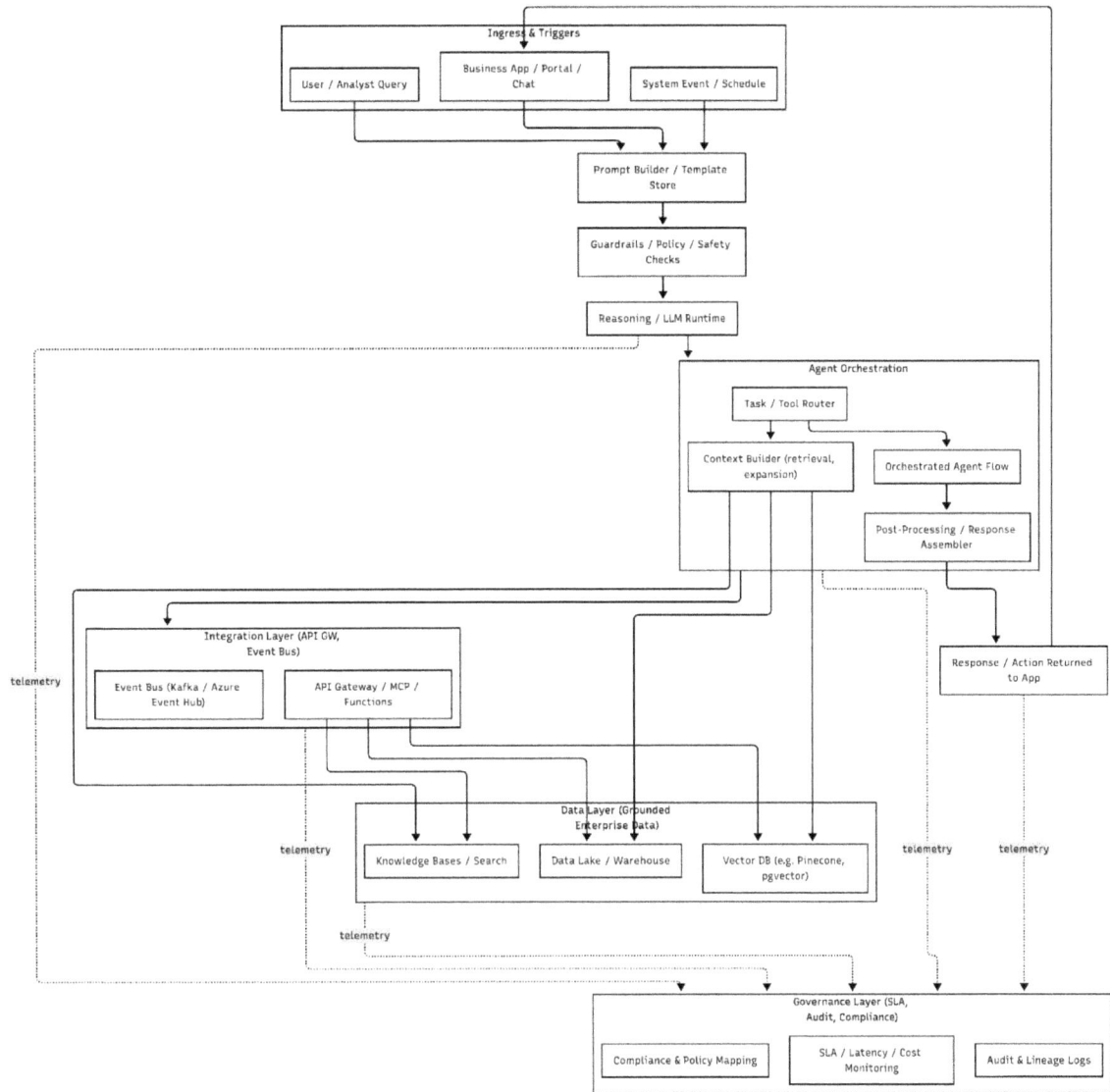

Figure 24: End-to-End Enterprise LLM Data Flow.

## 5.2 Integration Patterns

Enterprise LLM agents integrate via three primary patterns, consistent with Chapter 4's multi-agent system (MAS) frameworks:

- **Agent-to-System**: Secure API gateways connect LLMs to enterprise systems (e.g., SAP, Salesforce) for data access and updates.

- **Agent-to-Agent**: Event-driven buses (e.g., Kafka, RabbitMQ) enable asynchronous collaboration between agents.

- **Hybrid**: Combines LLM reasoning with legacy systems and human oversight, using middleware for seamless data flow.

## 5.2.1 Graph-Based Workflows

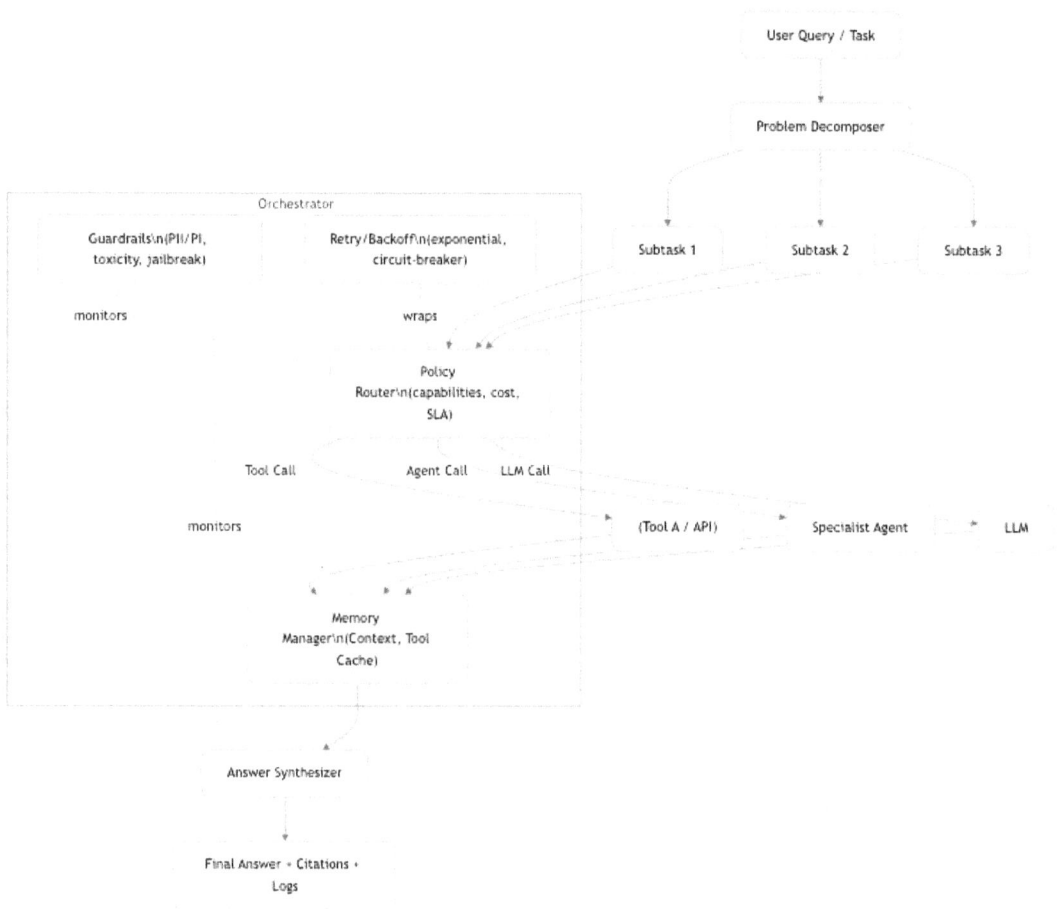

Figure 25: Multi-step Orchestration Pipeline for LLM-Powered Agents.

Figure 25 illustrates a multi-step orchestration pipeline for LLM-powered agents, detailing how user queries are decomposed, routed, and resolved through a combination of tools, specialist agents, and language models. The diagram emphasizes the role of guardrails, retry logic, and policy routing in ensuring safe, cost-effective, and SLA-compliant execution. Memory management preserves context across subtasks, while the final output includes synthesized answers, citations, and observability logs, demonstrating how enterprise-grade agentic systems achieve both operational precision and governance.

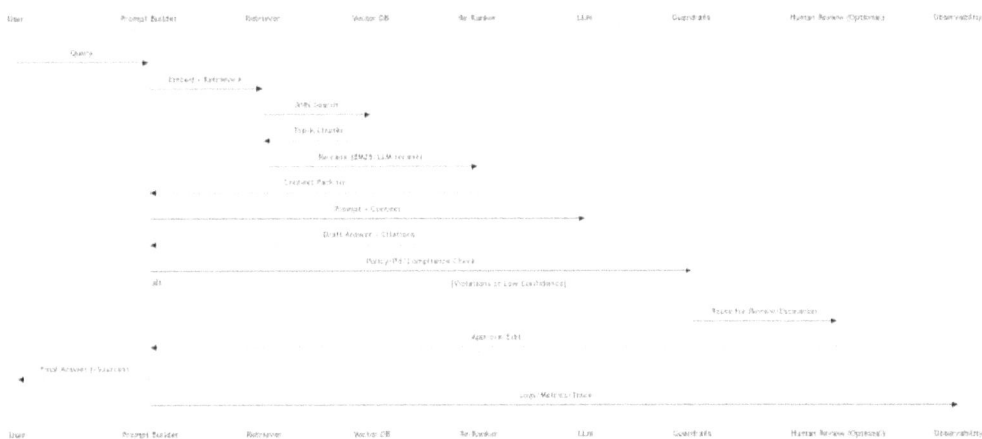

Figure 26: RAG + Guardrails Response Pipeline.

Figure 26 outlines a Retrieval-Augmented Generation pipeline enhanced with guardrails and optional human review, illustrating how enterprise systems generate reliable, compliant responses. The flow begins with a user query, which is embedded and retrieved from a vector database, re-ranked for relevance, and passed to an LLM for draft generation. Guardrails assess the output for policy violations or low confidence, triggering human review when necessary. Observability mechanisms log each step, ensuring traceability and auditability across the entire response lifecycle.

This section outlines three primary integration patterns for enterprise LLM agents: agent-to-system, agent-to-agent, and hybrid. Each pattern reflects a distinct approach to embedding LLM capabilities within existing enterprise ecosystems, balancing automation, scalability, and compliance. Supporting diagrams illustrate multi-step orchestration pipelines and Retrieval-Augmented

Generation (RAG) workflows, emphasizing the role of guardrails, memory management, and observability in ensuring safe, auditable operations. Together, these patterns form the backbone of scalable, governed agentic systems.

With integration patterns established, the next step is seeing how they perform in the real world. Section 5.3 presents case studies from leading enterprises that showcase how agentic architectures deliver measurable impact across healthcare, finance, manufacturing, and more.

## 5.3 Case Studies

### 5.3.1 Pfizer and Microsoft – Healthcare R&D

Pfizer deployed Azure OpenAI to accelerate drug discovery by integrating LLMs with research databases.

**Architecture Diagram (Described)**: Queries flow through a prompt builder to Azure OpenAI's reasoning layer, augmented by RAG pipelines querying proprietary datasets. Guardrails enforce IP protection and HIPAA compliance.

**Quantified Outcome**: Reduced data retrieval time by 75%, accelerating R&D cycles by 30%.

**Executive Quote**: "LLMs have transformed our research velocity, enabling faster hypothesis testing." – Pfizer CTO.

**Lesson Learned**: RAG integration grounds LLM outputs in domain-specific data, enhancing accuracy and compliance.

### 5.3.2 HSBC – Financial Services Compliance

HSBC implemented LLM-powered compliance assistants fine-tuned on regulatory corpora and transaction logs.

**Architecture Diagram (Described)**: CrewAI orchestrates fine-tuned LLMs, with API gateways connecting to compliance systems and audit logs ensuring traceability.

**Quantified Outcome**: 30% reduction in compliance query handling costs; 20% faster regulatory reporting.

**Executive Quote**: "Agents deliver scalable, accurate compliance, reducing manual overhead." – HSBC CIO.

**Lesson Learned**: Fine-tuning on proprietary data minimizes hallucinations in regulated environments.

### 5.3.3 Siemens – Manufacturing Maintenance

Siemens built conversational copilots for predictive maintenance, integrating with PLM and ERP systems.

**Architecture Diagram (Described)**: Multi-modal agents on Vertex AI process IoT sensor data, routing maintenance recommendations to ERP systems, with SLA monitoring for performance.

**Quantified Outcome**: 25% improvement in equipment uptime; 15% reduction in maintenance costs.

**Executive Quote**: "Conversational agents optimize operations with real-time insights." – Siemens VP of Engineering.

**Lesson Learned**: Tool integration transforms LLM reasoning into actionable maintenance decisions.

### 5.3.4 JPMorgan – Fraud Detection

JPMorgan enhanced fraud detection by using LLM agents to query transaction databases.

**Architecture Diagram (Described)**: AWS Bedrock-hosted LLMs in a hybrid setup, with RAG for real-time data access and observability for auditability.

**Quantified Outcome**: 35% faster anomaly detection; 95% reduction in false positives.

**Executive Quote**: "LLMs provide explainable fraud insights, enhancing trust and efficiency." – JPMorgan Head of Risk.

**Lesson Learned**: Observability ensures traceability in high-stakes financial applications.

## 5.3.5 Mayo Clinic – Clinical Decision Support

Mayo Clinic piloted LLM agents for patient triage and clinical decision support.

**Architecture Diagram (Described)**: Federated architecture with HIPAA-compliant RAG pipelines on Azure, orchestrated via LangGraph, with human-in-the-loop for high-risk cases.

**Quantified Outcome**: 40% reduction in triage processing time; 10% improvement in patient satisfaction.

**Executive Quote**: "Agents augment clinician expertise safely, improving care delivery." – Mayo Clinic CIO.

**Lesson Learned**: Guardrails and human oversight mitigate risks in healthcare applications.

## 5.4 Cutting-Edge Advancements (2023–2025)

As enterprise adoption of LLM agents matures, the pace of innovation continues to accelerate. Between 2023 and 2025, several breakthroughs have reshaped how organizations deploy, govern, and scale agentic systems. These advancements span model capabilities, fine-tuning efficiency, interoperability protocols, and security frameworks, each contributing to more powerful, compliant, and cost-effective AI operations.

## Multi-Modal Intelligence

- **GPT-4o (2024)**: Combines text and vision capabilities, enabling agents to interpret diagrams, documents, and visual inputs for richer diagnostics and contextual understanding.
- **Claude 3.5 (2025)**: Adds voice interaction, expanding use cases to real-time support, voice-enabled copilots, and multimodal chatbots.
- Together, these models unlock new interfaces for enterprise agents, bridging the gap between human and machine collaboration across modalities.

## Security, Governance, and Compliance

- **Runtime Querying**: Enterprises are shifting from Retrieval-Augmented Generation (RAG) to runtime querying, which allows agents to access data in place without duplicating or exposing sensitive information. Enhancing compliance with GDPR, HIPAA, and the EU AI Act.
- **BlockA2A (2024)**: Introduces blockchain-based auditability for agent-to-agent interactions, supporting zero-trust environments and immutable logging.
- **Defense Orchestration (2025)**: Real-time adversarial risk mitigation frameworks now integrate with LLM pipelines, enabling proactive threat detection and drift prevention.

These innovations reinforce the enterprise imperative for secure, traceable, and policy-aligned AI operations.

## Interoperability and Agent Protocols

- **MCP 2.0 (2025)**: The Multi-Agent Communication Protocol standardizes secure tool invocation across platforms like Azure, GitHub Copilot, and LangGraph, enabling seamless orchestration across heterogeneous systems.

Protocol-level interoperability ensures that agents can collaborate across tools, vendors, and environments without compromising governance or performance.

**Networking and Infrastructure Resilience**

- **Adaptive Network Management**: LLM agents now support dynamic routing, load balancing, and proactive fault detection in enterprise networks, improving resilience by up to 30% (Accenture, 2025).

This shift positions agents not just as reasoning engines, but as infrastructure-aware collaborators capable of optimizing digital ecosystems in real time.

With these advancements shaping the technical frontier, enterprises face a new challenge: making informed, strategic decisions about how to deploy agentic systems. Section 5.5 offers actionable guidance: frameworks, models, and governance strategies to align integration choices with operational goals and regulatory demands.

---

# 5.5 Strategic Enterprise Guidance

As agentic systems mature, enterprises must move beyond experimentation and toward disciplined deployment. This section provides actionable frameworks for integration, deployment, ROI modeling, and governance. This ensures that LLM-powered agents align with operational priorities, regulatory mandates, and long-term scalability.

## 5.5.1 Integration Decision Frameworks

Choosing the right integration mode depends on workload characteristics, system architecture, and compliance needs. The following decision tree outlines three primary modes:

- **Event-Driven Integration**: Ideal for real-time, high-throughput workflows such as fraud detection or network monitoring. Agents respond to triggers via event buses (e.g., Kafka, RabbitMQ), enabling asynchronous execution and scalability.
- **API-Driven Integration**: Best suited for structured business logic and CRUD operations, such as compliance reporting or customer onboarding. Agents interact with enterprise systems via secure API gateways (e.g., SAP and Salesforce).

- **Hybrid Integration**: Combines LLM reasoning with legacy systems and human oversight. Middleware ensures seamless data flow while preserving manual checkpoints. Ideal for clinical triage or regulated decision support.

## 5.5.2 Deployment Models

Deployment choices reflect trade-offs between scalability, latency, and data sovereignty. Enterprises typically choose among:

- **Cloud-Native Platforms**: Offer elasticity and rapid scaling (e.g., AWS Bedrock, Azure OpenAI). Suitable for global operations with centralized governance.
- **On-Premises or Hybrid Models**: Prioritize data control and low-latency access, especially in healthcare, defense, or financial services. Hybrid setups balance cloud flexibility with local compliance.
- **Federated Architectures**: Enable multi-region autonomy with synchronized governance. Agents operate across edge devices or regional nodes, supporting localized compliance and resilience.

## 5.5.3 ROI Modeling and Maturity Assessment

To justify investment and guide scaling, organizations must quantify impact and assess readiness.

### Sample ROI Metrics

- Compliance audit savings: 40% reduction in manual reviews.
- Operational efficiency: 25–75% reduction in process latency.
- Error mitigation: 90–95% reduction in false positives.
- Scale: Agent deployment growth (e.g., 100 to 1,000 agents in 18 months).

### Maturity Checklist

- **Data Readiness**: Unified data fabric, no silos, governed access.

- **Infrastructure Readiness**: GPU clusters, microservices, MCP/A2A support.
- **Governance Readiness**: Audit trails, SLA dashboards, compliance mappings.

## 5.5.4 Governance, Compliance, and Risk Management

Governance must be embedded from inception, not bolted on post-deployment. Key strategies include:

- Aligning with GDPR, HIPAA, SOX, and the EU AI Act through guardrails and audit logs.
- Embedding **BlockA2A** for immutable logging and traceability.
- Implementing SLA dashboards for latency, accuracy, and bias detection.
- Mitigating drift and adversarial risks via real-time defense orchestration.

With strategic frameworks and governance models in place, it's time to distill the chapter's core insights. Section 5.6 consolidates key takeaways across technical depth, integration patterns, and enterprise impact, providing a clear reference point for decision-makers and practitioners alike.

---

## 5.6 Key Takeaways

- ROI Proven: Agentic and LLM architectures deliver 25–75% time savings and 15–50% cost reductions across industries.
- Governance First: Traceability, compliance, and domain adaptation are essential for scalable enterprise AI.
- Secure Integration: Agent-to-system patterns rely on event-driven APIs for safe, auditable data access.
- Balanced Control: Hybrid models pair automation with human oversight to ensure trust and accountability.
- Architectural Resilience: Federated and layered stacks enhance scalability, sovereignty, and observability.
- LLMs as Reasoning Cores: Fine-tuned LLMs power adaptive reasoning but require orchestration and governance.

- Compliance by Design: Runtime querying and protocols like MCP and BlockA2A strengthen auditability.

- Cross-Industry Adoption: Finance (55%), Healthcare (45%), and Manufacturing (52%) lead in agentic deployment.

- Enterprise Integration: Multi-modal LLMs and API-driven frameworks align AI agents with business workloads.

- Strategic Imperative: Governance, ROI modeling, and scalable orchestration define competitive success by 2027.

## 5.7 Discussion Questions / Exercises

1    **Workflow Mapping Exercise**: Identify three enterprise workflows where LLM agents could reduce manual effort by >30%. Describe the tasks, data sources, and expected outcomes.

2    **Architecture Review**: Sketch your organization's API/data flow and identify where an LLM reasoning layer could be embedded, specifying integration points and the tools used.

3    **Compliance Risk Assessment**: List applicable compliance frameworks (e.g., GDPR, HIPAA, SOX) and evaluate whether your conversational agent design includes sufficient guardrails.

4    **ROI Calculation**: Develop a FinOps model to project annual GPU/API costs versus labor/time savings, using metrics such as audit reductions or latency improvements.

As Large Language Models become the cognitive core of enterprise AI, their true impact depends not just on reasoning, but on coordination. Chapter 6 explores how agentic workflow orchestration transforms isolated intelligence into synchronized execution. Aligning autonomous agents with enterprise goals, timing, and governance.

# CHAPTER 6

# Agentic Workflow Orchestration

Modern enterprises increasingly depend on intelligent agents to perform reasoning, prediction, and decision support across highly distributed environments. Yet even the most capable agents cannot operate in isolation. They require coordination, governance, and resilience.

*An orchestration layer converts individual reasoning into collective intelligence.*

Agentic Workflow Orchestration is, therefore, the connective tissue of the enterprise AI stack. It coordinates autonomous components, aligns their goals with organizational intent, and ensures that every agent executes tasks in the right order, at the right time, with the right data.

Earlier generations of workflow automation were linear and deterministic: one system called another in a fixed chain. By 2025, however, enterprises began adopting Multi-Agent Orchestration (MAO) platforms that enabled adaptive scheduling, contextual awareness, and policy-driven decision-making. Gartner (2025) projects that by 2027, half of all organizations deploying generative or reasoning AI will operate at least one orchestrated multi-agent pipeline. Deloitte's AI Enterprise Report notes that orchestration maturity correlates directly with RO. Companies with coordinated agent workflows achieve 40% higher automation efficiency than those using isolated bots.

Across industries, the momentum is clear:

- **Finance**: In financial services, orchestrated agents conduct anti-fraud checks, manage compliance reporting, and reconcile transactions in real time. These systems reduce latency and ensure auditability across regulatory frameworks.
- **Healthcare**: Within healthcare networks, orchestration aligns diagnostic workflows, billing operations, and research coordination, allowing secure information exchange while maintaining patient privacy and HIPAA compliance.
- **Manufacturing**: In manufacturing environments, distributed orchestration synchronizes sensors, robots, and analytics at the industrial edge, supporting predictive maintenance and adaptive production lines.

---

*Orchestration has become the invisible conductor of digital transformation.*
*A discipline of systems thinking, software engineering, and governance fused into one.*

---

## 6.1 Core Technical Foundations

### 6.1.1 The Role of the Orchestrator

In an agentic system, the Orchestrator mediates between intent and execution. It interprets a high-level plan often produced by a large-language-model planner (Chapter 5) and transforms it into a directed set of executable tasks. Each task is then assigned to the most capable agent or service. The orchestrator enforces order, dependencies, and policy compliance, ensuring that local autonomy does not compromise global coherence.

### 6.1.2 Directed Acyclic Graphs (DAGs) as the Execution Model

The canonical structure for representing these relationships is the Directed Acyclic Graph (DAG). A DAG encodes tasks as nodes and dependencies as edges, guaranteeing that execution proceeds forward without cycles. In agentic systems, each node can represent a reasoning step, data transformation, or API call. DAGs are preferred because they make workflow logic transparent, auditable, and parallelizable.

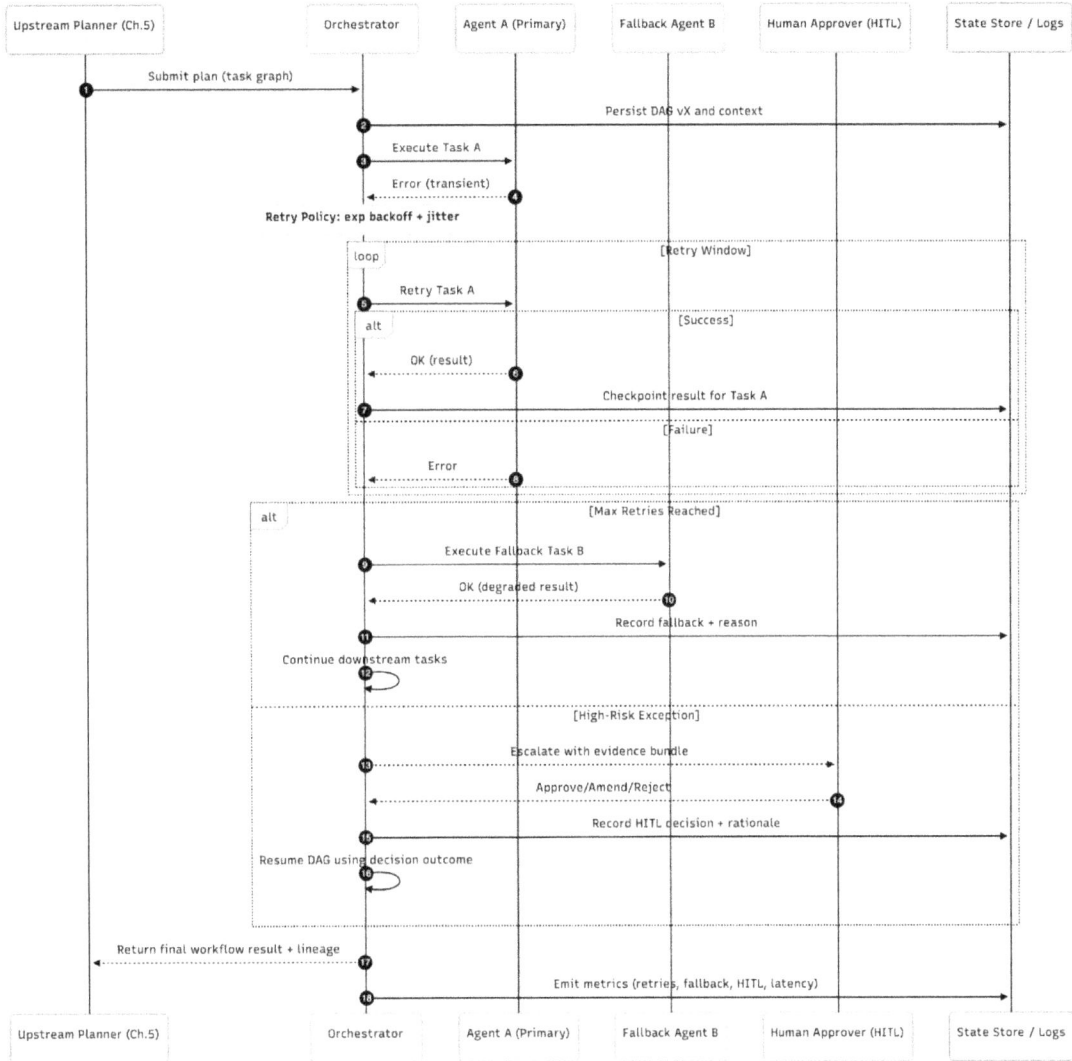

Figure 27: Orchestration DAG Lifecycle.

Figure 27 traces the conversion of a high-level plan into a resilient execution path. The orchestrator persists the DAG and delegates an initial task (Task A) to the primary agent. Transient errors trigger a retry window governed by exponential backoff with jitter, preventing thundering herd effects. When retries are exhausted, the workflow follows one of two controlled branches: a degraded but safe fallback to an alternate agent, or a HITL escalation for high-risk exceptions, where a human approves, amends, or rejects with a recorded rationale. Checkpoints, lineage, and metrics (retries, fallbacks, HITL, latency) are continuously written to state and observability systems so execution can resume deterministically and improvements can be learned over time.

## 6.1.3 Architectural Layers

A well-engineered orchestration stack typically contains five layers:

- **Infrastructure Layer**: Cloud-native microservices (Kubernetes and Docker) providing scalability and fault isolation.
- **Coordination Layer**: Message brokers (Kafka and RabbitMQ) for asynchronous communication between agents.
- **State Management Layer**: Persistence stores (Redis, PostgreSQL, and vector DBs) retaining agent context and checkpointing results.
- **Agent Layer**: Specialized executors: compliance, forecasting, and security communicating through standardized APIs or the MCP/A2A protocols.
- **Governance Layer**: Dashboards, audit logs, and policy enforcement providing visibility and accountability.

These layers create separation of concerns while maintaining end-to-end traceability. While these layers define the structural anatomy of an orchestration stack, how they are deployed across an enterprise environment varies significantly. The next consideration is architectural topology, specifically, whether orchestration is centralized for unified control or federated for distributed autonomy.

## 6.1.4 Centralized versus Federated Models

Centralized orchestration platforms (e.g., AWS Step Functions and Temporal) excel at governance and uniform policy control but can create bottlenecks. Federated orchestration distributes coordination across domains or geographies, enhancing resilience and data sovereignty but introducing synchronization challenges.

> *Most enterprises adopt a **hybrid approach**, keeping compliance-sensitive logic centralized while delegating operational workloads to regional orchestrators.*

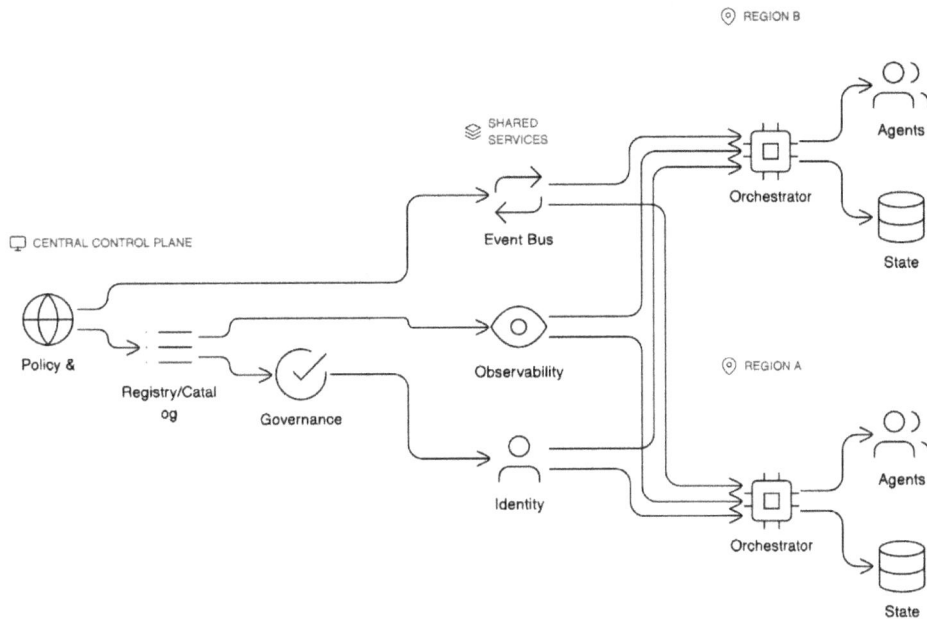

Figure 28: Hybrid Orchestration Architecture

## 6.1.5 Hybrid Orchestration Architecture

This architecture shows a central control plane that distributes policy, capability metadata, and governance while regional orchestrators execute workloads close to data and users. Shared services like message bus, identity/secrets, and observability provide standardized plumbing for secure, auditable coordination. Regional domains host specialized agents and local state stores, enabling low-latency operation and data-sovereign processing. Policies and registries flow top-down to ensure conformance; metrics and traces flow bottom-up to close the loop on SLOs, cost/FinOps, and compliance. Results are delivered to enterprise applications, giving a single pane of glass without sacrificing regional autonomy.

## 6.2 Failure Management and Resilience

Reliability is paramount in any orchestration framework. Unlike deterministic pipelines, agentic workflows must anticipate partial failures, network latency, and probabilistic model behavior:

- **Retry Mechanisms**: When a task fails due to transient issues (e.g., API timeouts, token limits), the orchestrator triggers a retry policy. This is often an exponential back-off with jitter to prevent cascading load. Metrics such as retry count, interval, and success ratio after retry, feed directly into operational dashboards.

- **Fallback Paths**: If retries are exhausted, the DAG diverts execution to a fallback task, an alternate agent, or a simplified heuristic. For example, a failed deep learning forecast might revert to a rule-based estimator, ensuring continuity rather than termination. Fallbacks represent design humility: the recognition that "good enough and complete" is often superior to "perfect but stalled."

- **Human-in-the-Loop (HITL) Escalation**: Certain high-risk failures, such as financial transactions, medical diagnoses, or security incidents, demand human oversight. When a predefined risk threshold is exceeded, the orchestrator suspends execution and routes the task to a human approver. Once reviewed, results are reintegrated into the DAG so that learning systems can refine future behavior.

- **Observability and Feedback Loops**: Resilience is inseparable from observability. Logs, metrics, and traces feed monitoring dashboards (e.g., Grafana, Prometheus), enabling real-time anomaly detection and adaptive optimization. Observability data also trains meta-agents that predict failure patterns and propose pipeline adjustments.

## 6.3 Case Study: Scaling Claims Processing with Agentic Orchestration

### 6.3.1 Background

Alight, a global leader in human capital and benefits services serving over 4,300 clients, including 70% of the Fortune 100, faced a claims processing challenge. The company handled approximately twenty million claims annually, with nearly six million still processed manually. This manual load caused delays, higher operational costs, and inconsistent customer experiences. Fragmented rule sets and legacy systems required over two hundred staff members to manage workflows, resulting in more than half a million customer inquiries each year.

## 6.3.2 Challenge

The claims process was constrained by legacy systems that lacked orchestration and adaptability. Each rules engine operated in isolation, creating bottlenecks when exceptions occurred. Management sought a unified orchestration layer that could dynamically route claims, consistently apply business logic, and escalate edge cases through human-in-the-loop oversight to preserve compliance and quality.

## 6.3.3 Solution Architecture

Alight partnered with Automation Anywhere and AWS AI Services to design an agentic orchestration solution centered on Automation Anywhere's Process Reasoning Engine (PRE). PRE coordinates multiple automation agents that understand workflows and make context-sensitive decisions without brittle scripting. The architecture integrated several layers:

- **Process Reasoning Engine (PRE)**: Served as the orchestrator, decomposing complex claim-handling workflows into modular tasks and coordinating them across agents.

- **Automation Co-Pilot**: Embedded human-in-the-loop (HITL) functionality, allowing staff to intervene during exceptions and approve or reject claims in real time.

- **AWS AI Stack**: Amazon Textract extracted structured data from claim documents, while Amazon Comprehend provided natural language understanding to categorize and validate claims.

- **Integration Layer**: API-driven connections integrated PRE outputs with Alight's ERP and CRM systems, enabling straight-through processing and reducing latency.

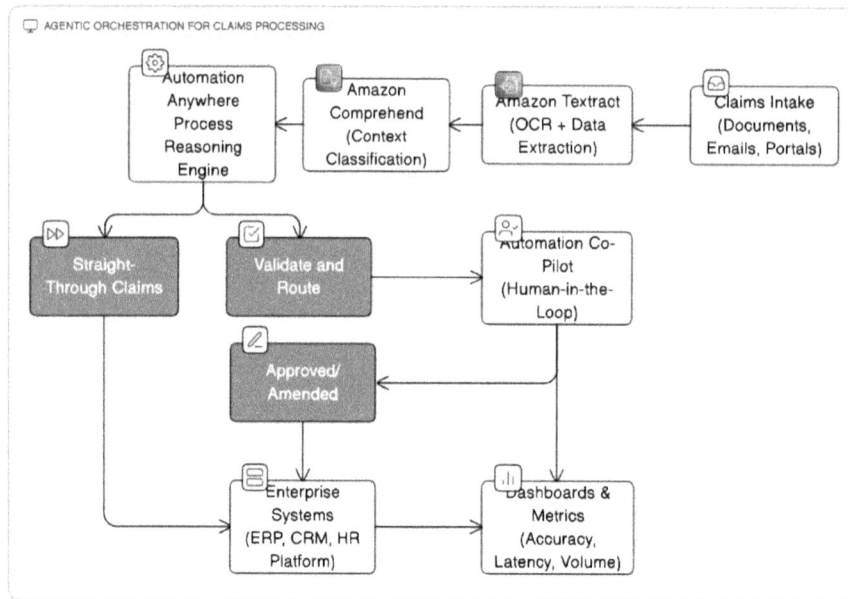

Figure 29: Agentic Orchestration Architecture for Claims Processing (Verified). Source: Automation Anywhere and AWS (2025), "Alight cuts claims processing from days to hours with AI agents."

The reconciliation pipeline begins with batch ingestion and partitioning, then validates records against schema, control totals, FX rules, and cutoffs. Validation failures are retried under an explicit policy; persistent errors route to a fallback rule engine that provides bounded, explainable outcomes. Matched items proceed straight through to posting, while high-risk exceptions trigger HITL review with an evidence bundle attached. Human decisions (approve/amend/reject) are captured and the DAG resumes accordingly. Every step emits metrics to dashboards and writes an immutable audit trail for regulatory reporting, enabling faster end-of-day close with full traceability and controlled operational risk.

## 6.3.4 Results

Deployment of the PRE-based orchestration transformed claims management within eight weeks. The program achieved 95% accuracy in claims validation and a sixfold improvement in processing speed, reducing cycle times from three days to under one. Customer call volume dropped by 50% due to faster payouts and greater transparency. These measurable gains demonstrated the value of orchestrated AI governance and automation convergence.

## 6.3.5 Lessons Learned

Alight's experience illustrates that orchestration delivers the greatest value when paired with governance and HITL oversight. Automation Anywhere's PRE allowed Alight to unify rule-based and intelligent automation within a single orchestrated framework. By embedding human checks for exceptions, the system balanced autonomy with compliance, achieving both operational efficiency and trustworthiness. As Vineet Kumar, a senior leader at Automation Anywhere, noted, "PRE enables agents to understand complex workflows and make intelligent decisions without relying on brittle scripts." The case underscores how agentic orchestration scales reliably across regulated enterprise environments, combining AI-driven precision with human judgment.

## 6.4 Metrics and Implementation Guidance

| Category | Example Metric | Typical Target | Interpretation |
|---|---|---|---|
| Reliability | Success Rate after Retries | ≥ 98% | Indicates stability of transient failure handling. |
| Efficiency | Average Task Latency | < 1 s | Directly correlates with user experience and ROI. |
| Resilience | Fallback Activation Rate | < 5% | High rate may signal upstream quality issues. |
| Governance | HITL Intervention Rate | 2 – 5% | Balances automation with compliance control. |
| Financial | Cost per Transaction | –30% YoY | Measures economic benefit of orchestration. |

### Implementation priorities for CTOs

- Define measurable SLOs before deployment.
- Instrument every node in the DAG for observability.
- Simulate failure scenarios monthly.
- Automate rollback and versioning (see Chapter 8).

## 6.5 Strategic Enterprise Guidance

### 6.5.1 Integration Mode Decision Tree

Agentic orchestration can be configured in multiple integration modes depending on workload and responsiveness. In an event-driven model, the system reacts to real-time alerts such as cybersecurity breaches or IoT sensor events, ensuring minimal latency. An API-driven mode is better suited to structured, transactional environments such as finance and human resources, where well-defined interfaces guarantee consistency. A hybrid mode blends both approaches, enabling orchestration across legacy systems that still require human oversight or sequential approval.

### 6.5.2 Deployment Models

Enterprises also choose deployment models based on regulatory, operational, and scalability requirements. A cloud-native deployment leverages the elastic scaling capabilities of platforms such as AWS Step Functions or Google Cloud Composer. On-premises orchestration remains common in healthcare, defense, and other regulated sectors that require strict data residency and security controls. A federated deployment distributes orchestration responsibilities across multiple geographic regions, maintaining shared governance and localized autonomy.

Strategically, orchestration maturity becomes a competitive advantage. It transforms IT from a service provider into an intelligence platform that continuously optimizes itself.

## 6.6 Key Takeaways

- Orchestration converts autonomous agents into coherent, goal-aligned enterprises.
- DAGs are the canonical representation of workflow execution.
- Resilience mechanisms, retries, fallbacks, and HITL are mandatory, not optional.
- Observability and governance close the loop between autonomy and accountability.

- Real-world deployments (e.g., financial reconciliation) achieve 20–40% efficiency gains.
- Strategic design choices (centralized versus federated) must align with risk and regulation.

## 6.7 Discussion Questions / Exercises

1   **Conceptual Reflection**: How does agentic orchestration differ from traditional workflow automation? Discuss the implications for governance and accountability.

2   **Design Exercise**: Draft a simplified DAG for a three-stage customer-onboarding workflow. Specify where retries, fallbacks, and HITL interventions should occur.

3   **Scenario Analysis**: Imagine your orchestration system handles one million daily tasks with a 1% failure rate. Calculate how improving the success after retry from 80% to 95% affects overall throughput.

4   **Cross-Chapter Integration**: Using Chapter 5's LLM planner as the input layer, describe how your orchestrator (Chapter 6) would communicate with the state storage mechanisms of Chapter 7.

5   **Ethical Consideration**: When should a workflow orchestrator escalate to human review rather than automated fallback? Identify three governance criteria that trigger HITL involvement.

6   **Quantitative Exercise**: Build a simple ROI model using the metrics in Table 6.1. How does reducing average task latency from three seconds to one second affect cost per transaction and user experience?

7   **Implementation Challenge**: Propose a monitoring dashboard layout that summarizes retry rates, fallback usage, and HITL activity in real time. How would you visualize bottlenecks?

8   **Research Prompt**: Review open-source orchestration frameworks such as Airflow or LangGraph. Compare their handling of DAG versioning and failure recovery. Cite sources using APA style.

9   **Strategic Discussion**: Consider the trade-offs between centralized and federated orchestration for a global enterprise. Which model better balances control and resilience?

While orchestration enables agents to act in concert, true intelligence demands continuity. Chapter 7 explores how memory architectures give agentic systems the capacity to recall, adapt, and persist, transforming fleeting decisions into durable, auditable cognition.

# CHAPTER 7

# Modern Agent Storage and Processing for Enterprise AI

In an enterprise landscape increasingly defined by autonomous decision-making, memory has become the backbone of intelligence. If orchestration, explored in Chapter 6, represents the nervous system of agentic AI, then memory is its enduring consciousness. The mechanism that allows an agent to recall, reason, and refine its behavior over time. Without a persistent state, even the most sophisticated reasoning engine collapses into amnesia, unable to learn from experience, preserve context, or meet the reliability standards of enterprise operations.

The shift from stateless automation to stateful autonomy marks a pivotal transformation. Gartner (2025) and Deloitte (2024) note that enterprises now demand AI systems capable of contextual recall, error recovery, and replayable reasoning for audit and compliance. Whether managing customer journeys, predicting equipment failures, or processing financial transactions, memory enables agents to connect moments across time, transforming isolated interactions into a coherent understanding of the world.

This chapter examines how memory and state persistence are implemented within enterprise agent systems. It defines the three canonical tiers of agent memory, analyzes architectures for durability and idempotency, and presents a real-world case study from Petrobras that demonstrates how these mechanisms drive compliance and resilience. Chapters 4 and 5 introduce retrieval-augmented generation (RAG) for grounded reasoning, and Chapter 7 expands into durable cognition of how agents remember, forget, and recover at scale. The discussion also bridges to Chapter 8, which addresses governance and performance frameworks that ensure those memories remain reliable, explainable, and ethically constrained.

## 7.1 The Three Tiers of Agent Memory

Agent memory mirrors the layered organization of human cognition. Just as people rely on fleeting perceptions, working recall, and deep episodic retention, enterprise agents require differentiated mechanisms for information persistence, short-term, medium-term, and long-term memory that together define how an agent perceives, reasons, and learns in dynamic environments:

- **Short-Term Memory**: Short-term memory corresponds to the immediate conversational or computational context in which an agent operates. Implemented as in-memory caches (Redis and Memcached), it retains task parameters, dialogue turns, or system variables for seconds or minutes. Optimized for latency rather than durability, this layer ensures coherence across reasoning loops without introducing persistent storage overhead.

- **Medium-Term Memory**: Medium-term memory extends awareness beyond a single interaction, storing episodic traces of recent experiences. Architecturally, it is realized through vector databases such as Pinecone, Qdrant, or PostgreSQL pgvector, which capture embeddings of prior events and enable semantic retrieval. This substrate enables agents to recall prior dialogues, tasks, or anomalies, which is fundamental to personalization and auditability. However, it also demands governance: vector index maintenance, embedding refresh, and semantic drift control.

- **Long-Term Memory**: Long-term memory anchors an agent's enduring knowledge base of structured knowledge graphs, relational databases, and immutable logs that persist across sessions and versions. It demands durability, idempotency, and recoverability, achieved via append-only ledgers, transaction logs, or distributed consensus protocols. In regulated sectors, this memory layer becomes the legal substrate of trust, underpinning reproducible audits and explainable AI.

To prevent storage inflation, enterprises employ memory-compaction pipelines that summarize episodic traces into distilled knowledge, ensuring both compliance and efficiency.

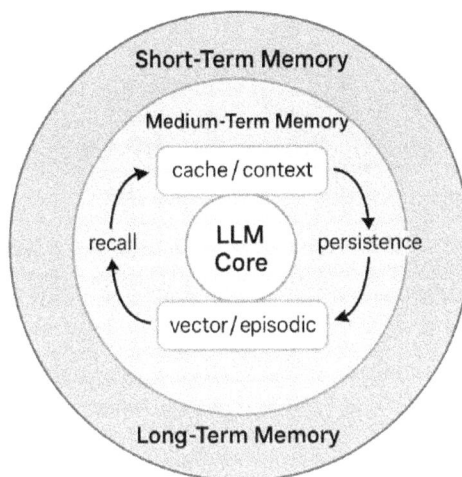

Figure 30: Agent Memory Hierarchy.

In Figure 30, we see the hierarchical nature of agent memory, depicting how information is processed and retained across different temporal layers. At the base, short-term memory (Contextual State) represents transient information for immediate use. Building upon this, medium-term memory (Episodic and Working Context) stores recent experiences and interactions. Finally, long-term memory (Knowledge and Durability) forms the apex, encompassing the enduring knowledge base and immutable logs crucial for persistent understanding and compliance. This layered structure ensures that agents can operate with both immediate responsiveness and deep, lasting cognition.

## 7.2 Architectures for Durability and State Persistence

### 7.2.1 Durability as Enterprise Mandate

Durability ensures that once a system acknowledges an operation, transaction, embedding update, or learning event, it persists even after failure. For enterprise agents, durability is a compliance requirement. Redundant replicas, write-ahead logs, and quorum-based protocols such as Raft (Ongaro and Ousterhout, 2014) provide fault-tolerant confirmation of each write.

## 7.2.2 Idempotency and Replay

Idempotency guarantees that repeated operations yield identical results. Multi-agent workflows rely on unique transaction IDs, checkpointing, and sequence numbers to prevent duplication during retries. Deterministic replay underpins agentic auditability: the ability to reproduce any prior decision path for regulators or internal governance (Microsoft Azure Architecture Center, 2025).

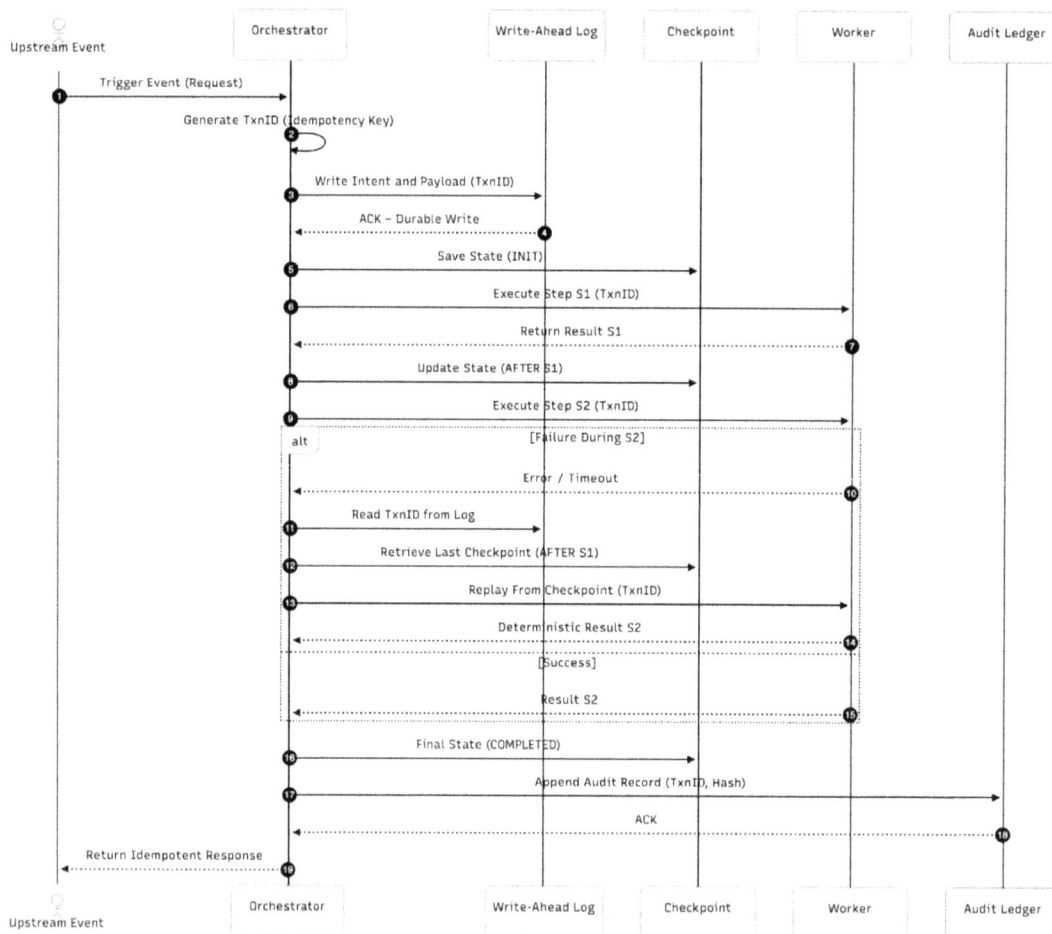

Figure 31: Idempotent Replay Architecture.

Figure 31 depicts a sequence of operations designed for idempotent replay, ensuring that each step, even when repeated, leads to a consistent, singular outcome. It illustrates the critical role of transaction IDs and checkpointing in establishing a reliable audit trail, allowing for the precise reproduction of agent decisions and state changes. This architecture is fundamental to achieving fault tolerance, enabling systems to recover safely from interruptions while maintaining data integrity and regulatory compliance.

## 7.2.3 State Persistence and Resumability

Beyond data durability, agents must persist cognitive state plans, goals, and reasoning traces so they can resume after interruption. Serialization frameworks (JSON-LD, Protocol Buffers) and orchestration checkpoints (LangGraph, CrewAI) externalize cognition, enabling elastic scaling and forensic replay.

## 7.2.4 The RAG Continuum

RAG evolves here from retrieval to dynamic memory management. Each retrieval updates vector relationships, refining context for future reasoning. Enterprises monitor index freshness, latency, and cost via FinOps dashboards to balance precision and efficiency (Accenture, 2025).

## 7.2.5 Integrated Memory Fabric

A modern enterprise deploys a composite stack: operational stores (Redis and PostgreSQL), analytical stores (BigQuery and Snowflake), vector stores (Pinecone and Weaviate), knowledge graphs (Neo4j and Ontotext), and object archives (AWS S3 and Azure Blob). Unified by governance and observability, this distributed memory lattice delivers durability without sacrificing scalability.

Figure 32 presents a conceptual diagram of a distributed memory fabric, showing how various storage layers are integrated to provide a robust, scalable memory solution for enterprise agent systems. It shows the interconnectedness of operational, analytical, vector, and knowledge graph stores, alongside object archives, all working in concert. This unified approach, underpinned by strong governance and observability, ensures agents have access to durable, consistent memory that is essential for resilient, intelligent operations without compromising scalability.

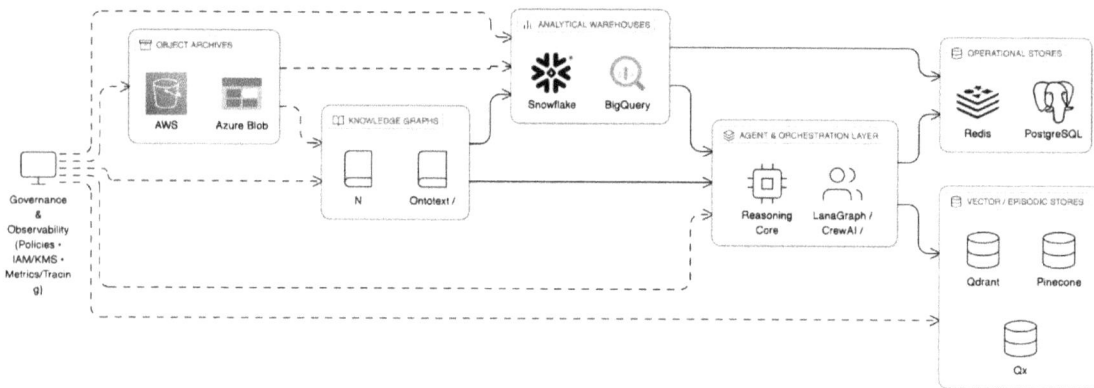

Figure 32: Distributed Memory Fabric for Agent Systems.

These architectural principles come to life in Petrobras's deployment of agentic memory for tax compliance. A real-world case study that demonstrates how durable state, idempotent replay, and orchestration checkpoints translate into measurable impact across regulated enterprise workflows.

## 7.3 Case Study: Petrobras and Automation Anywhere: Agentic Memory in Tax Compliance

### 7.3.1 Context

Petrobras, a South American energy leader with 45,000 employees and over 70 years of experience in ultra-deep-water exploration, faced an immense tax-compliance challenge. Each filing cycle required reconciling 150 pages of complex Brazilian regulations while paying roughly $54 billion USD in annual taxes. Manual cross-checks left room for error, overtime, and regulatory risk.

## 7.3.2 Implementation

Under CIO Carlos Barreto, Petrobras partnered with Automation Anywhere to modernize tax operations using Generative AI and Agentic Process Automation (APA), built on the Process Reasoning Engine (PRE). This orchestration layer provides persistent state, rule memory, and reasoning traceability.

Key elements included PRE-driven orchestration, Bedrock-based generative models, SageMaker predictive modeling, and Automation Co-Pilot for human oversight. Each workflow carried unique transaction IDs enabling idempotent replay: if a process failed mid-execution, PRE resumed from the last confirmed checkpoint, ensuring deterministic recomputation.

Figure 33 showcases the architectural blueprint of Petrobras's agentic tax system, powered by Automation Anywhere's Process Reasoning Engine (PRE). It visually illustrates how PRE orchestrates generative AI tax agents, integrating persistent, auditable memory to manage complex tax compliance workflows. The diagram highlights the interconnectedness of various components, demonstrating how the system achieves reliable, traceable, and efficient tax operations through intelligent automation.

## 7.3.3 Results and Lessons Learned

Within three weeks, Petrobras uncovered $120 million USD in verified savings, achieved a 40% efficiency increase, and eliminated 15 years of weekend overtime. Projected annual savings exceeded $1 billion. CIO Carlos Barreto stated, *"We saved $120 million in just three weeks with Automation Anywhere's generative AI-powered solutions. This is just the beginning."* Victor Pace, General Manager of Taxes and Government Participations, added: *"For the first time in 15 years, we did not have to work over the weekend to file taxes."*

Petrobras demonstrates that durable memory and idempotent agentic workflows enable compliance-grade automation and reproducible traceability, transforming static rules into a persistent knowledge base that reasons autonomously yet accountably. *(Source: Automation Anywhere, 2025.)*

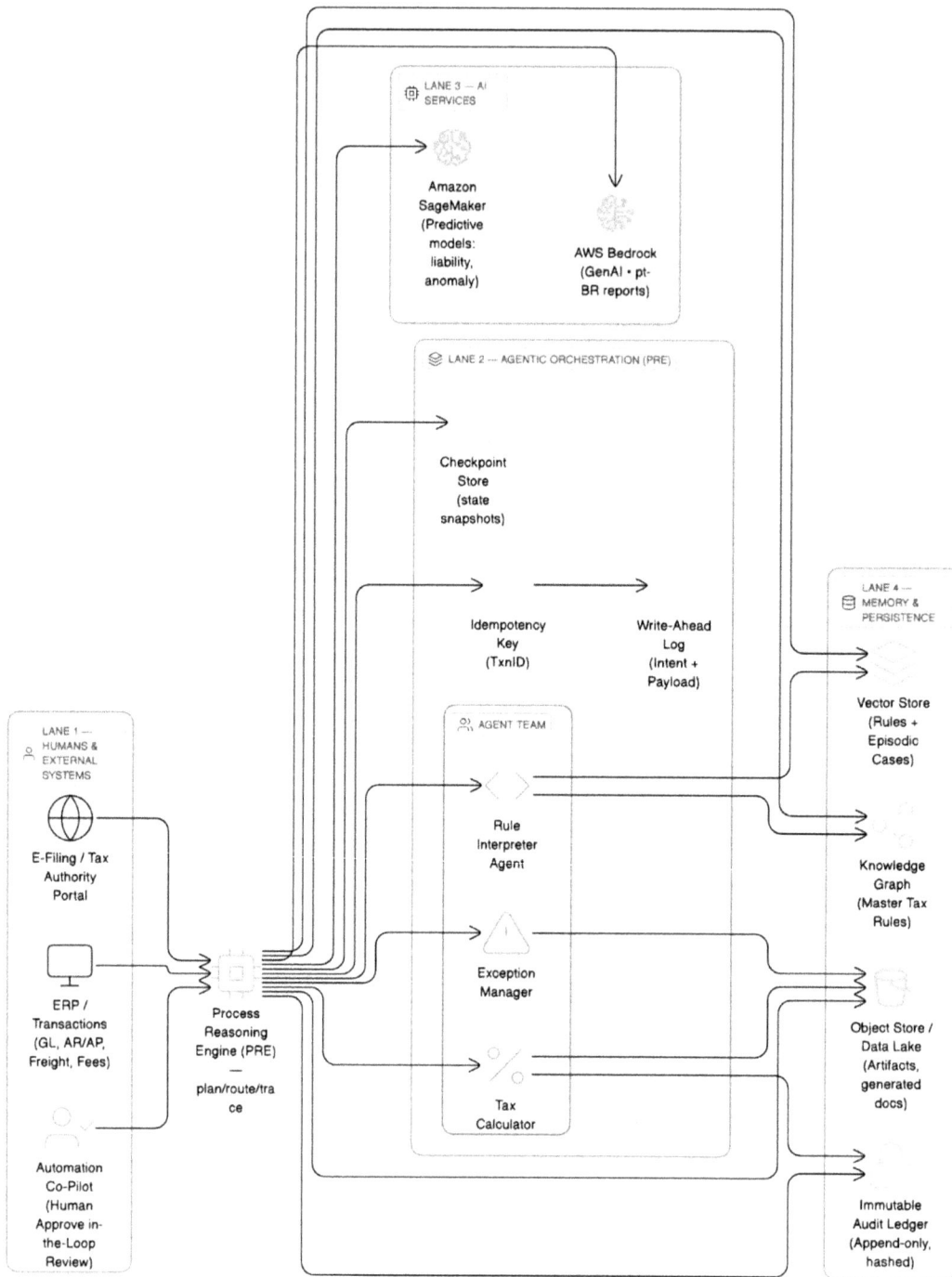

Figure 33: Petrobras Agentic Tax Architecture.

## 7.4 Strategic Guidance for CTOs

### 7.4.1 Memory as a Governance Surface

Each memory layer constitutes a governance surface. Enterprises must define Service Level Objectives (SLOs) for latency, durability, and retention. Example: *"95% of vector queries respond within 250 ms with 99.999% record durability."*

### 7.4.2 FinOps and Cost Efficiency

Persistent memory introduces ongoing storage and compute costs. FinOps metrics help sustain balance: Storage Efficiency Ratio (SER), Recall Latency Percentile (RLP), and Durability Cost Index (DCI).

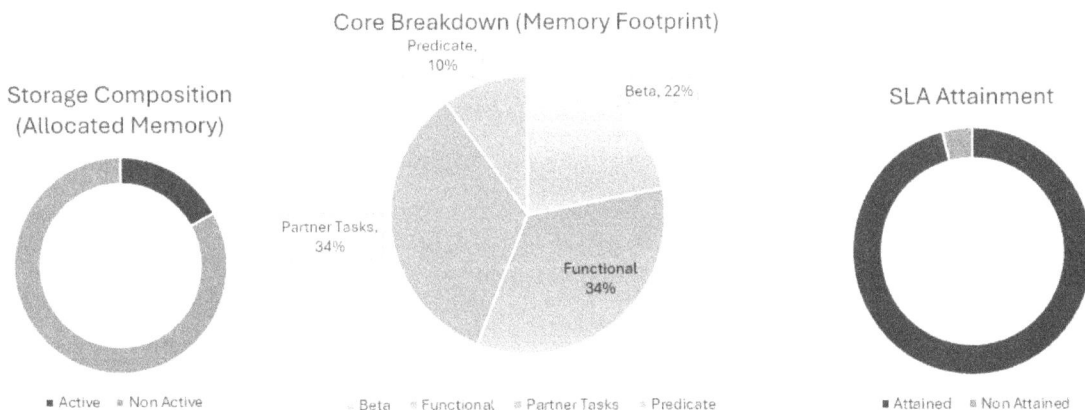

Core Breakdown (Memory Footprint)

Predicate, 10%

Beta, 22%

Storage Composition (Allocated Memory)

Partner Tasks, 34%

Functional 34%

SLA Attainment

■ Active  ■ Non Active

Beta  Functional  Partner Tasks  Predicate

■ Attained  ■ Non Attained

Figure 34: FinOps Metrics Dashboard for Agent Memory.

Figure 34 illustrates a sample FinOps dashboard that provides a comprehensive overview of agent memory health, linking key performance indicators (KPIs) to governance and cost performance. It visually represents metrics such as Storage Efficiency Ratio, Recall Latency Percentile, and Durability Cost Index, allowing enterprises to monitor and optimize the balance between precision, efficiency, and the financial implications of persistent memory solutions. This dashboard serves as a critical tool for strategic decision-making in managing the operational and economic aspects of agentic AI systems.

This framework naturally extends into defining concrete metrics and Service Level Objective (SLO) templates that provide tangible targets for each aspect of memory management.

| Category | Metric | Target |
|---|---|---|
| Durability | Write-ahead log ack latency | < 50 ms |
| Idempotency | Replay divergence rate | < 0.1% |
| Resilience | Mean time to recover (MTTR) | < 5 min |
| Cost | Storage per agent per month | ≤ $0.10 / GB |
| Compliance | Audit replay success rate | 100% |

Table 7: Agentic Orchestration Metrics and SLO Targets.

Table 7 outlines key performance indicators and service-level objectives (SLOs) for agentic orchestration systems, spanning durability, resilience, cost efficiency, and compliance. Each metric is paired with a target threshold to guide operational monitoring and governance alignment across enterprise deployments.

## 7.5 Key Takeaways

**Agent Memory Fundamentals**

- Memory is the backbone of agentic intelligence, enabling recall, reasoning, and refinement over time.
- Stateless automation is giving way to stateful autonomy, driven by enterprise needs for contextual recall and auditability.
- Memory enables agents to connect interactions across time, supporting personalization, compliance, and resilience.

### The Three Tiers of Agent Memory

- **Short-Term Memory**: In-memory caches (e.g., Redis, Memcached) for immediate context; optimized for latency.
- **Medium-Term Memory**: Vector databases (e.g., Pinecone, Qdrant) for episodic recall; supports personalization and auditability.
- **Long-Term Memory**: Durable stores (e.g., knowledge graphs, transaction logs) for persistent, explainable knowledge.

### Architectures for Durability and Persistence

- **Durability**: Ensures operations persist post-failure using write-ahead logs and quorum protocols like Raft.
- **Idempotency**: Guarantees consistent outcomes for repeated operations via transaction IDs and checkpointing.
- **Replayability**: Enables deterministic recomputation for audit and governance.
- **State Persistence**: Agents externalize cognitive state using serialization frameworks (e.g., JSON-LD, Protocol Buffers).
- **RAG Continuum**: Retrieval evolves into dynamic memory refinement, monitored via FinOps dashboards.
- **Integrated Memory Fabric**: Combines operational, analytical, vector, and archival stores under unified governance.

### Case Study: Petrobras Tax Compliance

- Petrobras used Automation Anywhere's Process Reasoning Engine (PRE) to modernize tax workflows.
- PRE enabled persistent state, idempotent replay, and human-in-the-loop oversight.
- Results: $120M saved in 3 weeks, 40% efficiency gain, and elimination of 15 years of weekend overtime.

**Strategic Guidance for CTOs**

- **Governance Surfaces**: Each memory layer requires SLOs for latency, durability, and retention.
- **FinOps Metrics**: Track cost-performance balance using SER, RLP, and DCI.
- **Dashboarding**: Visual tools link memory health to operational and financial KPIs.

---

# 7.6 Discussion Questions / Exercises

1. Map your organization's agent memory stack; identify durability gaps.
2. Design an idempotent replay mechanism for a critical workflow.
3. Build a FinOps model for embedding refresh frequency versus latency cost.
4. Draft data-retention policies that satisfy both GDPR and SOX compliance.

Durable memory is the substrate for governance and performance management. The logs, traces, and checkpoints captured here feed directly into the Agent Governance Loop discussed next. Without a trustworthy memory, no audit or ethical assurance can hold. As Chapter 8 will show, the enterprise that governs its memory governs its intelligence.

# CHAPTER 8

# Agent Governance and Performance Management

Enterprise AI agents cannot be left to run on trust alone. As orchestration (Chapter 6) and distributed processing (Chapter 7) bring autonomy to scale, a new requirement emerges: governance. Governance is the control plane that keeps autonomous systems accountable, auditable, and financially sustainable. This chapter introduces two complementary frameworks, Master Agent Management (MAM) and AgentOps/Quality Assurance (QA), and situates them alongside resilience patterns and FinOps principles. We conclude with a real-world case study of Tanium's Autonomous Endpoint Management (AEM), one of the most concrete examples of large-scale, governed autonomy in production.

## 8.1 Why Governance Matters Now

The enterprise AI surge of 2024–2025 brought not only innovation but also operational exposure: rogue prompt versions, cost blowouts from unmanaged token use, and compliance risks under GDPR and the EU AI Act. Gartner's AI Governance Forecast (2025) notes that 70 percent of organizations deploying AI agents cite governance, auditability, or cost control as their top risk areas.

Governance provides the "safety rail" that converts raw autonomy into enterprise reliability. It defines what agents exist, how they behave, and how performance, cost, and compliance are verified. As we progress through this chapter, MAM and AgentOps form the twin pillars of this system: the first handles registration and lineage; the second ensures quality, rollback, and resilience. Together, they link every stage of the agent lifecycle from code to cost.

## 8.2 Master Agent Management (MAM): The Registry of Governance

To achieve this governance, every enterprise needs a source of truth for its agents. Master Agent Management (MAM) is that registry: the canonical repository where each agent's identity, purpose, prompt version, lineage, and policy bindings are stored.

A centralized MAM ensures uniform governance within a single domain, simplifying audit trails and approvals. In contrast, a federated MAM distributes control across regions or business units to comply with data-sovereignty laws. In either case, no agent can enter production without a registered version ID, QA certificate, and rollback lineage.

This registry also enables traceability. When a compliance audit asks, "Which model made this decision?", MAM provides an immutable record of the agent, its reasoning version, and associated data policies.

Figure 35 illustrates a comprehensive, closed-loop lifecycle conceptualized as a dual-plane system for robust, continuous operational management. This model distinctly separates and integrates two critical operational spheres: the Governance Plane and the Execution Plane. The Governance Plane is positioned as the strategic and oversight layer, responsible for the initial stages of development and quality assurance. Within this plane, key activities include agent authoring, where the core logic and parameters for automated processes are designed and implemented. Following this, rigorous QA testing is conducted to ensure the reliability, accuracy, and security of these agents before they are deployed. The final stage in the Governance Plane is registry approval, a formal process that certifies an agent's readiness for operational use and ensures compliance with established standards and policies.

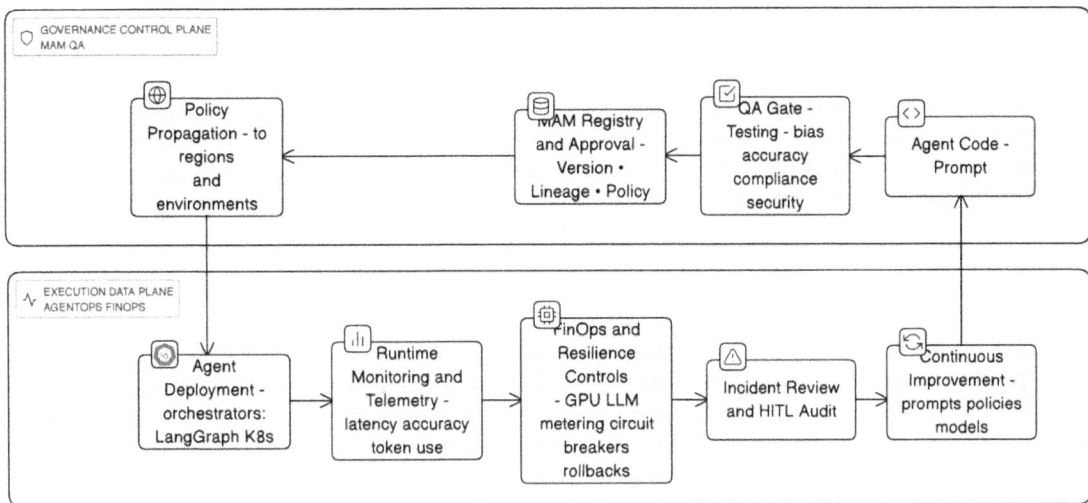

Figure 35: Governance Operating Model (MAM / QA).

In contrast, the Execution Plane represents the operational and reactive layer, focused on the real-world deployment and ongoing management of approved agents. This plane encompasses several crucial stages, beginning with deployment, where agents are integrated into the live operational environment. Post-deployment, continuous monitoring is paramount, involving active observation of agent performance and resource utilization, and the identification of any anomalies or issues. A vital component of the Execution Plane is FinOps feedback, which involves analyzing the financial implications and cost-efficiency of agent operations to provide data-driven insights for optimization. Finally, the principle of continuous improvement ensures that feedback from monitoring and FinOps is systematically used to refine and enhance agent performance and efficiency.

The dynamic interplay between these two planes forms a closed-loop control system. Arrows between the planes symbolize this continuous flow of information and action: control originating from the Governance Plane above, guiding the execution processes below, and feedback from the Execution Plane iteratively informing and refining the governance processes. This synergistic relationship ensures agility, accountability, and a perpetual cycle of enhancement across the entire operational lifecycle.

With governance architecture in place through MAM, the focus shifts to operational assurance. That is, how agents are tested, monitored, and refined once deployed. AgentOps provides the executional discipline that ensures agents behave reliably and ethically in dynamic environments.

## 8.3 AgentOps and Quality Assurance

Where MAM defines what can exist, AgentOps defines how agents behave in the wild. It extends DevOps and MLOps practices to adaptive reasoning systems whose outputs may vary by context.

The lifecycle begins with sandboxed authoring: developers craft agent prompts and code fragments annotated with metadata. Automated QA gates then test for bias, accuracy, and security vulnerabilities. Passing agents are committed to MAM; failing ones trigger correction cycles.

Once in production, AgentOps activates telemetry for latency, accuracy, and token utilization. It incorporates resilience patterns circuit breakers that pause failing agents, canary deployments that release to limited rings, and shadow testing that compares new versions against baselines. Each anomaly generates a rollback workflow linked back to the registry.

Human-in-the-loop audits remain essential: operators inspect exceptions, approve restarts, and refine QA rules from post-incident analysis. This closes the feedback loop between governance and execution. These elements appear in Figure 36. Beginning with automated QA and validation, the loop progresses through phased deployment, real-time monitoring, rollback mechanisms, and iterative improvement before returning to QA. Each stage reinforces resilience, traceability, and operational integrity, ensuring that agents not only launch safely but also evolve responsibly in production environments. This closed-loop design reflects the enterprise imperative for adaptive, accountable automation.

While AgentOps ensures behavioral reliability through testing and rollback, resilience alone is not enough. Enterprises must also govern the financial footprint of agent operations. Enter FinOps, the discipline that brings cost visibility and control to autonomous systems.

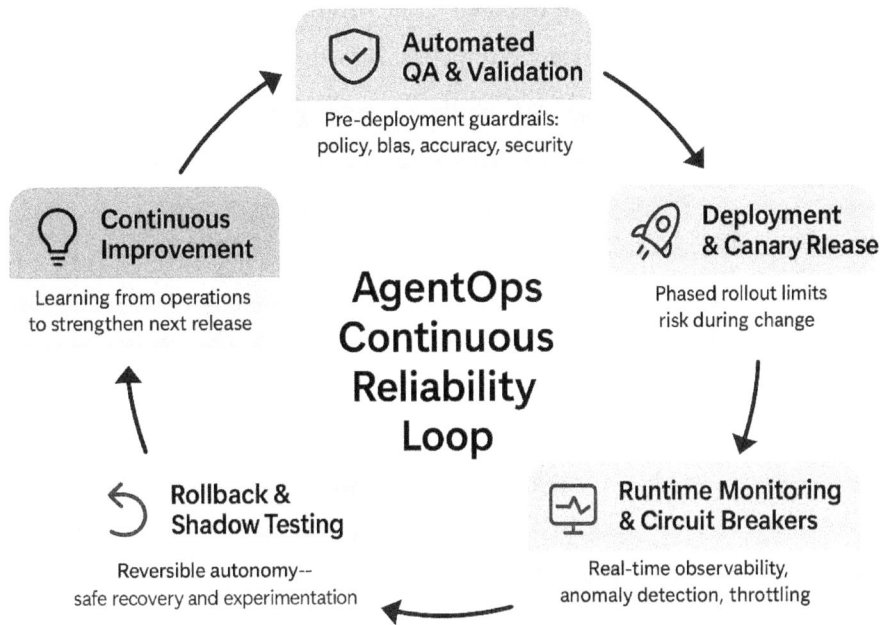

Figure 36: AgentOps Lifecycle and Resilience Controls.

## 8.4 Resilience and FinOps: Governing Cost and Availability

Even the most elegant orchestration collapses if cost visibility is lost. In generative-AI workloads, each agent invocation consumes variable compute, GPU time, and tokens. FinOps brings fiscal accountability to this dynamic environment.

According to the FinOps Foundation AI Cost Optimization Guide (2024), enterprises overspend by 20–35 percent on unmanaged inference and training costs. Integrating FinOps into governance means tagging every agent call with usage data, attributing spend to business functions and enforcing quotas through automated controls.

Microsoft's governance architecture provides a live example. In Administering and Governing Agents in Copilot Studio (2024), Microsoft describes audit logging through Purview and Sentinel, permission-based publishing, and analytics dashboards that track token usage across tenants, effectively a FinOps-enabled control plane for its Copilot ecosystem.

Resilience and FinOps are two halves of reliability: one protects uptime, the other sustains budgets. Agents that exceed error thresholds trigger circuit breakers; those that exceed cost thresholds trigger throttling or rollback. Figure 37 brings together these core issues.

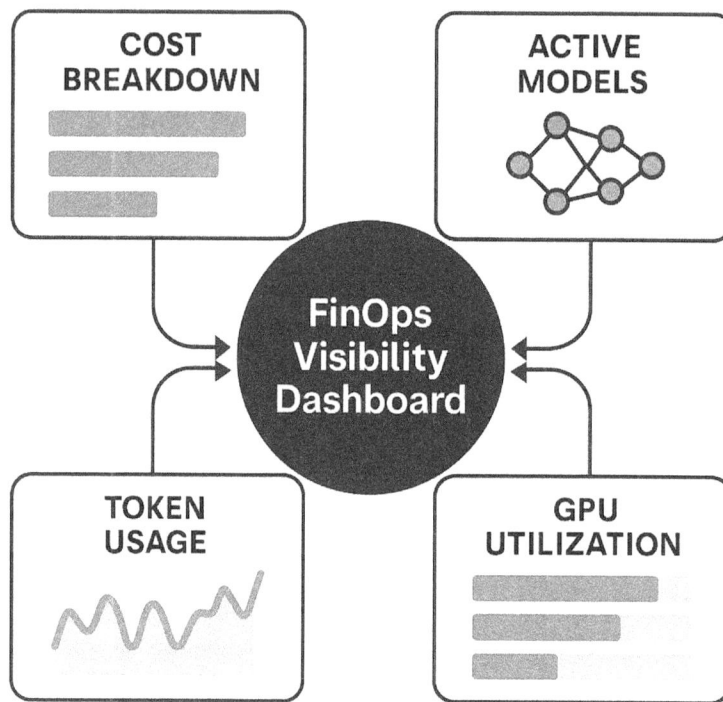

Figure 37: FinOps Visibility Dashboard for Agentic Systems.

Figure 37 visually depicts the integrated governance architecture of Tanium's Autonomous Endpoint Management (AEM) platform, illustrating how centralized oversight and control are applied to autonomous-agent operations. The diagram typically depicts a multi-layered system where Tanium agents manage endpoints (devices). These agents perform autonomous actions, which are then routed through a governance layer that includes components for "Action Oversight," "Deployment Rings," and "Phased Rollouts."

This architecture emphasizes a closed-loop system where real-time insights from endpoints feed into the AEM platform, enabling automated changes. However, these changes are subject to human-governed reversibility and auditability through the oversight mechanisms. This ensures that while agents operate autonomously, they remain accountable and controllable, aligning with the MAM and AgentOps principles discussed in this chapter.

The convergence of resilience and FinOps principles sets the foundation for governed autonomy. But theory alone is not enough. To see these mechanisms in action, we now turn to Tanium's Autonomous Endpoint Management (AEM) platform. This real-world implementation operationalizes MAM, AgentOps, and cost-aware governance at enterprise scale.

## 8.5 Case Study Tanium Autonomous Endpoint Management (AEM)

Few enterprises demonstrate governed autonomy as concretely as **Tanium**. In November 2024, Tanium launched its Autonomous Endpoint Management (AEM) platform, a fusion of agentic automation with centralized oversight.

According to CTO Matt Quinn, "Tanium AEM leverages real-time insights from millions of Tanium cloud-managed endpoints to recommend and automate changes … giving IT and security teams a safe, scalable, and automated platform to deliver increasingly efficient operations and an improved security posture." (Help Net Security, 2024)

The platform introduces Action Oversight, which "puts the user firmly in control of all aspects of the platform's autonomous functions. Every system is tied into this centralized governance component. Operators can inspect autonomous activity and swiftly isolate or remediate as needed." (Help Net Security, 2024)

Tanium couples oversight with deployment rings and phased rollouts, allowing administrators to stage updates through confidence-scored waves before full release. Its public solution brief highlights that "each autonomous action maintains a complete record of past, current, and scheduled activities," enabling full rollback and audit. (Tanium AEM Solution Brief, 2025)

These capabilities together form a real-world MAM + AgentOps ecosystem: registry-driven control, runtime telemetry, cost-aware execution, and human-governed reversibility.

Figure 38 illustrates the integrated governance architecture of Tanium's Autonomous Endpoint Management (AEM) platform, highlighting how telemetry and FinOps feedback form a closed loop for agent oversight. At the top, the governance components of Action Oversight, Governance

Registry, and Policy Engine define the control plane. This sets the boundaries for agent behavior and cost attribution. These components interface directly with the Tanium platform, which orchestrates agentic rollout stages across enterprise endpoints.

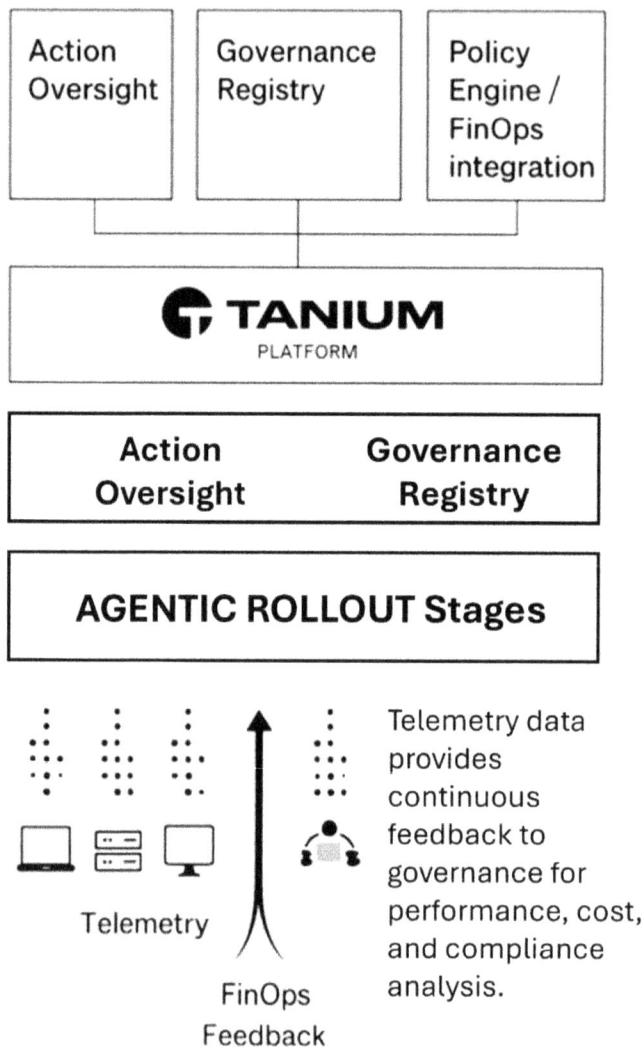

Figure 38: Tanium AEM Governance Architecture. Adapted from Tanium Platform Overview (2024) and Tanium Autonomous Endpoint Management Solution Brief (2025). Conceptualized by the authors for illustrative purposes based on publicly available Tanium architecture and product documentation.

The lower half of the diagram shows how telemetry flows upward from devices, feeding real-time performance, cost, and compliance data into the governance layer. This feedback loop enables dynamic throttling, rollback, and policy refinement, ensuring that autonomous actions remain accountable and reversible. By embedding FinOps into the operational lifecycle, Tanium aligns agent autonomy with fiscal discipline and regulatory assurance.

This architecture exemplifies the principles of MAM and AgentOps in practice, where every autonomous action is traceable, auditable, and governed by policy. It demonstrates how enterprise platforms can scale agentic automation without sacrificing control, making Tanium's AEM a compelling model for governed autonomy in endpoint management.

Tanium's AEM platform exemplifies how governed autonomy can be operationalized. But, to sustain trust and accountability, enterprises must quantify performance through governance metrics and service-level objectives (SLOs) that translate agent behavior into actionable insights. We will discuss this in the next section.

## 8.6 Governance Metrics and SLOs

Governance is only as effective as its ability to be measured. To ensure reliability, cost control, and operational accountability, CTO dashboards should surface a core set of quantitative indicators that reflect both system health and fiscal discipline. These metrics serve as the backbone of enterprise oversight, enabling leaders to track performance across engineering, compliance, and finance:

- **QA Pass Rate (≥ 98%):** Percentage of agents that successfully pass automated validation checks for bias, accuracy, and security.

- **Rollback Success Rate (≥ 95%):** Rate at which system reversions are executed without residual error or data corruption.

- **FinOps Variance (< 10%):** Difference between projected and actual compute spend, highlighting cost predictability.

- **Mean Time to Remediate (MTTR) (< 2 hours):** Average time from anomaly detection to successful correction.

- **Drift Detection Lag (< 15 minutes):** Time elapsed between behavioral drift and alert generation.

These service level objectives (SLOs) create a unified performance vocabulary across technical and business domains. Their trends should be visualized in enterprise BI platforms such as Power BI or Tableau, ensuring transparency and alignment across leadership teams.

To operationalize governance, enterprises must move beyond policy and architecture into measurable performance. Figure 39 presents a dashboard view of key governance indicators. This includes capturing trends in agent validation, rollback reliability, cost control, and remediation speed. These metrics offer a real-time lens into the health and accountability of agentic systems.

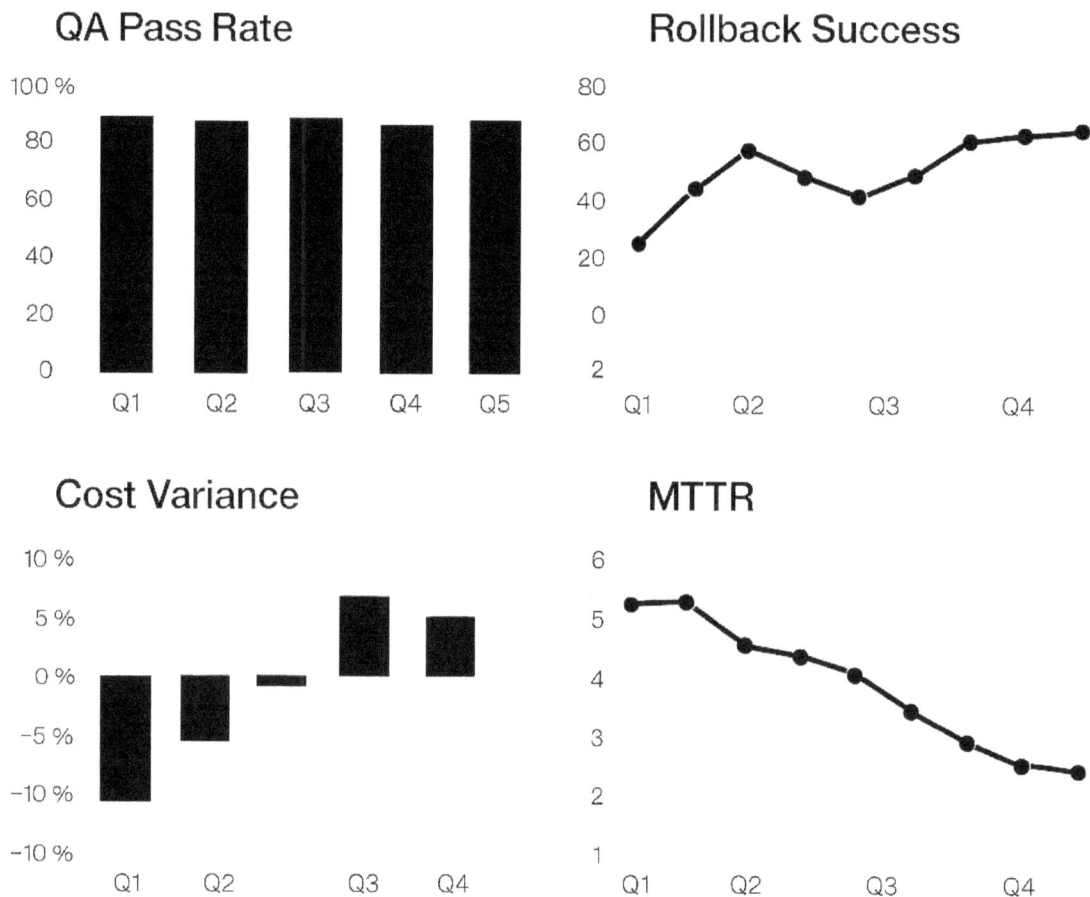

Figure 39: Governance KPIs Dashboard. Conceptualized by the authors for illustrative purposes, based on industry-standard AI governance and FinOps frameworks (FinOps Foundation 2024; NIST AI RMF 2023; Tanium AEM Solution Brief 2025; Microsoft Copilot Governance Whitepaper 2024).

Figure 39 visualizes quarterly performance across four critical governance metrics:

- The QA Pass Rate chart shows consistently high validation success, indicating strong pre-deployment quality.
- Rollback Success reveals a steady upward trend, reflecting improved resilience and error recovery.
- Cost Variance highlights fiscal discipline, with fluctuations narrowing over time.
- Finally, the MTTR chart demonstrates accelerated remediation, with recovery times dropping significantly.

---

*Together, these trends provide actionable insight into the reliability and efficiency of enterprise agent operations.*

---

## 8.7 Key Takeaways

- MAM and AgentOps together form a closed-loop governance system where every agent is registered, tested, monitored, and cost-controlled. FinOps adds fiscal discipline; resilience patterns ensure uptime; and platforms like Tanium AEM and Microsoft Copilot Studio prove that autonomy and accountability can scale together.
- Governance is not a brake on innovation. It is the architecture of trust. As enterprises move from experimentation to production, agent governance must evolve from reactive oversight to proactive design. The organizations that master this shift will not only avoid risk, they will also define the future of responsible AI.
- Governance provides the scaffolding; observability provides the sightlines. With MAM and AgentOps in place, the next frontier is real-time transparency. Seeing agent behavior as it unfolds, correlating telemetry across systems, and delivering traceable decisions at scale.

With governance metrics in place, the next step is action. To move from insight to implementation, CTOs must pressure-test their systems: map oversight, simulate failures, and pilot dashboards that turn theory into operational discipline. The following exercises offer a practical starting point:

## 8.8 Discussion Questions / Exercises

1   **Map your governance chain**: Identify where agent registration, QA, and rollout are enforced, and where blind spots remain.

2   **Conduct a FinOps baseline**: Quantify LLM and GPU expenses; simulate a 25 percent reduction scenario via token optimization.

3   **Perform a rollback drill**: Pick an agent version, simulate failure, and measure MTTR from alert to recovery.

4   **Define SLOs**: Select three governance metrics and run a pilot dashboard for one fiscal quarter.

As agentic systems scale across enterprise environments, governance ensures they remain accountable, performant, and financially sustainable. Chapter 9 deepens this imperative by addressing the ethical foundations of trust, exploring how privacy, explainability, and regulatory compliance must be embedded into every layer of autonomous decision-making.

CHAPTER 9

# Ethics, Privacy, and Explainability in Agentic AI

In enterprise-class agent systems, capability is not enough: the system must also command trust. For CTOs and technical leaders, the Trust Mandate means ensuring that autonomous agents operate under rigorous accountability, transparency, and privacy constraints while delivering high performance. This chapter centralizes the principles of ethics, privacy, explainability, and auditability, and describes how they must be embedded into architecture, reasoning, data, and governance.

From a regulatory perspective, jurisdictions are converging on high-stakes AI governance: the European AI Act classifies certain autonomous systems as "high risk," requiring demonstrable transparency, human oversight, and logging. Similarly, GDPR (EU), CCPA (California), and sectoral regulations like HIPAA (healthcare) all embed rights to explanation, data minimization, and accountability. These legal regimes increasingly treat explainability and auditability as technical, rather than merely legal requirements.

Within our book's architecture, this chapter interfaces deeply with:

- **Chapter 8 (Governance and Performance)**: Where policy, oversight, and governance mechanisms are defined, here we operationalize them at the technical level.

- **Chapter 4 (Data Architecture and Sovereignty)**: Federated, decentralized, or privacy-aware data architectures are key enablers of compliance and sovereignty, and now serve as foundations for audit and tracing.
- **Chapter 5 (Reasoning and Agent Logic)**: We must layer explainability over these logic systems; proof traces or post hoc explanations must align with reasoning flows.

By the end of this chapter, the reader will see that ethics, privacy, and transparency are not add-ons or afterthoughts; they are core technical disciplines and cross-cutting constraints.

## 9.1 Ethical Frameworks for Agentic AI

### 9.1.1 Foundations of AI Ethics

At a high level, AI ethics seeks to ground autonomous systems in human values: fairness, non-maleficence, autonomy, and justice. In the AI systems domain, several reference frameworks exist:

- **IEEE 7000 series** (e.g., IEEE 7001 for transparency, IEEE 7002 for data privacy) prescribe that system design must integrate ethical considerations from the start.
- **OECD AI Principles** (2019) emphasize inclusive growth, transparency, and accountability.
- **NIST AI Risk Management Framework (RMF 1.0, 2023)** positions explainability and resilience as core pillars of trustworthy AI.

One often uses the concept of value-aligned autonomy: the agent's utility functions and decision boundaries must reflect stakeholder values and constraints, rather than purely performance metrics.

### 9.1.2 The Oversight Flow

To operationalize ethics, we propose the canonical Ethical Oversight Flow (see Figure 40).

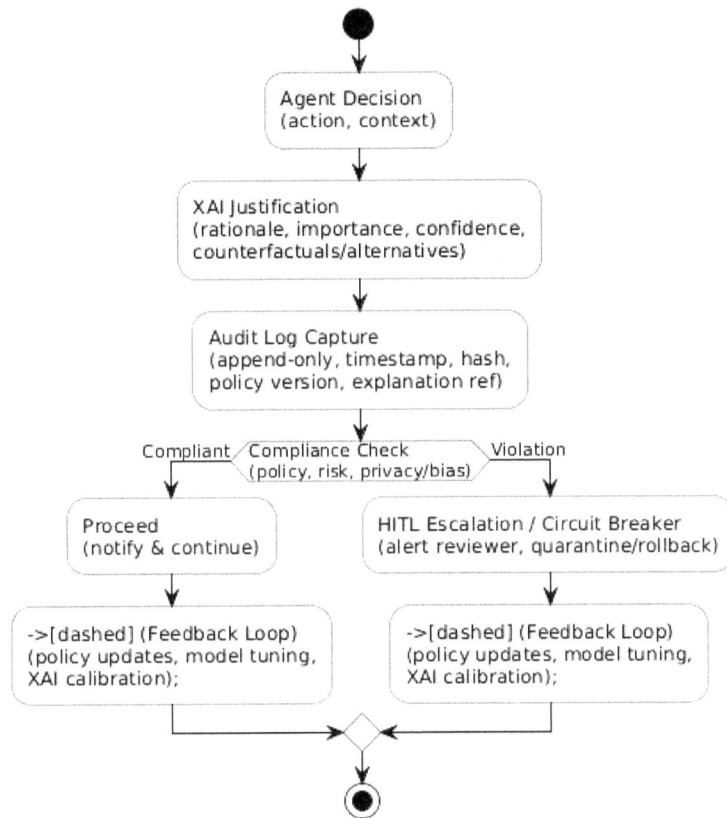

Figure 40: Ethical Oversight Flow.

This flow ensures every autonomous decision is justified, logged, checked, and, if necessary, overridden by human-in-the-loop (HITL) mechanisms.

In practice, the compliance check module references policy rules (e.g., governance constraints) and may trigger circuit breakers or escalate to human operators. This mechanism forms the technical backbone of governance.

## 9.1.3 Cross-Chapter Interactions

- From Chapter 8, the policy definitions and governance rules feed directly into the compliance-check module.

- From Chapter 5, the reasoning engine must produce not just decisions but explanation artifacts that the XAI layer uses.
- From Chapter 4, the underlying data's provenance and governance constraints must support tracing of audit logs.

This integrated chain ensures the agent does not act as a black box; each decision is accountable, interpretable, and traceable.

Ethical oversight defines the boundaries of responsible agent behavior. Those boundaries are only meaningful if they protect sensitive data. As agents increasingly operate across jurisdictions and handle regulated information, privacy and sovereignty become core design constraints. The next section explores how federated architectures and explainable AI can work together to meet these demands.

## 9.2 Data Privacy and Sovereignty in Federated Architectures

### 9.2.1 The Privacy Challenge in Agent Systems

Modern agentic systems often require rich, sensitive datasets (customer behavior, device telemetry, and health data). Over-centralization can conflict with data sovereignty laws (e.g., data must remain in-country), increase regulatory risk, and create single points of failure. The solution lies in federated or decentralized data planes, which enable model training without moving raw data.

Such topologies directly support data minimization, anonymization, and differential privacy constraints.

### 9.2.2 Federated Learning + Explainability

Recent works explore the intersection of Federated Learning (FL) and XAI. The scoping review by Lopez-Ramos et al. (2024) identifies 37 studies that combine FL and explainability; most focus on feature-relevance explanations (e.g., SHAP) in horizontal federated settings, but only one quantitatively analyzes how FL alters explanations relative to centralized models.

Another study adapted FL-XAI for healthcare, achieving 99% accuracy in liver disease prediction while preserving privacy constraints. However, challenges remain: aggregating explanation metrics across nodes may dilute localized patterns, or nodes may require node-specific explainability that global aggregation cannot capture.

Thus, architectural choices must consider:

- **Hierarchical Explanation Aggregation**: Each node (data silo) produces local explainability that is aggregated upward.
- **Privacy-preserving Explanation Methods**: Ensuring that published explanations do not leak sensitive details (e.g., via differential privacy noise).
- **Synchronization of Explanation Semantics:** Across nodes so that the global model and local explanations align.

### 9.2.3 Case Study: Federated XAI in Healthcare

In one practical instantiation, researchers designed an ECG monitoring framework that combined federated transfer learning with explainable AI. The system trained CNN-based classifiers across hospitals without centralizing patient data, and, on top of the classifiers, added explainability modules to produce human-interpretable explanations of cardiac arrhythmias. The model achieved ~94-98% accuracy in arrhythmia detection across noisy and clean data environments.

This demonstrates that even in real-world, regulated domains, one can co-design learning and explanation layers without violating privacy constraints.

### 9.2.4 Architectural Implications and Cross-Linking

- From Chapter 4, the data fabric must be federated or hybrid so that local data remains under jurisdictional control.

- A privacy-aware agent system must propagate not only decision logs but also explain metadata without leaking sensitive elements.
- The compliance check module must reason over both local and aggregated data policies, sometimes reconciling conflicting privacy constraints across silos.

In this way, federated explainable AI becomes a central pattern for responsible agentic AI in regulated environments.

While federated architectures safeguard privacy and sovereignty, they also introduce complexity in how decisions are explained and understood. To maintain trust across distributed systems, explainability must be embedded directly into the agent pipeline. The next section explores how explainable AI (XAI) techniques serve as technical enablers of transparency, interpretability, and oversight.

## 9.3 Explainable AI (XAI) as a Technical Enabler

### 9.3.1 Defining Explainability and Interpretability

Explainability encompasses techniques that render AI decisions understandable to humans, either via intrinsic interpretability (e.g., simple models like decision trees) or via post hoc explanation (e.g., LIME, SHAP). The DARPA XAI program articulates a vision: AI systems should produce rationales, self-assess their weaknesses, and allow human oversight.

In modern discourse, some authors argue that XAI is not merely a transparency tool but the foundation of responsible AI: explainability must intersect with fairness, privacy, robustness, and security.

In high-stakes domains like healthcare, explainability is non-negotiable. Clinicians demand an understanding of predictions to trust AI recommendations.

## 9.3.2 XAI Techniques and Trade-Offs

Key XAI methods include:

- **LIME (Local Interpretable Model-agnostic Explanations)**: Approximates local decision regions using interpretable surrogate models.
- **SHAP (SHapley Additive exPlanations)**: Uses a game-theoretic approach to allocate feature importance contributions.
- **Counterfactual Explanations**: Identify minimal changes to inputs that flip outputs (e.g., "If feature X had been five units less, the decision would change").
- **Partial Dependence Plots (PDPs) and ICE Plots**: Show marginal relationships between features and outcomes.
- **Surrogate Models**: Globally approximate black-box models using simpler interpretable models like decision trees.

Each method brings trade-offs: LIME is intuitive but may be unstable; SHAP is mathematically principled but computationally intensive in high dimensions; counterfactuals are user-friendly but may not fully capture model internals.

Figure 41 illustrates how explainability is architected as a layered system within agentic AI. Raw inputs, including features, context, and identifiers, flow through the agent's reasoning core, which may include classifiers, planners, or LLMs. Surrounding this core is an explanation layer that applies techniques like LIME, SHAP, and counterfactuals to extract interpretable insights.

These insights are then surfaced through dashboards and APIs, providing rationale text, feature importances, and quality metrics such as stability and faithfulness. Telemetry feeds into this interface, enabling real-time monitoring of explanation coverage and latency. This stack ensures that every decision is not only made but made transparent, bridging model logic with human oversight.

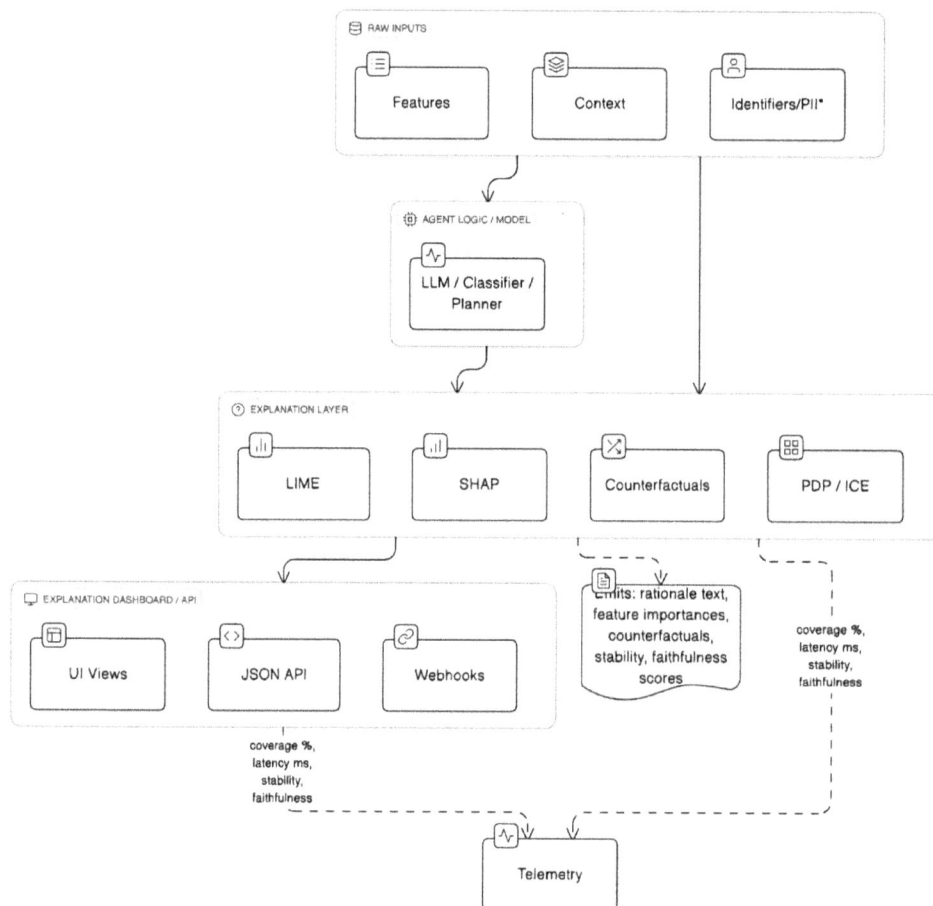

Figure 41: Explainability Stack.

## 9.3.3 Measuring Explanation Coverage and Quality

CTOs must define explanation coverage (the percentage of decisions accompanied by rationales) and explanation latency (the time from decision to explanation availability). Additional metrics include:

- **Stability of explanations**: How much explanations vary under small perturbations.
- **Faithfulness**: How well the explanation reflects the internal model logic.
- **Comprehensibility**: How well human stakeholders understand explanations (often measured via user studies).

These metrics should be tied to SLOs within the governance layer.

## 9.3.4 XAI in Production: Case Studies and Outcomes

- The DARPA XAI program produces prototypes combining high-performing models with explainability to support human decision-making.
- In healthcare, a recent survey outlines multiple deployments of XAI in imaging, diagnostics, and multimodal systems, each emphasizing the need for transparent reasoning to support clinical decisions.
- In the finance sector, explainable credit scoring models using SHAP are now favored to satisfy regulatory demands in the EU and U.S. (though less publicly documented, the pattern is widespread).

These real-world cases underline that explainability is not a theoretical accessory: it materially shapes adoption, trust, and regulatory compliance.

Explainability makes agent decisions interpretable, but interpretation alone doesn't guarantee accountability. To enforce compliance and traceability, those decisions must be recorded, verified, and auditable. The next section introduces immutable audit trails and continuous compliance pipelines as the backbone of trustworthy agentic systems.

## 9.4 Immutable Audit Trails and Continuous Compliance

## 9.4.1 Why Audit Trails Are Non-Negotiable

To satisfy regulators and governance bodies, agent systems must record every decision, input, explanation, and override in a non-erasable, tamper-resistant log. These audit trails serve as forensic records, compliance proofs, and debugging backbones. Without them, transparency and accountability collapse into mere rhetoric. From a technical perspective, audit logs should be:

- **Append-only** and **cryptographically timestamped** (e.g., using blockchain or Merkle tree structures).

- **Correlated** with policy versions, system state snapshots, and input provenance.

- **Queryable** for compliance checks, anomaly detection, and rollbacks.

## 9.4.2 Audit Pipeline Design

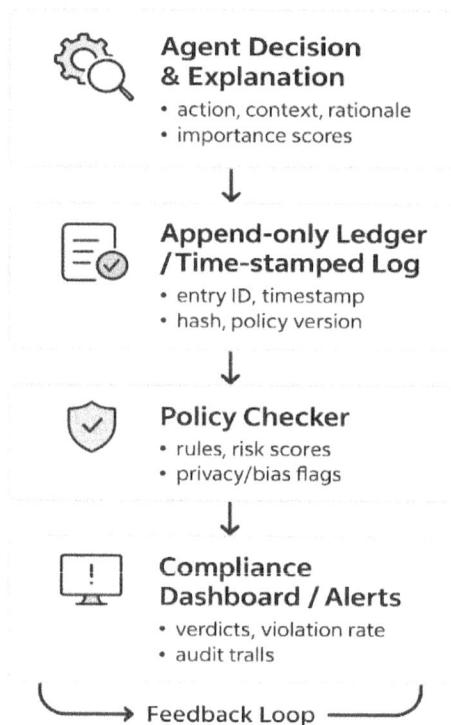

Figure 42: Audit and Compliance Pipeline.

Figure 42 depicts the end-to-end flow of decision auditing and compliance verification in agentic systems. Each agent decision, along with its rationale and importance scores, is captured in an append-only, time-stamped ledger, preserving integrity and traceability. This log is then evaluated by a policy checker that applies governance rules, risk scores, and privacy/bias flags.

The results of this evaluation are displayed in a compliance dashboard that shows verdicts, violation rates, and audit trail summaries. A feedback loop closes the system, allowing policy updates, model tuning, and escalation protocols to be refined based on observed violations. This architecture ensures that every autonomous action is not only explainable but continuously verified against enterprise and regulatory standards.

At ingestion, each log entry must include:

- Decision metadata (timestamp, agent identity, and context)
- Explanation artifact (feature importances or counterfactuals)
- Policy check results and verdict
- Any override or HITL escalation data.

These ingestion elements form the foundation of traceable autonomy. By capturing not just what the agent did, but why it did so, under which policy, and with what human oversight, the audit pipeline transforms raw decisions into accountable records. This level of granularity is essential for forensic analysis, regulatory response, and continuous governance refinement, ensuring that agentic systems remain transparent, reversible, and aligned with enterprise trust mandates.

### 9.4.3 Blockchain or Ledger Use Cases

To ensure audit trails are truly immutable, some organizations are turning to blockchain and distributed ledger technologies. These systems offer cryptographic guarantees that logs cannot be altered retroactively, making them ideal for high-stakes agentic environments.

For instance, EY's Blockchain Assurance Platform (2024) demonstrated real-time audit logging anchored to distributed ledgers, enabling continuous auditability and external verification by regulators. While the implementation did not focus specifically on agentic AI, the architectural pattern is highly relevant.

Similarly, several AI consortia have proposed using platforms like Hyperledger Fabric or Corda to anchor autonomous system logs. These approaches allow external auditors to verify decision histories without relying on centralized control, reinforcing transparency and trust.

## 9.4.4 Challenges and Mitigations

Despite their promise, immutable audit systems introduce new technical challenges that must be addressed to scale responsibly:

- **Scalability** remains a key concern. High-frequency agent decisions can overwhelm append-only systems, requiring thoughtful design strategies such as batching, compression, or tiered logging.
- **Privacy leakage** is another risk. Logs must avoid embedding sensitive data directly; instead, they should reference hashed or redacted pointers to full context stored under strict access controls.
- **Versioning drift** complicates historical audits. As governance policies evolve, audit logs must record the exact policy version applied at the time of each decision to enable accurate retrospective compliance checks.

These mitigations are essential to preserving the integrity and utility of audit infrastructure in dynamic agentic systems.

## 9.4.5 Compliance as a Continuous Loop

Auditability is not a one-time event; it must be embedded into a continuous governance cycle. Effective systems treat compliance as an active feedback loop, not a passive archive.

Alerts from compliance violations should feed directly into governance controllers (as outlined in Chapter 8), enabling real-time response. Detection of anomalous logs may trigger automated circuit breakers that roll back or quarantine agent actions before harm propagates. Over time, aggregated audit statistics inform policy refinement, model retraining, and escalation protocols. This closed-loop architecture ensures that compliance is perpetual, adaptive, and deeply integrated into the operational fabric of agentic AI. With governance architecture and operational controls in place, the final pillar of trust is auditability. To sustain accountability at scale, agentic systems must record, verify, and respond to every autonomous action. The next section explores how Microsoft has implemented unified auditability across its ecosystem, offering a real-world blueprint for policy-driven governance.

## 9.5 Microsoft: Policy-Driven Governance with Unified Auditability

Microsoft serves as an exemplary model for production agent governance, with a comprehensive, end-to-end approach that aligns perfectly with the Ethical Oversight Flow. This includes tenant-wide, append-only auditing, detailed trails of device/admin and security actions, and robust policy evaluation and remediation supported by dashboards and human-in-the-loop operations.

Microsoft exemplifies strong production agent governance through its comprehensive, end-to-end strategy, which fully adheres to the Ethical Oversight Flow. This strategy incorporates tenant-wide, append-only auditing, extensive logging of device/admin and security actions, and powerful policy evaluation and remediation capabilities, all supported by interactive dashboards and human-in-the-loop interventions.

### Key Components of Microsoft's Governance Model

- **Unified, Append-Only Auditing (Purview)**: Microsoft Purview Audit systematically captures and retains thousands of user and administrative operations across all Microsoft 365 services within a single, unified audit log. The Premium version offers extended retention periods, increased API bandwidth, and "intelligent insights," with capabilities for searching and exporting data via the Purview portal and APIs.

- **Security and Endpoint Action Auditing**: Defender XDR and Defender for Endpoint meticulously record security-relevant changes and actions. This data is then searchable from both the Defender portal and Purview, providing critical forensic information on activities such as device isolation and indicator updates.

- **Device/Admin Activity Trails and Observability Streaming**: Intune audit logs, enabled by default for all tenants, document create, update, delete, assign, and remote operations. These logs can be streamed to Azure Storage, Event Hubs, or Log Analytics (KQL), enabling integration with SIEMs and other observability pipelines.

- **Continuous Compliance and Drift Remediation (Azure Policy)**: Azure Policy continuously assesses resources and displays their compliance status on a dedicated dashboard. It also supports both bulk and automated remediation tasks, ensuring that non-compliant resources are brought back into alignment with defined policies, effectively addressing the "Compliance Check → Proceed/Violation" stage.

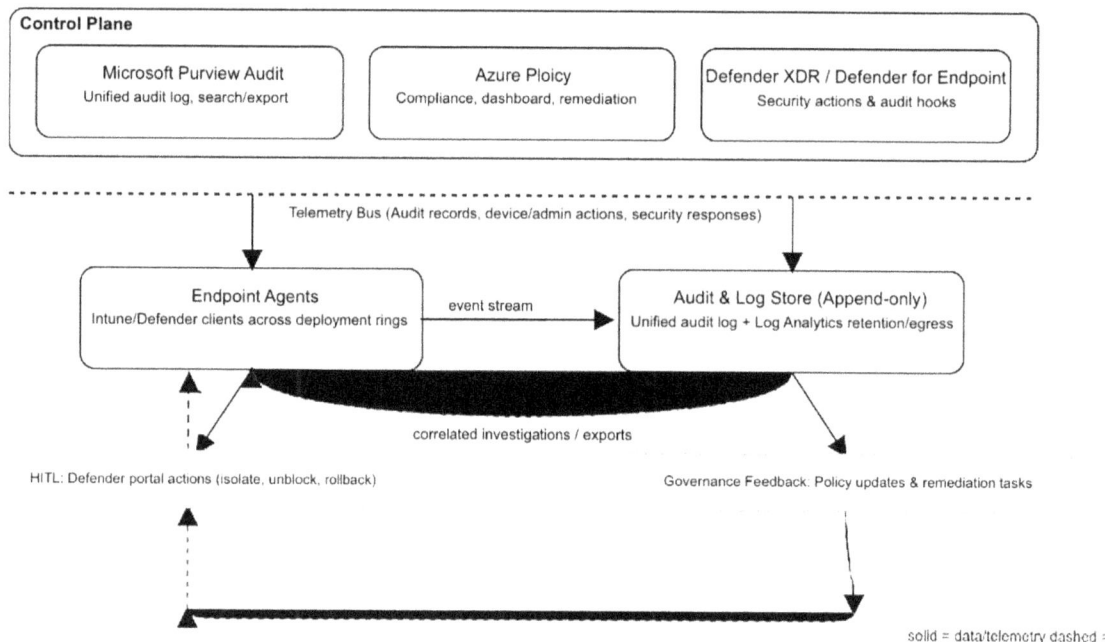

Figure 43: Microsoft Governance and Auditability Architecture. Author-created illustration. AI Agents at Work. Based on publicly documented Microsoft Purview Audit, Azure Policy, Microsoft Defender (XDR/for Endpoint), and Intune audit logging capabilities; not reproduced from any third-party figure.

Figure 43 illustrates Microsoft's integrated governance architecture for agentic systems, emphasizing how auditability and policy enforcement are operationalized across endpoints and cloud services. The control plane includes Purview Audit for unified logging, Azure Policy for compliance dashboards and remediation, and Defender XDR for security actions and audit hooks. These components stream telemetry through a centralized bus, capturing device activity, administrative actions, and security responses.

Endpoint agents, such as Intune and Defender clients, generate event streams that feed into an append-only audit and log store, enabling correlated investigations and long-term retention. Human-in-the-loop actions, such as isolate, unblock, or rollback, are surfaced through Defender portals, while governance feedback loops continuously update policies and trigger remediation tasks. This architecture exemplifies how enterprise-scale agent governance can be both automated and accountable, aligning with the Ethical Oversight Flow introduced earlier in the chapter.

## 9.6 ServiceNow

ServiceNow's IRM/GRC provides end-to-end workflows for policy/controls, evidence requests/collection, and exception handling. Evidence objects and attestations create a traceable audit trail, and dashboards surface control health; organizations often wire telemetry from Azure Policy/Defender/Intune into GRC evidence to operationalize CCM and maintain a ready-for-audit posture with human approvals where variance is detected.

Figure 44 presents the architecture of ServiceNow's IRM/GRC platform, showcasing how continuous controls monitoring is operationalized across cloud resources, applications, and endpoints. The execution surface generates telemetry on violations and events, which flows through integrations with platforms like Azure Policy, Defender, and SIEM into the control plane. Here, governance components, including policies, risk registers, and approval workflows, drive remediation tasks and change tickets.

The audit and log store captures time-stamped activity and exception decisions, supporting posture and drift detection. Human-in-the-loop actions, such as approval, rollback, and quarantine, are embedded throughout the workflow, ensuring that automated responses remain accountable. This architecture exemplifies how ServiceNow enables traceable, evidence-backed compliance across distributed environments, aligning with the principles of continuous auditability and governance feedback.

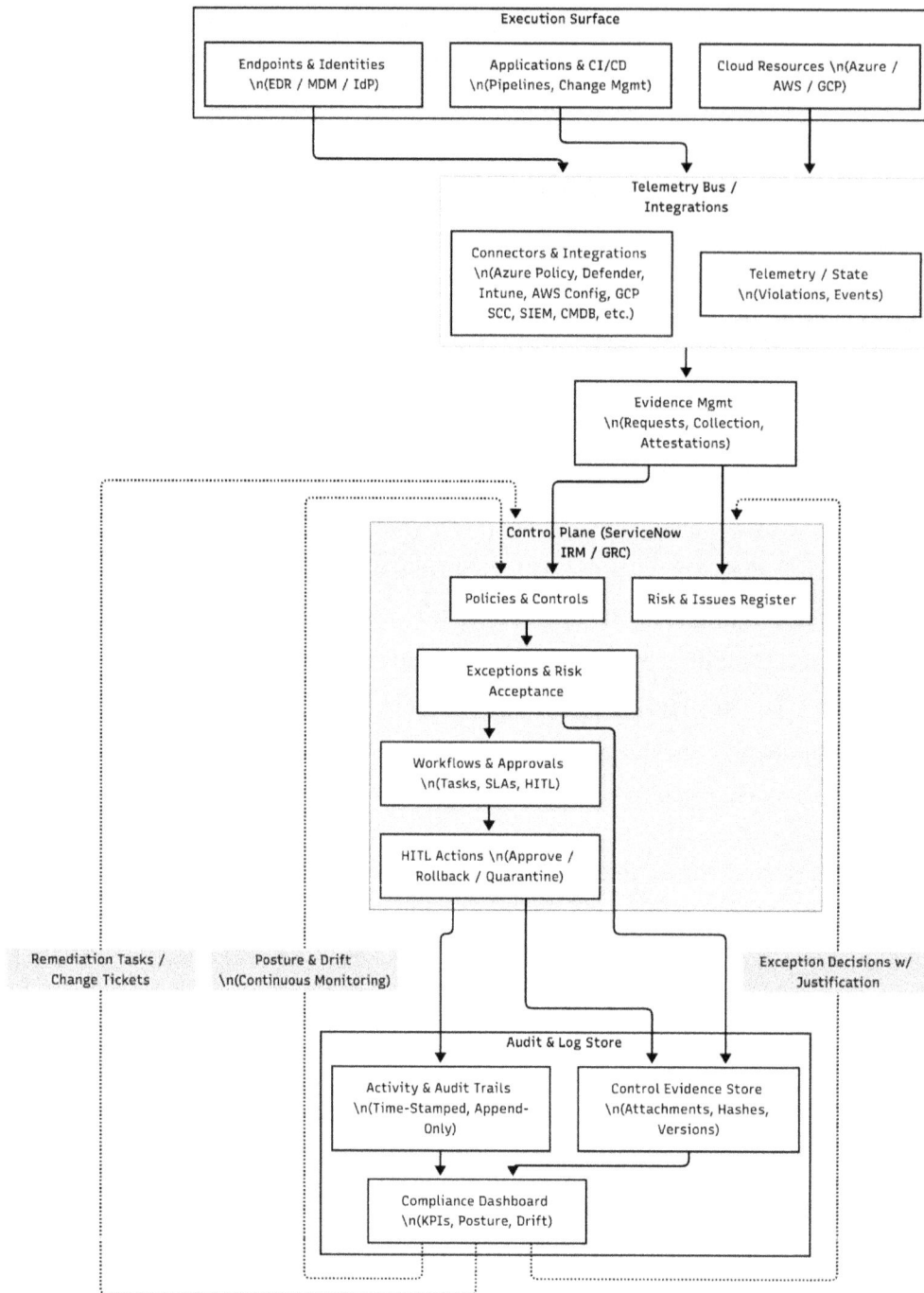

Figure 44: ServiceNow Governance and Auditability Architecture. Author-created illustrations. © AI Agents at Work. Based on publicly documented ServiceNow IRM/GRC capabilities and standard Continuous Controls Monitoring patterns, not reproduced from a third-party figure.

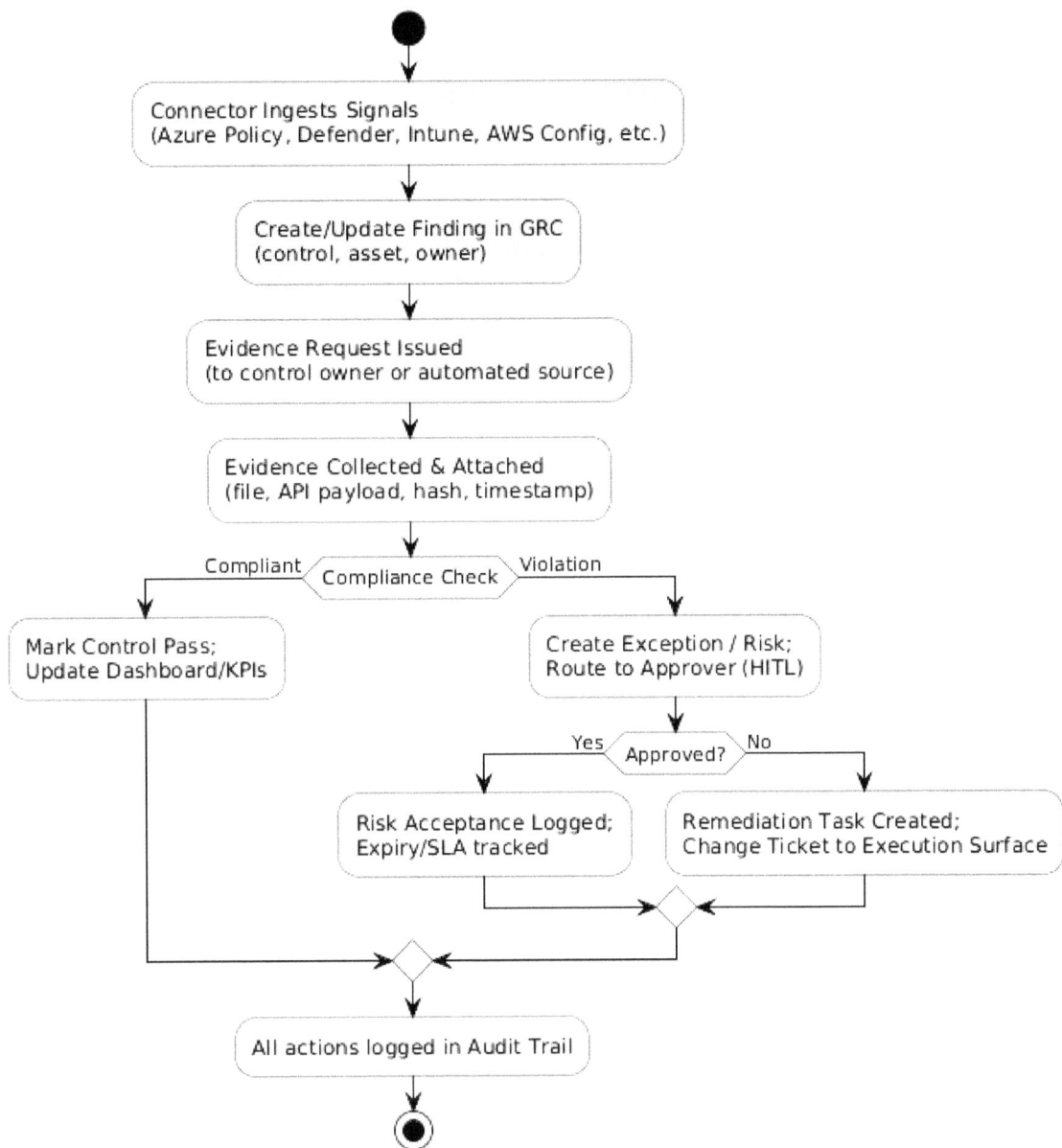

Figure 45: ServiceNow GRC Flow: Evidence-Backed Compliance. Author-created illustrations. © AI Agents at Work. Based on publicly documented ServiceNow IRM/GRC capabilities and standard Continuous Controls Monitoring patterns, not reproduced from a third-party figure.

Figure 45 illustrates the operational flow of ServiceNow's GRC system, emphasizing how compliance is enforced through evidence-backed workflows. Signals from platforms such as Azure Policy, Defender, Intune, and AWS Config are ingested by connectors, triggering the creation or update of findings linked to specific controls, assets, and owners. Evidence requests are issued and fulfilled either manually or automatically, with collected artifacts such as API payloads, hashes, and timestamps attached to the compliance record.

The flow then branches based on compliance outcomes: if the control passes, dashboards and KPIs are updated; if a violation occurs, a human-in-the-loop (HITL) process initiates exception handling. Approved exceptions are logged with SLA tracking, while rejected ones trigger remediation tasks and change tickets. Every action is recorded in an audit trail, ensuring traceability and accountability across the entire compliance lifecycle. This architecture exemplifies how automated and human oversight can co-exist in scalable, enterprise-grade governance systems.

Real-world platforms like Microsoft and ServiceNow demonstrate that governance and auditability are not abstract ideals. They are operational realities. But visibility alone isn't enough. To sustain trust, organizations must quantify it. The next section introduces key metrics, KPIs, and service-level objectives (SLOs) that translate ethical oversight into measurable performance.

## 9.7 Metrics, KPIs, and SLOs for Responsible Agentic AI

Trust in agentic AI is not a sentiment. It's a measurable system property. To ensure that ethics, privacy, and explainability are not just aspirational, organizations must define and track key performance indicators that reflect governance health. These metrics serve as the connective tissue between oversight and execution, enabling leaders to monitor compliance, detect drift, and refine policy in real time.

To operationalize trust, you must measure it. Figure 46 contains a recommended KPI dashboard structure. This figure presents a quarterly dashboard view of six core governance metrics that quantify trust, transparency, and operational discipline in agentic AI systems.

The Trust Index reflects the percentage of decisions that pass compliance checks. At the same time, Audit Latency measures the time between the decision and log capture, which is critical for real-time oversight. Explainability Coverage tracks how many decisions are accompanied by human-readable rationales.

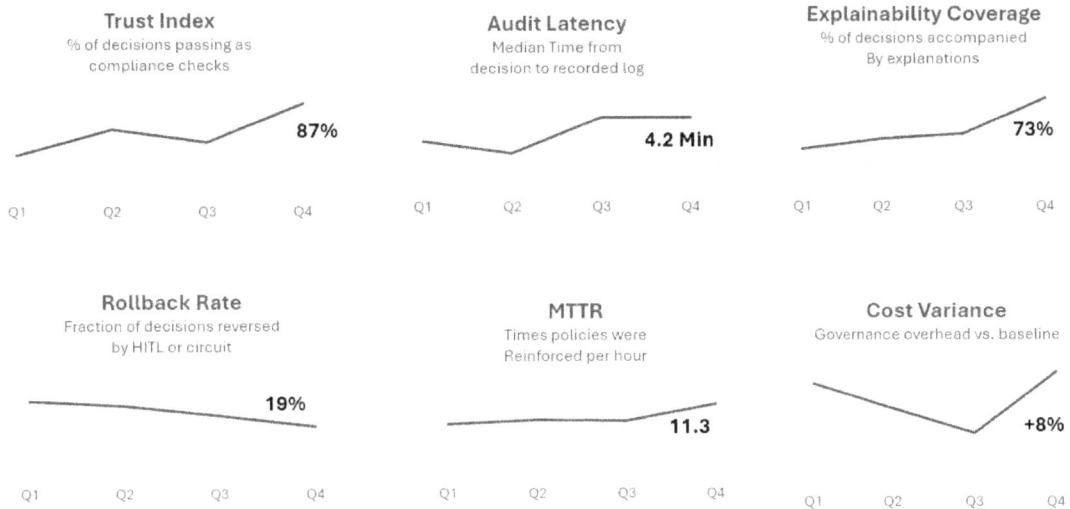

**Trust Index**
% of decisions passing as
compliance checks
87%

Q1  Q2  Q3  Q4

**Audit Latency**
Median Time from
decision to recorded log
4.2 Min

Q1  Q2  Q3  Q4

**Explainability Coverage**
% of decisions accompanied
By explanations
73%

Q1  Q2  Q3  Q4

**Rollback Rate**
Fraction of decisions reversed
by HITL or circuit
19%

Q1  Q2  Q3  Q4

**MTTR**
Times policies were
Reinforced per hour
11.3

Q1  Q2  Q3  Q4

**Cost Variance**
Governance overhead vs. baseline
+8%

Q1  Q2  Q3  Q4

Figure 46: Governance KPI Dashboard.

The Rollback Rate indicates the frequency of human or automated reversals. MTTR (Mean Time to Remediate) captures the speed of policy enforcement after violations, and Cost Variance highlights the financial overhead of governance relative to baseline operations.

Together, these indicators offer a multidimensional lens into system health, enabling leaders to monitor reliability, responsiveness, and fiscal stewardship over time.

## 9.7.1 Metric Definitions and SLOs

Trust Index:

$$\text{Trust Index} = \frac{\text{Decisions passing compliance checks}}{\text{Total decisions}} \times 100\%$$

**Audit Latency SLO**: For instance, 99% of decisions must appear in audit logs within 200 ms.

- **Explainability Coverage**:

$$\text{Coverage} = \frac{\text{Decisions with explanations}}{\text{Total decisions}} \times 100\%$$

- **Rollback Rate**: Ideally < 0.1% in stable systems; spikes indicate policy or model drift.
- **MTTR**: Track time from detection of violation to remediation.
- **Policy Drift Count**: Number of policy iterations per quarter indicates system dynamism.
- **Cost Variance**: Delta between governance overhead and baseline operational costs.

## 9.7.2 Interpretations and Targets

- A **Trust Index** above 99% is a pragmatic target in mature systems; below 98% may indicate governance gaps.
- **Audit Latency** must be low to avoid data staleness; batch logging for performance must not violate timeliness SLOs.
- **Tracking rollback rate** over time may surface bias or unmodeled edge cases.
- **Policy drift** should be infrequent but deliberate; constant changes imply instability.

These metrics should feed back into the governance cycle (Chapter 8), triggering audits, retraining, or policy revision. Metrics provide the lens, but execution requires a plan. To embed trust into enterprise systems, CTOs must move from measurement to implementation. The following roadmap outlines how to build, monitor, and evolve a responsible agentic AI stack.

# 9.8 Strategic Guidance for CTOs

## 9.8.1 Implementation Roadmap

Building responsible agentic AI systems requires more than technical excellence. It demands a governance-first mindset. The following ten steps offer a practical roadmap for CTOs to embed trust, transparency, and auditability into every layer of their AI infrastructure:

- **Governance and Ethics Council Formation**: Establish a cross-functional ethics and trust committee comprising legal, privacy, compliance, ML, and operations leads.

- **Policy Specification and Encoding**: Translate high-level rules into machine-executable policy languages (e.g., OPA, Rego, Drools) tied to governance modules.

- **Instrumented Agent Design**: From the agent logic (Chapter 5), require that every decision emits explanatory metadata and policy-check hooks.

- **Audit Log Infrastructure**: Design a cryptographically anchored append-only log (e.g., Merkle tree, DLT ledger) and integrate with compliance tooling.

- **Explainability Engine Integration**: Choose or build LIME, SHAP, counterfactual modules; define coverage, latency, and quality SLOs.

- **Federated Data and Privacy Layer**: If data sovereignty is required, architect federated or hybrid data layers (see Chapter 4) with an explanation of compatibility.

- **Continuous Monitoring and Feedback**: Deploy KPI dashboards (Figure 9.5), anomaly detection, and closed-loop governance escalation.

- **Audit and Simulation Testing**: Run simulated violations (policy breaches) to validate circuit breakers, escalation, and rollback mechanisms.

- **External Audit and Certification**: Engage third-party auditors (e.g., independent AI audit firms) to validate fairness, transparency, and log integrity.

- **Iterative Policy Refinement**: Use audit logs and drift statistics to refine policies, retrain models, and evolve governance.

Together, these steps form a repeatable blueprint for operationalizing trust. They ensure that agentic systems are not only performant but governable, capable of adapting to new risks, regulations, and ethical expectations without compromising transparency or control.

## 9.8.2 Organizational Considerations

To support this roadmap, organizations should establish a dedicated **Trust Ops Team A** group, responsible for monitoring, auditing, and tuning the trust infrastructure. Maintain **separation of duties** between model development, policy governance, and audit review to prevent conflicts of interest and ensure accountability.

Invest in **training and culture**: engineers must treat ethics, transparency, and privacy as first-class requirements, not post-hoc add-ons. And plan for **governance budgeting.** Expect that the trust infrastructure may consume 10-20% of the total AI system overhead during early deployment phases.

## 9.8.3 Link to Resilience and Risk (Chapter 10)

Trust is not just a compliance imperative. It's a risk mitigation strategy. Failures in explainability or auditability can escalate into operational, legal, and reputational crises. In the next chapter, we explore how governance connects to resilience, adversarial threats, and fallback strategies that ensure agentic systems remain safe under pressure.

---

## 9.9 Key Takeaways

- Ethics, privacy, explainability, and auditability are core technical disciplines, not optional add-ons.
- The Ethical Oversight Flow establishes a chain of accountability from decision to human oversight.
- Federated data architectures support data sovereignty and privacy-aware explanations.
- Explainability methods (LIME, SHAP, counterfactuals) must be carefully integrated and measured by coverage, latency, and fidelity.
- Immutable audit logs and ledger systems underpin traceability and compliance.
- Real systems like Tanium offer architectural analogies for governance and control in distributed-agent environments.

- Trust metrics and dashboards operationalize governance into SLOs.
- CTOs must treat trust infrastructure as a core component of their AI stack, managed, monitored, and iterated continuously.

## 9.10 Discussion Questions / Exercises

1   **Audit Flow Mapping**: Draw a detailed audit flow (similar to Figure 9.1) for your system's agent decisions, identifying all loggable events, fallback branches, and human-escalation paths.

2   **KPI Design**: Define a custom metric set for your domain (e.g., financial, healthcare) and propose target SLOs. How do you calibrate thresholds for rollback or escalation?

3   **Explanation Coverage Analysis:** Given a test agent workload of 1M decisions per day, propose sampling strategies (e.g., 1% full explanations, 100% minimal explanations) to manage cost without compromising trust.

4   **Policy and Versioning Scenario**: Suppose you update a policy mid-quarter (e.g., stricter constraint). Design a mechanism to reconcile pre-update log entries versus new policy decisions. How do you enable retroactive audits?

5   **Federated Explainability Challenge**: Consider your data resides across five geographic silos. Propose a mechanism that preserves per-silo local explanations while aggregating global explanations without violating sovereignty constraints.

6   **Tanium-Inspired Architecture Adaptation**: Using Figure 44 as a template, map how your agent fleet would integrate with a governance plane, telemetry buses, and audit store. Identify scaling and latency bottlenecks.

# CHAPTER 10

# How Agents Coordinate
# in AI-Powered Organizations

## 10.1 Technological Solutions for Addressing Agent System Failures

In most enterprise discussions about agentic AI, the spotlight tends to fall on the agent itself; its reasoning, autonomy, and ability to interact with users or systems. That's understandable.

Designing a capable agent is no small feat. But in practice, agents rarely operate in isolation. They are part of a larger choreography. One that involves messaging, coordination, and real-time orchestration across distributed systems, legacy infrastructure, and human workflows.

This chapter shifts the focus from the individual agent to the connective tissue that binds agents into operational ecosystems. It's about how agents communicate with each other, synchronize across time and space, and plug into enterprise platforms that manage workflows, enforce policies, and ensure reliability at scale.

We'll begin by exploring the technologies that underpin agent communication. These are message brokers, event streaming platforms, and coordination protocols. These systems allow agents to publish signals, subscribe to events, and negotiate shared state. They form the nervous system of agentic organizations, enabling responsiveness, resilience, and distributed decision-making.

From there, we'll examine the integration platforms that enable seamless agent coordination. These include middleware solutions, workflow engines, and semantic tools that help agents interpret data consistently across domains. We'll look at how agents participate in long-running business processes, how they escalate when thresholds are breached, and how they remain observable and governable within enterprise boundaries.

Throughout the chapter, we'll anchor these concepts in real-world patterns. How logistics agents reroute deliveries in response to traffic data, how compliance agents monitor transactional anomalies, and how customer-facing agents personalize experiences based on behavioral signals.

The goal is not just to describe the technology, but to show how coordination becomes a differentiator. Turning isolated intelligence into synchronized action.

*Agentic AI is not just about autonomy. It's about alignment.*

In enterprise environments, alignment requires communication, orchestration, and trust. This chapter is your guide to building that foundation.

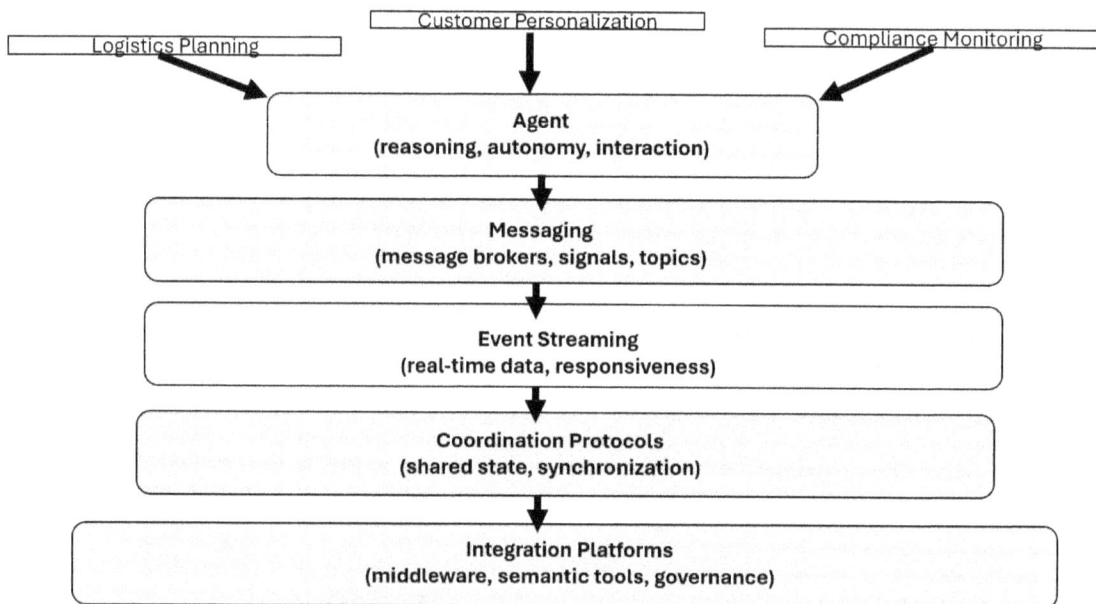

Figure 47: Agentic AI Coordination Overview.

This layered architecture illustrates how agentic intelligence becomes operationally aligned through messaging, streaming, and integration. It shows that agents are not standalone entities. They rely on a responsive infrastructure to interpret signals, synchronize decisions, and embed themselves into enterprise workflows. Coordination is the backbone of scalable autonomy, and includes:

- **Messaging, Streaming, Coordination**: The nervous system that allows agents to signal, respond, and synchronize.
- **Integration Platforms**: The connective tissue of middleware, workflows, and semantic tools that embed agents into enterprise operations.
- **Real-World Patterns**: Logistics, compliance, and personalization, where coordination becomes a business differentiator.

To move from concept to implementation, we begin with the foundational technologies that enable agents to communicate and coordinate at scale. These include messaging systems, event-streaming platforms, and protocols that enable agents to synchronize decisions across distributed environments.

## 10.2 How Companies Use Agent Messaging, Event Streaming, and Coordination Protocols

In traditional software systems, communication is often rigid and defined by APIs, scheduled jobs, and brittle integrations. But agentic environments demand something more fluid. Agents must be able to signal intent, respond to events, negotiate shared state, and recover from failure, all in real time, and often across distributed infrastructure. This section explores how companies enable that fluidity through three foundational layers: messaging, streaming, and coordination.

### 10.2.1 Messaging: The Language of Agentic Intent

At the heart of agent communication lies messaging. Not just emails or chatbots but structured, machine-readable signals. These signals express what agents have observed, what they intend to do, or what they need from others.

In enterprise settings, this messaging is mediated by broker systems like Apache Kafka, RabbitMQ, Azure Service Bus, or Google Pub/Sub. These platforms decouple senders from receivers, allowing agents to publish and subscribe to topics without knowing who's listening or responding. It's a model built for scale, resilience, and loose coupling.

Consider a fulfillment agent monitoring inventory levels. When stock drops below a threshold, it might publish a message to the topic "inventory.low". That message could trigger:

- A procurement agent to initiate a reorder.
- A pricing agent to adjust dynamic pricing.
- A customer experience agent to update availability messaging.

Each agent listens for signals relevant to its domain. And because messages are timestamped, versioned, and often schema-validated (using formats like JSON, Protobuf, or Avro), they carry context.

Messaging also supports escalation. A risk agent might publish "transaction.flagged" to alert compliance systems. A scheduling agent might emit "delivery.delayed" to trigger customer notifications. These aren't just events. Their decisions are encoded as messages.

---

*Messaging lets agents speak in verbs, not just nouns. They don't just describe, they act.*

---

## 10.2.2 Event Streaming: Real-Time Responsiveness at Scale

While messaging handles discrete signals, event streaming manages continuous flows. It's the difference between receiving a memo and monitoring a live feed. In agentic systems, both are essential.

Streaming platforms such as Apache Kafka, AWS Kinesis, and Azure Event Hubs enable agents to ingest and respond to high-velocity data, including telemetry, user interactions, sensor readings, and system logs. These streams are partitioned, replicated, and durably stored, enabling agents to process events in real time or replay them later for analysis.

Imagine a logistics agent tracking delivery vehicles. GPS coordinates stream in every few seconds. The agent doesn't just log them. It analyzes velocity, route deviation, and estimated arrival. If a delay is detected, it might publish a "delivery reroute" message or escalate to a human dispatcher.

Streaming also supports pattern detection. A fraud agent might monitor transaction velocity across accounts. A surge in activity could trigger anomaly detection, risk scoring, and escalation. All within milliseconds.

To coordinate effectively, agents rely on temporal metadata, such as timestamps, watermarks, and sequence IDs. These markers help maintain causality, detect out-of-order events, and ensure that decisions reflect the most current state.

And because events are stored durably, agents can replay history. This is critical for debugging, compliance audits, and training new agents on historical patterns.

In short, streaming turns agents from reactive responders into proactive orchestrators.

## 10.2.3 Coordination Protocols: Negotiating Shared State and System Integrity

Messaging and streaming enable communication. But coordination is about agreement. In multi-agent systems, agents often need to negotiate shared state, elect leaders, or synchronize actions. This requires protocols that go beyond simple signaling.

Consensus algorithms like Raft and Paxos help agents reach agreement on decisions, whether selecting a master node, committing a transaction, or updating a shared ledger. These protocols are designed for fault tolerance, ensuring that even in the face of network partitions or node failures, agents can reach quorum and proceed safely.

Other coordination primitives include:

- **Distributed Locks**: Prevent agents from simultaneously modifying the same resource.
- **Semaphores**: Control concurrency across agent tasks.
- **Heartbeats**: Monitor agent availability and trigger failover or rebalancing.

These mechanisms are especially important in environments with shared dependencies, such as databases, APIs, or physical assets. Without coordination, agents risk race conditions, deadlocks, or inconsistent states.

Consider a manufacturing floor with multiple agents controlling robotic arms. If two agents try to access the same conveyor belt simultaneously, the result could be a collision or downtime. Coordination protocols ensure that access is serialized, prioritized, and recoverable.

Coordination also supports escalation. If an agent detects a failure in its peer, it can trigger a fallback routine, notify a human operator, or reassign tasks to a backup agent. It is more than just resilience. It's operational maturity. In agentic organizations, coordination is what turns distributed intelligence into coherent action.

Figure 48 summarizes this section. It reveals the three foundational layers that transform agent communication into enterprise-grade orchestration. Messaging enables intent-driven signaling, streaming delivers real-time responsiveness, and coordination protocols ensure system integrity. Together, they form a resilient communication stack that allows agents to act independently without acting in isolation.

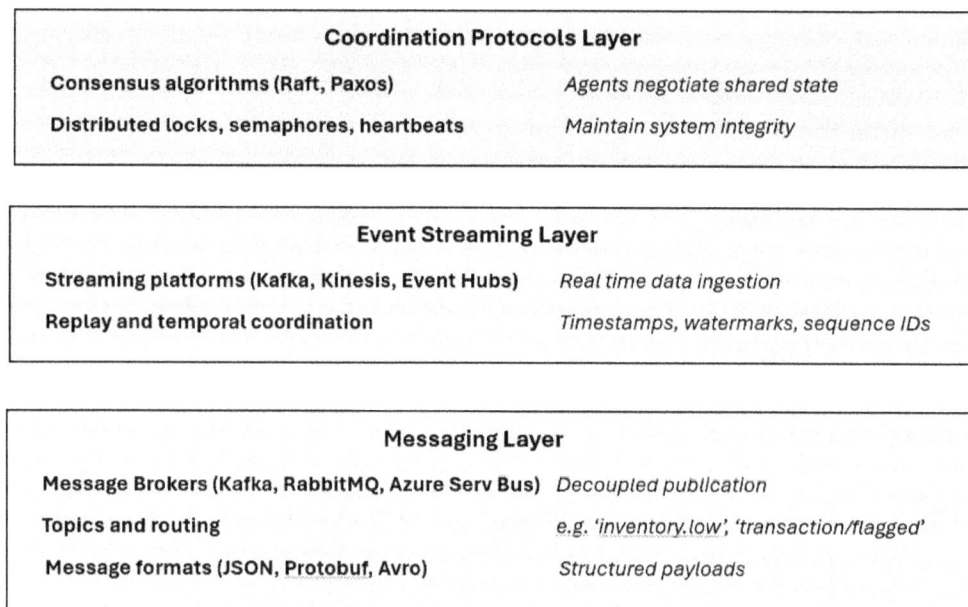

**Coordination Protocols Layer**

| | |
|---|---|
| **Consensus algorithms (Raft, Paxos)** | *Agents negotiate shared state* |
| **Distributed locks, semaphores, heartbeats** | *Maintain system integrity* |

**Event Streaming Layer**

| | |
|---|---|
| **Streaming platforms (Kafka, Kinesis, Event Hubs)** | *Real time data ingestion* |
| **Replay and temporal coordination** | *Timestamps, watermarks, sequence IDs* |

**Messaging Layer**

| | |
|---|---|
| **Message Brokers (Kafka, RabbitMQ, Azure Serv Bus)** | *Decoupled publication* |
| **Topics and routing** | *e.g. 'inventory.low', 'transaction/flagged'* |
| **Message formats (JSON, Protobuf, Avro)** | *Structured payloads* |

Figure 48: Enterprise Agent Communication and Coordination Layers.

While messaging, streaming, and coordination protocols enable agents to communicate and synchronize, they don't operate in a vacuum. To drive real business outcomes, agents must be embedded within the systems, workflows, and governance frameworks that define enterprise execution. We will discuss this in the next section.

## 10.3 Agent Integration Platforms for Seamless Enterprise Workflows

If messaging and coordination are the nervous system of agentic organizations, integration platforms are the connective tissue. They bind agents to the systems, data, and workflows that define enterprise operations.

*Without integration, agents remain isolated.*

They may be intelligent, but they are operationally inert. This section explores how companies use integration platforms to embed agents into business processes, orchestrate multi-step workflows, and ensure semantic consistency across domains.

### 10.3.1 Middleware and Workflow Engines: Orchestrating Agentic Action

Enterprise environments are rarely clean. They're a patchwork of cloud services, legacy systems, APIs, spreadsheets, and human approvals. Agents must navigate this complexity without becoming brittle or tailor-made. That's where integration middleware comes in.

Platforms like MuleSoft, Boomi, and Azure Logic Apps offer prebuilt connectors to common enterprise systems, including ERP, CRM, and data lakes. They allow agents to trigger workflows, retrieve data, and post updates without custom code. This low-code orchestration is critical for scale: it lets agents participate in business processes without requiring deep integration engineering.

Workflow engines like Camunda, Temporal, and Apache Airflow take it further. They manage long-running tasks, retries, compensation logic, and escalation paths. Agents can initiate a workflow, monitor its progress, and intervene when thresholds are breached. For example:

- A procurement agent might launch a multi-step approval flow for a high-value purchase.
- A compliance agent might monitor a transaction workflow for anomalies.
- A customer service agent might escalate a ticket based on sentiment analysis and SLA timers.

These platforms don't just connect agents; they choreograph them.

## 10.3.2 Semantic Interoperability: Making Meaning Portable

Communication is easy. Understanding is hard. In multi-agent environments, semantic consistency is essential. Agents must interpret data consistently, even if they operate in different domains, use different models, or were built by different teams.

Ontologies and schemas provide that consistency. Whether it's schema.org for web data, HL7 for healthcare, or FIBO for finance, these shared vocabularies help agents reason about meaning. Not just syntax. They define entities, relationships, constraints, and context.

Knowledge graphs take it further. By representing data as nodes and edges, agents can infer relationships, detect anomalies, and personalize responses. A customer agent might use a graph to understand purchase history, support interactions, and product preferences. A logistics agent might use it to model supply chain dependencies and risk propagation. Semantic tools also support translation. If one agent emits "customer.intent" and another expects "user.goal", a semantic layer can reconcile the difference. This provides operational integrity.

## 10.3.3 Governance and Observability: Trusting the Choreography

Coordination without oversight is chaos. Enterprises need visibility into agent behavior. Who did what? When? Why? They also need guardrails to ensure agents operate within policy boundaries.

Observability platforms like OpenTelemetry, Prometheus, and Grafana provide metrics, traces, and logs that make agentic systems transparent. They help teams monitor latency, throughput, error rates, and decision paths. If an agent misbehaves, engineers can trace its actions, diagnose the issue, and adjust its logic or permissions.

Security is equally critical. Agents authenticate via OAuth, JWT, or mutual TLS. They communicate over encrypted channels. And they operate within defined scopes, such as data access, escalation thresholds, and audit trails. Governance frameworks ensure that agents don't overstep, leak data, or make unauthorized decisions.

Policy enforcement can be dynamic. A compliance agent might block a transaction based on real-time risk scoring. A privacy agent might redact sensitive fields before sharing data with external systems. These aren't static rules. They are adaptive, context-aware, and enforceable.

*In mature organizations, governance isn't bolted on. It's embedded. It's what makes agentic intelligence trustworthy, auditable, and aligned with enterprise values.*

Figure 49 illustrates the Agentic AI Coordination paradigm. it highlights how agents become trustworthy participants in enterprise systems. Middleware and workflow engines allow agents to trigger and navigate complex business processes. Semantic tools ensure consistent interpretation across domains. Governance and observability enforce boundaries and transparency. The stack reflects a shift from experimentation to operational maturity.

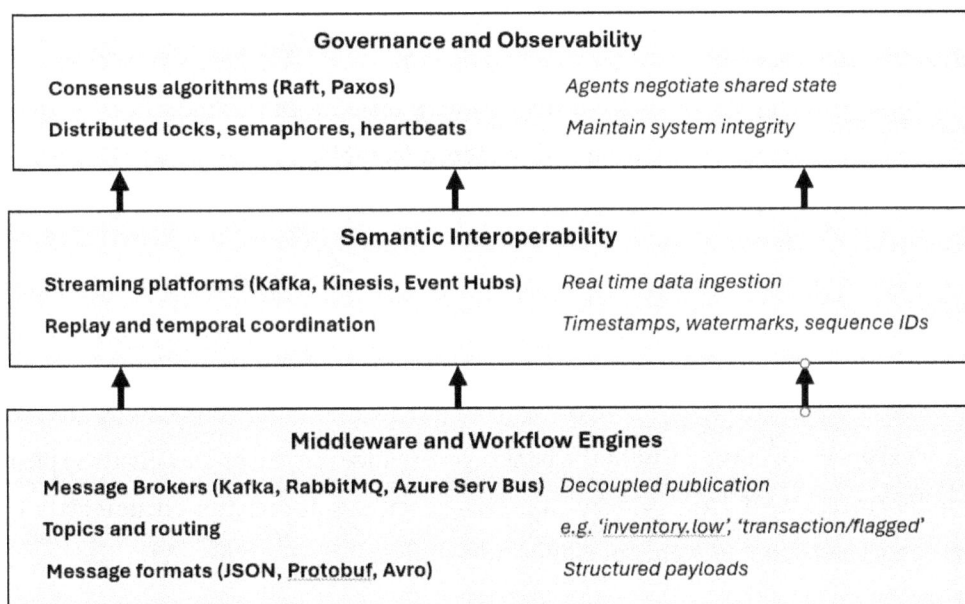

Figure 49: Agentic AI Coordination Overview.

## 10.4 Use Case Vignette: Coordinated Agents in Real-Time Financial Risk Monitoring

In the high-stakes world of financial services, speed and precision are everything. A multinational bank operating across retail, commercial, and investment divisions deploys a network of intelligent agents to monitor transactional activity, enforce compliance, and mitigate risk. These agents are embedded across systems.

Some are watching for fraud, others scanning for regulatory violations, and still others managing customer experience. On a typical day, they operate independently. But when a suspicious pattern emerges, coordination becomes critical.

Late one afternoon, a fraud detection agent monitoring retail transactions notices a burst of high-value transfers originating from a dormant account. The velocity, amount, and timing violate several behavioral thresholds. Within milliseconds, the agent publishes a "risk.alert" message to the enterprise event bus. An Apache Kafka stream routes signals across the organization.

That signal is picked up by multiple agents:

- A **compliance agent**, trained on jurisdictional rules and KYC (know your customer) profiles, cross-references the flagged account against known risk indicators. It identifies a mismatch in beneficiary location and triggers a "compliance.review" workflow via Camunda.

- A **customer experience agent**, integrated with the bank's CRM and mobile app, initiates a secure verification protocol. It temporarily freezes the account, sends a push notification to the customer, and offers a guided re-authentication path.

- A **legal agent**, operating within the bank's governance framework, evaluates exposure under current AML (Anti-Money Laundering) statutes. It prepares documentation for potential escalation to regulatory authorities and logs the event for audit.

Each agent operates within its domain, but they share context through semantic layers. The term "risk.alert" is mapped to "transaction.anomaly" and "account.freeze" across systems, ensuring consistent interpretation. Knowledge graphs help agents understand relationships between accounts, customers, geographies, and historical patterns.

Coordination protocols ensure that no two agents take conflicting actions. Distributed locks prevent simultaneous updates to the same account. Heartbeats confirm agent availability. If the fraud agent goes offline during the escalation, a backup agent resumes the workflow without losing state.

Observability tools like OpenTelemetry trace the entire response chain from detection to resolution. Engineers can see which agents acted, when, and why. Governance policies enforce access boundaries: the customer experience agent can freeze the account, but only the compliance agent can initiate a regulatory report.

The entire response unfolds in under 30 seconds. No human intervention is required until the final escalation. The customer is notified, the risk is contained, and the bank remains compliant.

This isn't just automation. It's orchestration. A distributed network of agents, each with its own intelligence, communicating, coordinating, and acting in concert.

---

*It's the operational maturity that agentic AI makes possible.*
*And the kind of responsiveness that modern financial institutions demand.*

---

Figure 50 demonstrates how a network of specialized agents responds to a high-risk event in real time. Each agent acts within its domain, shares context through semantic layers and coordination protocols. The result is not just automation, but synchronized intelligence that protects the enterprise without sacrificing speed or control.

A fraud detection agent initiates the alert, triggering coordinated actions across compliance, customer experience, and legal domains. Communication flows through Kafka topics, while coordination protocols ensure safe concurrency and failover. Integration platforms like Camunda orchestrate workflows, semantic layers reconcile terminology, and observability tools trace the full response chain.

Together, these components demonstrate how agentic AI transforms isolated detection into synchronized enterprise action.

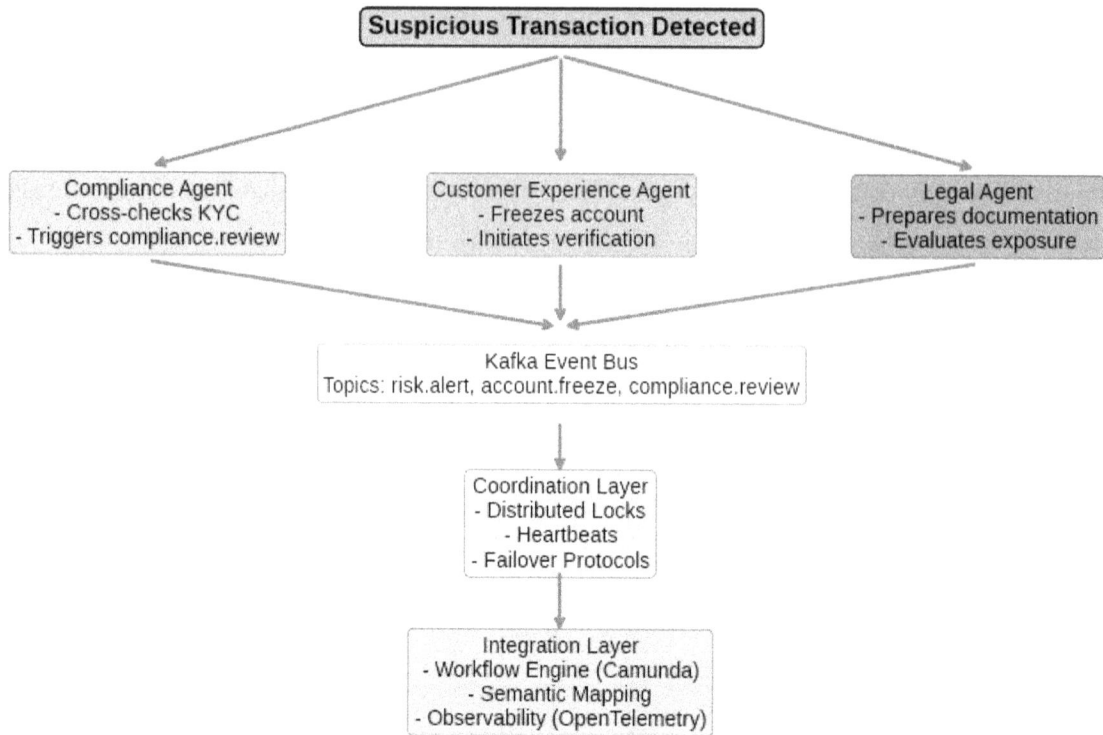

Figure 50: Coordinated Agents in Financial Risk Monitoring.

## 10.5 Key Takeaways

- **Agentic intelligence requires alignment**, not just autonomy achieved through communication, coordination, and integration.

- **Messaging systems** enable agents to signal intent and trigger domain-specific actions via decoupled channels.

- **Event streaming platforms** provide real-time responsiveness, allowing agents to monitor, react, and replay high-velocity data.

- **Coordination protocols** ensure agents negotiate shared state, maintain system integrity, and recover from failure.

- **Integration platforms** embed agents into enterprise workflows using middleware, workflow engines, and semantic tools.

- **Semantic interoperability** allows agents to interpret data consistently across domains and reconcile terminology differences.
- **Governance and observability frameworks** enforce policy boundaries, trace agent behavior, and ensure trustworthiness.

## 10.6 Discussion Questions / Exercises

**Conceptual Reflection**

1. Why is coordination considered a differentiator in agentic AI systems? How does it go beyond simple automation?
2. Compare and contrast messaging and event streaming. In what scenarios would each be more appropriate?
3. How do coordination protocols like Raft or distributed locks prevent system-level failures in multi-agent environments?

**Applied Analysis**

4. Imagine an agent network deployed in a hospital setting. Outline how messaging, streaming, and coordination would support patient monitoring and emergency response.
5. Select a workflow engine (e.g., Camunda, Temporal). Describe how it could be used to orchestrate a multi-agent process in supply chain management.
6. Evaluate the role of semantic interoperability in cross-departmental agent communication. What risks arise without it?

**Hands-On Exercise**

7. Design a simple agent coordination flow using Kafka topics and coordination primitives. Include at least three agents and their respective triggers.
8. Create a governance checklist for deploying agents in a financial institution. Include observability, authentication, and escalation protocols.

9. Draft a semantic mapping table that reconciles terminology between a customer service agent and a marketing analytics agent.

As agents become embedded in enterprise workflows, their coordination must be matched by visibility. The next frontier is not just how agents act, but how their actions are observed, understood, and governed in real time. Chapter 11 explores the dashboards, analytics, and monitoring frameworks that turn agentic behavior into actionable insight.

CHAPTER 11

# Making Agentic AI Operational

## 11.1 Monitoring Agent Systems with Real-Time Dashboards

Agentic AI systems are only as valuable as their ability to deliver actionable insights at the moment they're needed. While much attention has been given to agent design, orchestration, and deployment, the true business impact emerges when these systems are operationalized: monitored, visualized, and integrated into decision workflows with precision and reliability.

This chapter explores the technologies and strategies that enable real-time visibility into agent performance and decision-making. From streaming dashboards to embedded analytics, enterprises now have the tools to observe agent behavior, track outputs, and intervene when necessary. Real-time monitoring not only enhances trust and transparency but also supports governance, compliance, and continuous improvement.

We examine how visual business intelligence platforms are evolving to support agentic architectures, offering intuitive interfaces for tracking agent interactions, system health, and decision outcomes.

*These dashboards serve as both control panels and feedback loops, allowing human stakeholders to validate, adjust, and learn from autonomous systems in flight.*

Beyond visualization, this chapter addresses the delivery of agent-driven decisions into business applications. Whether it's routing a recommendation to a CRM, triggering a workflow in an ERP, or updating a knowledge graph, the integration layer is where agentic intelligence meets operational execution. We highlight best practices to ensure that decisions are not only accurate but also timely, traceable, and aligned with enterprise priorities.

Ultimately, operationalizing agentic AI means bridging the gap between autonomy and accountability. It's about making intelligent systems observable, governable, and useful so that their insights don't just exist in isolation but drive real-world outcomes across the enterprise.

To make agentic AI truly operational, visibility is a requirement. Before decisions can be trusted, integrated, or acted upon, organizations must be able to observe how agents behave, what outputs they generate, and how those outputs evolve in real time. That begins with the technologies that enable continuous reporting and monitoring tools that transform autonomous systems from opaque engines into transparent, accountable collaborators.

## 11.2 Technologies That Enable Real-Time Reporting and Monitoring of Agent Systems

As agentic AI systems transition from experimental prototypes to enterprise-grade solutions, the need for robust, real-time monitoring becomes paramount. These systems are no longer isolated tools; they are dynamic, autonomous entities interacting with data, applications, and human stakeholders across distributed environments. To ensure reliability, transparency, and business alignment, organizations must adopt technologies that provide continuous visibility into agent behavior, decision outputs, and system health.

At the core of this capability is a modern observability stack. Tools such as Prometheus, Grafana, and OpenTelemetry enable developers and operations teams to collect, visualize, and analyze telemetry data from agent orchestration frameworks. These platforms track metrics such as task completion rates, latency, error frequency, and resource utilization, offering a granular view of how agents perform in real time. As we have discussed, integrated with orchestration tools like

LangGraph, CrewAI, or AutoGen, they can also surface workflow-level insights, such as branching-logic outcomes, retry patterns, and inter-agent communication flows.

Beyond system metrics, enterprises increasingly rely on real-time dashboards built with business intelligence platforms like Power BI, Tableau, and Looker. These dashboards translate agent outputs into actionable insights for non-technical stakeholders. For example, a dashboard might display the confidence score of a recommendation, the provenance of a decision, or the sequence of agent interactions leading to a business outcome. This level of transparency fosters trust, supports governance, and enables human-in-the-loop oversight where needed.

Real-time monitoring also plays a critical role in operational resilience. Autonomous systems, by nature, can encounter unexpected scenarios such as data drift, model degradation, or external API failures. Monitoring tools equipped with alerting mechanisms can detect anomalies as they occur, triggering automated responses or notifying human operators before issues escalate. This is especially vital in regulated industries, where auditability and compliance are non-negotiable. Technologies that log agent decisions, track data lineage, and timestamp interactions provide the foundation for traceability and post-hoc analysis.

Another emerging capability is agent visualization, which provides graphical representations of agent workflows, decision paths, and system interactions. These visualizations help teams understand how agents navigate complex logic, collaborate with other agents, and adapt to changing inputs. Whether rendered as node graphs, flowcharts, or heatmaps, these tools make abstract agent behavior tangible, enabling faster debugging, optimization, and stakeholder communication.

Finally, real-time monitoring technologies are increasingly being integrated with business applications. Agent decisions can be routed directly into CRMs, ERPs, or workflow engines, with dashboards tracking not just what agents decide but how those decisions impact operations. This tight feedback loop between autonomous systems and enterprise platforms is what transforms agentic AI from a promising innovation into a reliable operational asset.

In summary, real-time reporting and monitoring technologies are the connective tissue between agent autonomy and enterprise accountability. They ensure that agentic systems remain observable, governable, and aligned with business goals, delivering insights not just with intelligence, but with integrity and impact.

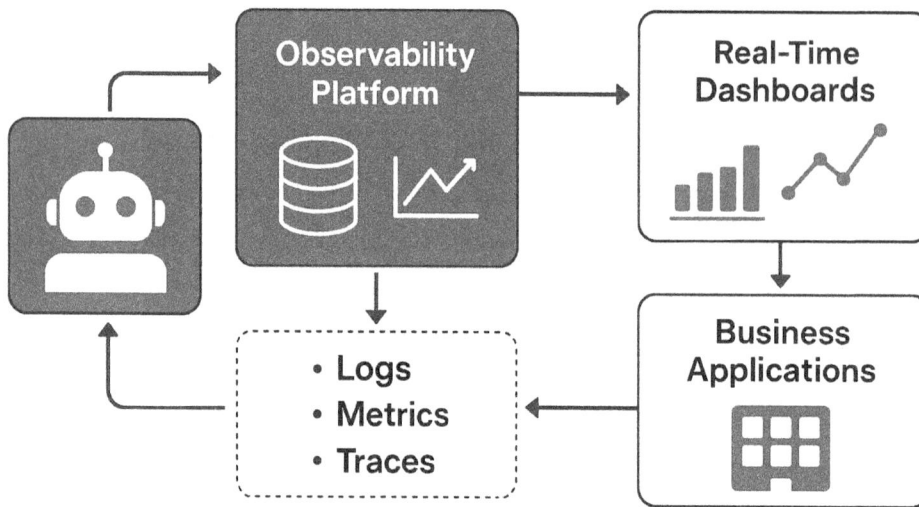

Figure 51: Real-Time Reporting and Monitoring Architecture.

Figure 51 illustrates the flow of real-time monitoring and reporting within an agentic AI system. At its core, autonomous agents generate outputs and telemetry data that are captured by observability platform tools like Prometheus or OpenTelemetry, which collect logs, metrics, and traces. These data streams feed into real-time dashboards, enabling stakeholders to visualize agent behavior, system health, and decision outcomes through intuitive interfaces.

From there, agent-driven insights are routed to business applications such as CRMs, ERPs, and workflow engines, ensuring that autonomous decisions are not only monitored but also operationalized. The diagram highlights how each layer from observability to visualization to integration works together to make agentic systems transparent, accountable, and enterprise-ready.

*Real-time monitoring technologies form the backbone of operational agentic AI.*

By capturing logs, metrics, and traces from autonomous systems, observability platforms and dashboards provide continuous visibility into agent behavior, system health, and decision latency. These tools enable organizations to detect anomalies, validate performance, and ensure that agent outputs remain aligned with enterprise goals and compliance standards.

Yet monitoring alone is not enough. To truly empower decision-makers and integrate agentic intelligence into business strategy, organizations must translate raw telemetry into meaningful, accessible insights. That's where visual business intelligence comes in, serving as the interpretive layer that transforms autonomous outputs into actionable narratives, bridging the gap between technical complexity and strategic clarity.

## 11.3 The Role of Visual Business Intelligence in Agentic AI Strategies

As agentic AI systems become more autonomous and embedded across enterprise functions, the need for interpretability and transparency grows in parallel. These systems are capable of generating complex decisions, recommendations, and insights, but without a mechanism to surface those outputs in a clear, accessible format, their strategic value remains underutilized. Visual business intelligence (BI) platforms serve as the connective tissue between autonomous agent behavior and human understanding, enabling organizations to monitor, validate, and act on agent-driven insights in real time.

Modern BI tools such as Power BI, Tableau, Looker, and Qlik are evolving to support agentic architectures. These platforms are no longer just passive reporting layers; they are dynamic interfaces that visualize agent workflows, decision paths, and system health across distributed environments. Dashboards can display key metrics such as agent confidence scores, task completion rates, branching logic outcomes, and even inter-agent communication patterns. For example, a dashboard might show how a team of agents collaborated to generate a market analysis, highlighting which agent performed research, which synthesized findings, and which delivered the final recommendation. This level of granularity transforms opaque agent behavior into a transparent, auditable process.

Visual BI also plays a critical role in decision traceability. In regulated industries such as finance, healthcare, and defense, organizations must be able to explain how decisions were made, what data was used, and whether any human oversight occurred. BI dashboards can log agent actions, timestamp decisions, and display the sequence of events leading to a particular outcome. This supports compliance with frameworks like HIPAA, GDPR, and FedRAMP, while also enabling post-hoc analysis and continuous improvement. When paired with observability platforms, BI tools can even correlate agent decisions with system-level telemetry, offering a holistic view of performance and reliability.

Another strategic function of visual BI is its ability to bridge technical and non-technical stakeholders. Engineers and data scientists may focus on orchestration logic and model performance, while business leaders care about outcomes, trends, and strategic alignment. BI dashboards serve as a shared interface, allowing both groups to engage with agentic AI from their respective vantage points. This fosters collaboration, accelerates feedback loops, and ensures that autonomous systems remain aligned with enterprise goals. In many cases, dashboards serve as the primary touchpoint for executives and decision-makers, providing a high-level overview of agent activity without requiring deep technical expertise.

Visual BI also supports governance and exception handling. Dashboards can be configured to flag anomalies, highlight outlier decisions, or trigger alerts when agents deviate from expected behavior. For instance, if an agent begins recommending actions outside of its defined scope, or if confidence scores drop below a threshold, the dashboard can notify human operators to intervene. This capability is essential for maintaining control over autonomous systems, especially in high-stakes environments where errors can have significant consequences.

Finally, visual BI enables strategic storytelling. As organizations scale their use of agents, they need to communicate the impact of these systems to internal and external audiences, including boards, regulators, partners, and customers.

---

*Dashboards can be used to demonstrate how agentic AI drives efficiency, improves decision quality, and uncovers new opportunities.*

---

They provide a visual narrative that complements technical documentation and performance reports, helping stakeholders understand not only what agents are doing but also why it matters.

In summary, visual business intelligence is a cornerstone of operationalizing agentic AI. It transforms raw outputs into meaningful insights, supports compliance and governance, bridges organizational silos, and empowers decision-makers to act with clarity and confidence. As agent systems become more sophisticated, the role of BI will only grow, serving as the lens through which autonomy becomes accountability, and complexity becomes clarity.

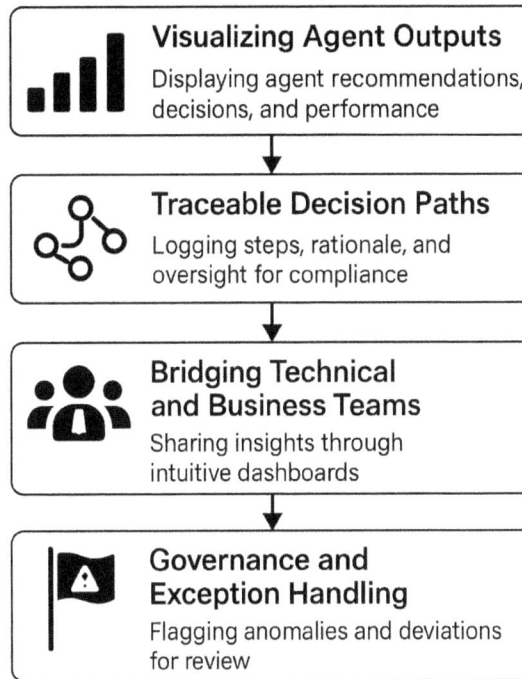

**Visualizing Agent Outputs**
Displaying agent recommendations, decisions, and performance

**Traceable Decision Paths**
Logging steps, rationale, and oversight for compliance

**Bridging Technical and Business Teams**
Sharing insights through intuitive dashboards

**Governance and Exception Handling**
Flagging anomalies and deviations for review

Figure 52: Key Functions of Visual Business Intelligence Within Agentic AI.

Figure 52 summarizes the key functions of visual business intelligence within agentic AI strategies, highlighting how BI platforms transform autonomous outputs into actionable insights. It illustrates four core roles: visualizing agent outputs through charts and performance metrics; enabling traceable decision paths for compliance and auditability; bridging technical and business teams via intuitive dashboards; and supporting governance through anomaly detection and exception handling. Together, these elements show how BI tools serve as the interpretive layer that makes agent behavior transparent, accountable, and strategically aligned with enterprise goals.

Real-time monitoring technologies form the backbone of operational agentic AI. By capturing logs, metrics, and traces from autonomous systems, observability platforms and dashboards provide continuous visibility into agent behavior, system health, and decision latency. These tools enable organizations to detect anomalies, validate performance, and ensure that agent output remains aligned with enterprise goals and compliance standards.

Yet monitoring alone is not enough. To truly empower decision-makers and integrate agentic intelligence into business strategy, organizations must translate raw telemetry into meaningful, accessible insights. That's where visual business intelligence comes in, serving as the interpretive layer that transforms autonomous outputs into actionable narratives, bridging the gap between technical complexity and strategic clarity.

## 11.4 Real-time Agent Visualization for System Monitoring

As agentic systems grow more autonomous and embedded across enterprise environments, the ability to monitor them in real time has shifted from a technical luxury to an operational necessity. Visualization is the lens through which we interpret agent behavior: what they're doing, why they're doing it, and whether their actions align with system goals or deviate in concerning ways.

At its core, real-time visualization offers a cognitive mirror into the agent's mind. Dashboards can surface internal states like memory usage, task queues, confidence scores, and environmental inputs. These views are foundational for building trust, interpretability, and rapid response in dynamic environments.

### Key Visualization Modalities

- **Agent State Dashboards**: These provide a live snapshot of each agent's operational metrics, helping teams assess performance, resource utilization, and responsiveness. When designed well, they reflect both internal reasoning and external stimuli in a way that's immediately actionable.

- **Interaction Graphs**: Mapping inter-agent communication and task handoffs reveals coordination patterns, bottlenecks, and emergent behaviors. These graphs help teams identify overloaded agents, redundant loops, or unexpected dependencies across distributed systems.

- **Temporal Activity Maps**: By tracking agent actions over time, these maps illuminate execution timelines, delays, and deviations from expected behavior. They're especially valuable in time-sensitive domains like manufacturing, logistics, or autonomous operations.

- **Decision Traceability Layers**: In regulated or high-stakes environments, it's not enough to know what an agent did; we need to understand why. Visualization tools that expose decision trees, model outputs, and rule-based triggers support transparency, compliance, and human oversight.

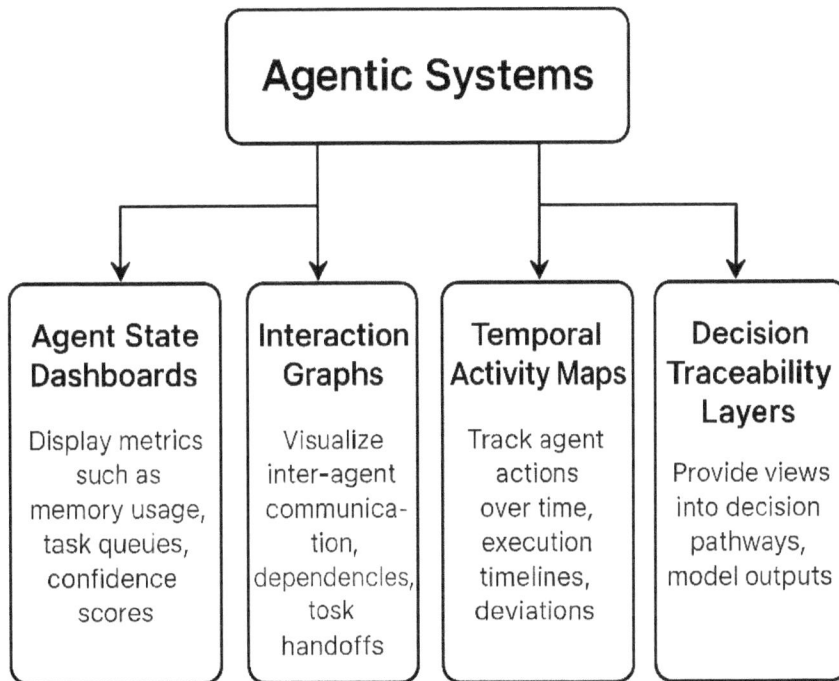

Figure 53: Real-Time Agent Visualization for System Monitoring.

Figure 53 illustrates how agentic systems are monitored through four core visualization components:

- Agent State Dashboards displaying internal metrics like memory and task queues.
- Interaction Graphs mapping communication and task handoffs.
- Temporal Activity Maps tracking actions and execution timelines.
- Decision Traceability Layers exposing reasoning and model outputs.

Each of these connects back to key implementation concerns: scalability, modularity, and security.

## Implementation Considerations

- **Scalability**: Tools must gracefully handle hundreds or thousands of agents without performance degradation. Techniques like data aggregation, sampling, and adaptive rendering are essential.

- **Modularity and Extensibility**: Systems should support plug-and-play modules for new agent types, behaviors, or monitoring protocols. API-first design and adherence to open standards accelerate integration and evolution.

- **Security and Access Control**: Real-time views often expose sensitive operational data. Role-based access, encryption, and audit trails are critical for enterprise-grade deployments.

Across industries, agent visualization is already delivering value. For example:

- In manufacturing, agents monitor robotic workflows, flag anomalies, and ensure synchronization across production lines.

- In customer service, dashboards track sentiment analysis, escalation triggers, and resolution paths for conversational agents.

- In cybersecurity, autonomous threat detection agents coordinate responses across network nodes, all monitored through intuitive, real-time interfaces.

Agent visualization will mature from raw metrics to semantically rich representations:

- **Semantic Visualization**: Tools that interpret agent cognition, like intent heatmaps or goal alignment scores, offer deeper insight into decision-making and behavioral alignment.

- **Mixed Reality Interfaces**: AR/VR environments are emerging as immersive platforms for agent monitoring, especially in high-stakes domains such as aerospace, defense, and remote operations.

Building on the ability to visualize agent behavior in real time, the next critical capability is to deliver those decisions directly into business applications, where insight becomes action.

---

*Real-time decision delivery ensures that agentic intelligence doesn't remain observational, but instead drives outcomes across operational systems, customer touchpoints, and enterprise workflows.*

---

## 11.5 Real-time Decision Delivery from Agent Systems to Business Applications

Once we can visualize what agents are doing in real time, the next step is to make those insights actionable. Visualization gives us awareness; decision delivery gives us impact. In agentic systems, this means ensuring that the decisions agents make, whether predictive, prescriptive, or reactive, are seamlessly transmitted to the business applications that execute them.

This isn't just about integration. It's about timing, trust, and precision. Decisions must arrive at the right moment, in the right format, and with the right level of confidence to be useful. Whether it's a recommendation engine updating a customer interface, a supply chain agent rerouting inventory, or a cybersecurity agent triggering a containment protocol, the delivery pipeline must be fast, reliable, and context-aware.

The architecture behind this capability often involves event-driven messaging, low-latency APIs, and decision orchestration layers that translate agent outputs into business logic. But the real challenge lies in harmonizing agent autonomy with enterprise governance. Agents may operate independently, but their decisions must align with business rules, compliance standards, and operational constraints.

In practice, this means embedding agents into workflows, not as passive observers, but as active participants. A marketing agent might adjust campaign parameters in real time based on engagement signals. A financial agent could rebalance portfolios in response to market volatility. A customer service agent might escalate or resolve issues based on sentiment and historical context. In each case, the agent's decision is not just logged. It's delivered, acted upon, and measured. As organizations adopt more agentic systems, the emphasis will shift from monitoring to mobilizing.

*The goal isn't just to know what agents are thinking, but to let them think on behalf of the business, and to do so with speed, clarity, and accountability.*

Figure 54 illustrates the architecture and flow of real-time decision delivery from agentic systems to business applications. On the left, agent systems generate decisions, whether predictive, prescriptive, or reactive, based on continuous analysis of data and environmental inputs. These decisions are then transmitted through a central delivery layer, which includes event-driven messaging, low-latency

APIs, and orchestration mechanisms that translate agent outputs into executable business logic. On the right, business applications receive and act on these decisions within operational workflows such as marketing, supply chain management, and customer service.

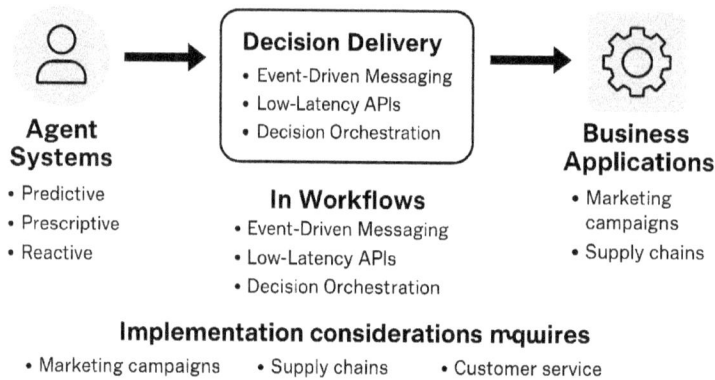

**Agent Systems**
- Predictive
- Prescriptive
- Reactive

**Decision Delivery**
- Event-Driven Messaging
- Low-Latency APIs
- Decision Orchestration

**In Workflows**
- Event-Driven Messaging
- Low-Latency APIs
- Decision Orchestration

**Business Applications**
- Marketing campaigns
- Supply chains

**Implementation considerations requires**
- Marketing campaigns
- Supply chains
- Customer service

Figure 54: Real-time Decision Delivery from Agent Systems to Business Applications.

The diagram emphasizes the importance of timing, trust, and precision in this pipeline, showing how agent autonomy is harmonized with enterprise governance to ensure decisions are not only made but mobilized with speed and accountability.

## 11.6 Operationalizing Agent-Driven Decisions

Once agentic systems can deliver decisions in real time, the final step is to embed those decisions consistently, securely, and with measurable impact into operational workflows. Operationalizing agent-driven decisions means moving beyond experimentation and dashboards. It's about ensuring that autonomous outputs become part of the business fabric: influencing actions, triggering processes, and adapting strategies on the fly. This requires more than technical integration. It demands governance, accountability, and alignment with enterprise objectives. Agents may operate independently, but their decisions must conform to business rules, regulatory constraints, and ethical standards.

*Whether the agent is adjusting pricing, rerouting logistics, or initiating a customer resolution, its output must be traceable, auditable, and explainable.*

To achieve this, organizations are embedding agents directly into decision loops, often through orchestration platforms, workflow engines, or rule-based middleware. These systems validate agent outputs, apply contextual filters, and route decisions to the appropriate endpoints. In some cases, human-in-the-loop mechanisms are retained for oversight; in others, agents operate autonomously within predefined guardrails. Key enablers of operationalization include:

- **Decision Governance Frameworks**: Define who can override, audit, or escalate agent decisions. These frameworks ensure that autonomy doesn't compromise accountability.

- **Feedback Loops and Learning Systems**: Capture outcomes from agent-driven actions to refine future decisions. This creates a virtuous cycle of performance improvement and contextual adaptation.

- **Cross-Functional Integration**: Align agent outputs with business units like marketing, finance, and operations. This ensures decisions are not siloed but synchronized across the enterprise.

- **Performance Monitoring and KPIs**: Track the impact of agent decisions using business metrics such as conversion rates, cost savings, resolution times, or risk mitigation. This quantifies value and builds trust.

In practice, operationalizing agentic AI often starts with narrow use cases like automated approvals, dynamic routing, or real-time personalization, and expands as confidence grows.

---

*The goal is not just automation, but augmentation:*
*letting agents act on behalf of the business with speed, precision, and contextual intelligence.*

---

As agentic systems mature, operationalization becomes the bridge between insight and impact. It's where autonomy meets accountability, and where AI begins to deliver on its promise. Not just to think, but to act. Figure 55 illustrates the process of operationalizing agent-driven decisions by embedding autonomous outputs into enterprise workflows. It begins with agents generating predictive or prescriptive decisions based on real-time data. These decisions are then routed through key enablers, such as governance frameworks, feedback loops, cross-functional integration, and performance monitoring, to ensure alignment with business rules, compliance standards, and strategic goals. The final stage shows these decisions being executed within operational workflows, where they influence actions across domains like marketing, supply chain, and customer service. The diagram emphasizes the transition from autonomous insight to accountable impact.

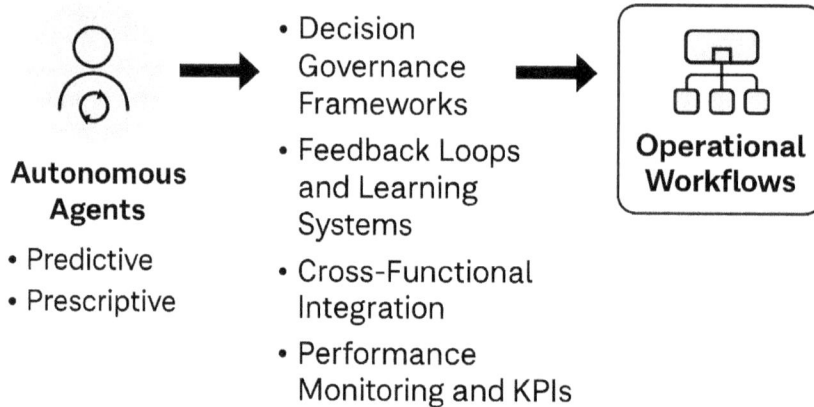

Figure 55: Operationalizing Agent-Driven Decisions.

## 11.7 Business Use Case: Dynamic Claims Processing in Insurance

A large insurance provider is modernizing its claims processing workflow using agentic AI. Traditionally, claims were routed through static rules and manual review, resulting in delays, inconsistent decisions, and limited transparency. The company aims to deploy autonomous agents to assess claims, detect anomalies, and recommend actions in real time while maintaining compliance and auditability. This includes:

- **Agentic AI Deployment**: Agents are embedded throughout the claims lifecycle, from intake and validation to fraud detection and payout recommendations. Each agent monitors structured and unstructured data (e.g., policy details, claim narratives, supporting documents) and collaborates with other agents to synthesize findings. Real-time dashboards visualize agent confidence scores, decision paths, and inter-agent communication, allowing supervisors to monitor system health and intervene when necessary.

- **Decision Delivery**: Once an agent recommends a payout or flags a claim for escalation, the decision is transmitted via low-latency APIs to the insurer's claims management platform. Event-driven messaging ensures that decisions are delivered at the right moment, with contextual metadata and traceability logs attached. This enables automated approvals for low-risk claims and immediate routing for complex or suspicious cases.

- **Operationalization**: The insurer implements governance frameworks to define override protocols, audit trails, and escalation thresholds. Feedback loops capture post-decision outcomes, such as customer satisfaction or fraud confirmation, and feed them back into the agent learning system. KPIs like claim cycle time, fraud detection rate, and payout accuracy are tracked to measure agent impact and refine behavior.

- **Outcome**: The company reduces average claim processing time by 40%, improves fraud detection by 25%, and enhances customer satisfaction through faster, more consistent decisions. Executives gain confidence in the system through transparent visualization and traceable decision delivery, while agents operate autonomously within well-defined business constraints.

## 11.8 Key Takeaways

- **Operationalizing agentic AI** requires real-time visibility into agent behavior, decision outputs, and system health.

- **Observability platforms** (e.g., Prometheus, OpenTelemetry) capture logs, metrics, and traces to monitor agent performance and orchestration.

- **Real-time dashboards** built with BI tools (e.g., Power BI, Tableau) translate agent outputs into actionable insights for technical and non-technical stakeholders.

- **Visualization components** such as interaction graphs, temporal maps, and decision traceability layers enhance interpretability and trust.

- **Decision delivery pipelines** ensure agent outputs are routed into business applications with speed, precision, and governance alignment.

- **Visual BI platforms** bridge technical and business teams, support compliance, and enable strategic storytelling around agentic impact.

- Together, these technologies transform autonomous systems from opaque engines into transparent, accountable collaborators.

## 11.9 Discussion Questions / Exercises

**Conceptual Reflection**

1. Why is real-time monitoring considered foundational to operationalizing agentic AI systems?

2. How do observability platforms differ from business intelligence dashboards in their role and audience?

3. What are the risks of deploying agentic systems without visualization or decision traceability?

**Applied Analysis**

4. Design a dashboard layout for monitoring a team of customer service agents. What metrics and visualizations would you include?

5. Compare two BI platforms (e.g., Tableau versus Power BI) in terms of their suitability for agentic system monitoring.

6. Evaluate how decision delivery pipelines can be governed to ensure compliance in regulated industries.

**Hands-On Exercise**

7. Create a mock interaction graph showing how three agents collaborate to resolve a logistics issue. Include task handoffs and coordination points.

8. Draft a temporal activity map for a manufacturing agent over a 24-hour cycle. Highlight deviations and escalation triggers.

9. Build a decision traceability checklist for a financial agent making investment recommendations. Include data lineage, model outputs, and oversight steps.

As organizations scale these systems, new risks emerge: silent failures, misaligned outputs, and unintended consequences that can undermine trust and performance. Chapter 12 turns attention to these critical concerns, exploring the technological safeguards, governance frameworks, and emerging trends that help enterprises avoid common pitfalls. It also looks ahead to the evolving role of agent-generated insights and how they will shape the future of intelligent business systems.

CHAPTER 12

# Avoiding Common Pitfalls
# and the Future of Agentic AI

## 12.1 Technological Solutions for Addressing Agent System Failures

As agentic AI systems become more autonomous and embedded in enterprise operations, the potential for system failures grows in both complexity and consequence. These failures can range from benign misalignments, such as agents pursuing suboptimal goals, to catastrophic breakdowns involving security breaches, ethical violations, or unintended real-world actions. The challenge is no longer just about building intelligent agents; it's about ensuring they remain aligned, accountable, and resilient in dynamic environments. This section explores the technological scaffolding that enables organizations to detect, prevent, and recover from agentic system failures.

At the heart of this effort are agent-monitoring tools that provide real-time visibility into agent behavior, decision pathways, and performance metrics. These tools serve as the nervous system of agentic infrastructure, enabling anomaly detection, behavioral logging, and human-in-the-loop interventions. By surfacing deviations early, monitoring platforms help prevent cascading failures and maintain operational integrity.

Complementing these tools are governance technologies that enforce boundaries on agent autonomy. These include policy engines, permissioning frameworks, and explainability modules that ensure agents operate within defined ethical and organizational constraints. Governance systems don't just limit risk. They also build trust, making agentic AI more transparent and auditable for stakeholders across legal, compliance, and executive domains.

To further safeguard agentic deployments, organizations are investing in safety detection platforms. These technologies are designed to identify and neutralize harmful, biased, or adversarial outputs. These platforms often include simulation environments for pre-deployment stress testing, red-teaming protocols to expose vulnerabilities, and embedded safety layers that act as circuit breakers during runtime. Together, they form a proactive defense against the unpredictable nature of autonomous systems.

*Red teaming in AI is a structured testing process that simulates adversarial attacks to identify flaws and vulnerabilities in artificial intelligence systems.*

While these technologies address immediate risks, they also lay the groundwork for long-term resilience. By integrating monitoring, governance, and safety into the agent lifecycle, enterprises can move beyond reactive troubleshooting toward strategic foresight. In doing so, they not only avoid common pitfalls. They create a foundation for scalable, ethical, and future-ready agentic ecosystems.

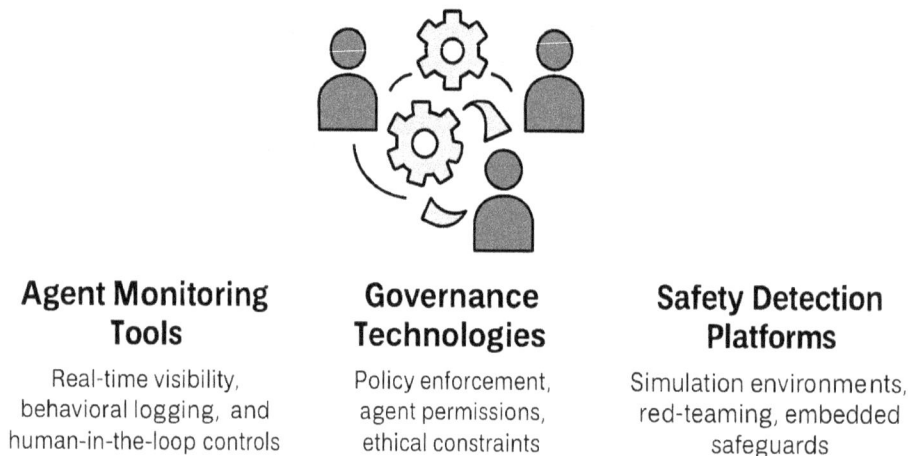

| **Agent Monitoring Tools** | **Governance Technologies** | **Safety Detection Platforms** |
|---|---|---|
| Real-time visibility, behavioral logging, and human-in-the-loop controls | Policy enforcement, agent permissions, ethical constraints | Simulation environments, red-teaming, embedded safeguards |

Figure 56: Technological Solutions for Addressing Agent System Failures.

Figure 56 highlights the triad of technologies essential for building resilient agentic systems. First, agent monitoring tools provide real-time oversight and behavioral transparency. Second, governance technologies enforce ethical and operational boundaries. Third, safety detection platforms proactively identify and mitigate risks before they escalate. Together, these components form a layered defense against system failures, ensuring that autonomous agents remain aligned, accountable, and safe within enterprise environments.

As agentic AI systems grow more capable and autonomous, the risks they introduce become more nuanced and harder to detect. These systems don't fail in the traditional sense; they drift, misalign, or behave in ways that are technically correct but contextually harmful. Avoiding these pitfalls requires more than patching bugs or tightening code. It demands a layered ecosystem of technologies that work in concert to provide visibility, enforce boundaries, and anticipate failures before they occur.

The first layer in this defense is agent monitoring. These tools act as the sensory system of agentic infrastructure, offering real-time visibility into what agents are doing, how they're reasoning, and whether their behavior aligns with expectations. Monitoring platforms log decision pathways, track resource usage, and flag anomalies such as goal drift, infinite loops, or unexpected output patterns. Crucially, they enable human-in-the-loop oversight, allowing operators to intervene when agents veer off course. This isn't just about catching errors. It's about maintaining situational awareness in systems that evolve and adapt on their own.

But visibility alone isn't enough. That's where governance technologies come in. These systems define the rules of engagement for autonomous agents, setting ethical, operational, and organizational boundaries. Through policy enforcement engines, role-based access controls, and explainability modules, governance frameworks ensure that agents act within the scope of their intended authority. They prevent unauthorized actions, enforce compliance standards, and make agent behavior auditable so that stakeholders can understand not just what an agent did, but why it made that decision.

*In a world where agents may operate across departments, jurisdictions, or even continents, governance is the glue that binds accountability.*

The third layer, safety detection platforms, takes a more anticipatory stance. These technologies are designed to identify and neutralize harmful or adversarial behaviors before they manifest in production. They include simulation environments for stress-testing agents under edge-case conditions, red-teaming protocols to expose vulnerabilities, and embedded safety layers that act as circuit breakers during runtime. These platforms are especially critical in high-stakes domains such as finance, healthcare, and infrastructure, where a single hallucinated output or misinterpreted signal can trigger cascading failures. By proactively modeling risk and embedding safeguards, safety platforms help organizations deploy agents with confidence, even in volatile or unpredictable environments.

Together, the three components of monitoring, governance, and safety form a resilient architecture for agentic systems. Each plays a distinct role, but their true power lies in how they reinforce one another.

*Monitoring provides the data, governance sets the rules, and safety ensures the system can withstand stress.*

When integrated thoughtfully, they enable enterprises to scale agentic AI without sacrificing control, integrity, or trust.

Figure 57 distills the three foundational layers of agentic system resilience: monitoring, governance, and safety. Each component plays a distinct role in preventing common failure modes, yet their true strength lies in how they interlock to form a comprehensive defense. Agent monitoring tools offer real-time visibility into agent behavior, enabling early detection of misalignment, resource overuse, or unintended loops. Governance technologies establish the ethical and operational boundaries within which agents must operate, ensuring that autonomy does not come at the expense of accountability. Safety detection platforms take a proactive stance, simulating edge cases and embedding safeguards to neutralize harmful or adversarial outputs before they reach production.

Together, these layers create a robust framework for deploying agentic AI in complex enterprise environments. They allow organizations to scale autonomy without sacrificing control, and to innovate with confidence even in high-stakes domains. As agentic systems become more integrated into business processes, this triad of visibility, constraint, and protection will be essential for building trust in the future of autonomous decision-making.

### Agent Monitoring Tools

Agentic obserrability flags misaligned goals, resource overuse, and allows for human override

### Governance Technologies

Policies, permissions, and explainability modules keep agents ethical and compliant

### Safety Detection Platforms

Simulations, stress tests, and safety layers neutralize harmful or adversarial behaviors

Figure 57: Three Technologies That Help Avoid Common Issues in Agentic Systems.

## 12.2 Ensuring Agent Integrity and Ethical Use of Autonomous AI

As agentic AI systems gain autonomy, their capacity to act independently introduces not only technical complexity but profound ethical responsibility. Unlike traditional software, agents are designed to interpret goals, make decisions, and adapt to changing environments, often without direct human oversight. This shift demands a new standard of integrity: one that ensures agents remain aligned with human values, organizational principles, and societal norms, even as they operate at scale.

Agent integrity begins with clarity of purpose. Agents must be designed with well-defined objectives, bounded autonomy, and transparent reasoning pathways. This means embedding ethical constraints directly into their decision logic. This may be through rule-based filters, value alignment models, or reinforcement learning frameworks that penalize harmful behavior. Integrity also requires identity: agents should be cryptographically verifiable, traceable across interactions, and resistant to spoofing or impersonation.

---

*In high-stakes environments, knowing not just what an agent did but which agent did it and why is essential for accountability.*

---

Equally important is the ethical use of autonomous AI. Organizations must ensure that agents are deployed in ways that respect privacy, avoid bias, and uphold fairness. This involves rigorous pre-deployment testing, diverse training data, and continuous monitoring for unintended consequences. It also calls for human-centered governance: escalation protocols for sensitive decisions, transparency in agent outputs, and clear communication about the role and limitations of AI systems. Ethical use isn't just about compliance; it's about trust. When agents make decisions that affect people's lives, reputations, or livelihoods, trust must be earned and maintained.

Ultimately, ensuring agent integrity and ethical use is not a one-time task. It's a discipline. It requires cross-functional collaboration between technologists, ethicists, legal experts, and domain specialists. It demands ongoing vigilance, adaptive safeguards, and a willingness to intervene when systems behave in unexpected ways. As agentic AI becomes more embedded in business, government, and society, the question is no longer whether we can build autonomous systems, but whether we can build them responsibly. The answer lies in our commitment to integrity, transparency, and the ethical stewardship of intelligence.

Figure 58 illustrates the three foundational pillars of agent integrity and ethical deployment: clarity of purpose, cryptographic identity, and human-centered governance.

At the core is the need for agents to operate with well-defined objectives and bounded autonomy. By embedding ethical constraints such as fairness, transparency, and value alignment directly into their decision logic, organizations can ensure agents act with intention and accountability. This clarity not only reduces the risk of misaligned behavior but also strengthens trust in autonomous systems.

Equally vital is the ability to verify and trace agent actions through cryptographic identity. In environments where agents interact across networks or make consequential decisions, it's essential to know which agent acted, under what conditions, and why. This traceability supports auditability and prevents spoofing or impersonation. Finally, ethical deployment depends on human-centered governance protocols that prioritize privacy, mitigate bias, and ensure oversight. These safeguards go beyond regulatory compliance; they reflect a deeper commitment to responsible innovation and the ethical stewardship of intelligent systems.

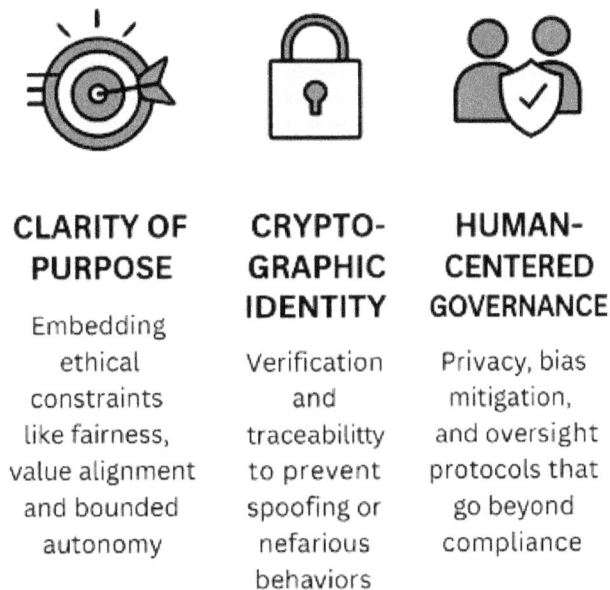

**CLARITY OF PURPOSE**

Embedding ethical constraints like fairness, value alignment and bounded autonomy

**CRYPTO-GRAPHIC IDENTITY**

Verification and traceabilitty to prevent spoofing or nefarious behaviors

**HUMAN-CENTERED GOVERNANCE**

Privacy, bias mitigation, and oversight protocols that go beyond compliance

Figure 58: Ensuring Agent Integrity and Ethical Use of Autonomous AI.

## 12.3 Emerging Trends in Enterprise Agentic Technologies

As agentic AI systems mature, their role within enterprise ecosystems shifts from experimental automation to strategic infrastructure. No longer confined to narrow tasks or isolated workflows, agents are increasingly designed to collaborate, adapt, and scale across departments, domains, and decision layers. This evolution is driven by a convergence of architectural innovation, operational tooling, and domain-specific specialization, each reshaping how organizations deploy and manage autonomous systems.

One of the most significant shifts is the rise of composable agent architectures. These modular frameworks allow organizations to build agents as interoperable components, each with defined capabilities, interfaces, and constraints. Rather than deploying monolithic agents with fixed behaviors, enterprises are assembling dynamic agent networks that can be reconfigured based on context, task complexity, or business priority. This composability enables agents to specialize, collaborate, and evolve, forming ecosystems that mirror the agility of human teams.

In parallel, we're seeing the emergence of domain-specific agent ecosystems tailored to the unique demands of vertical industries. In finance, agents are being used for fraud detection, portfolio optimization, and regulatory compliance, often operating in real time across volatile markets.

In healthcare, agents support clinical decision-making, patient triage, and medical coding, with an emphasis on accuracy, privacy, and explainability. Manufacturing environments are deploying agents for predictive maintenance, supply chain orchestration, and quality assurance, integrating sensor data and operational telemetry into closed-loop systems. These vertical applications demonstrate that agentic AI is not just a general-purpose tool. It's a strategic asset shaped by context.

Supporting this evolution is a new class of AgentOps platforms, end-to-end environments for deploying, monitoring, and managing agent lifecycles. These platforms offer integrated observability, policy enforcement, and performance analytics, allowing enterprises to treat agents as first-class operational entities. With built-in support for human-in-the-loop workflows, API orchestration, and compliance auditing, AgentOps platforms are transforming agent deployment from ad hoc experimentation into disciplined enterprise practice.

Together, these trends signal a new phase in agentic AI. One defined not by novelty, but by integration, specialization, and scale. As agents become embedded in core business systems, their design and governance must evolve accordingly.

> *The future of enterprise agentic technologies lies not in building smarter agents alone, but in building smarter ecosystems where agents collaborate, adapt, and deliver value across the full spectrum of enterprise decision-making.*

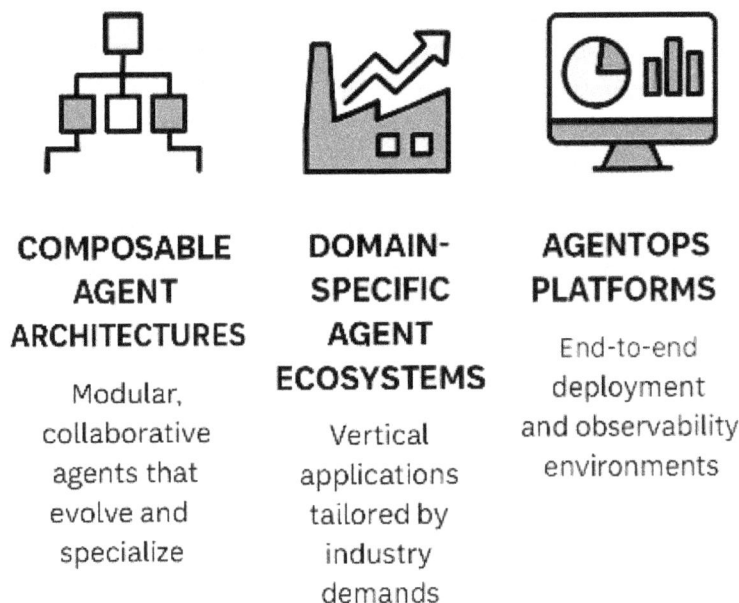

**COMPOSABLE AGENT ARCHITECTURES**

Modular, collaborative agents that evolve and specialize

**DOMAIN-SPECIFIC AGENT ECOSYSTEMS**

Vertical applications tailored by industry demands

**AGENTOPS PLATFORMS**

End-to-end deployment and observability environments

Figure 59: Emerging Trends in Enterprise Agentic Technologies.

Figure 59 highlights three transformative trends shaping the future of agentic AI in enterprise environments. First, composable agent architectures are redefining how organizations build and deploy autonomous systems. By assembling modular agents with specialized roles and interoperable interfaces, enterprises gain the flexibility to adapt agent behavior to changing business needs.

These architectures promote collaboration among agents, allowing them to evolve dynamically and operate as coordinated ecosystems rather than isolated tools. Second, the rise of domain-specific agent ecosystems reflects a growing emphasis on contextual intelligence. Whether in finance, healthcare, or manufacturing, agents are tailored to meet the unique demands of each industry, delivering precision, compliance, and strategic value.

Supporting this shift are AgentOps platforms, which provide the operational backbone for managing agent lifecycles. These platforms integrate deployment, monitoring, and governance into a unified environment, enabling organizations to scale agentic systems with confidence and control. Together, these trends signal a move toward more mature, integrated, and context-aware agentic infrastructures.

## 12.4 Agent-Generated Insights and Their Impact on Future Business Systems

As agentic AI systems evolve beyond automation and task execution, their ability to generate insights is emerging as a transformative force in enterprise strategy. These agents are no longer just operational tools. They are becoming analytical collaborators, capable of synthesizing data, modeling scenarios, and surfacing patterns that would otherwise remain hidden. This shift marks a new phase in business intelligence: one where insights are not passively extracted but actively generated by autonomous systems embedded within the decision-making fabric of the organization.

Agent-generated insights differ from traditional analytics in both speed and scope. Rather than waiting for human analysts to query data or build dashboards, agents can continuously scan enterprise systems, detect anomalies, and propose actions in real time. They can integrate signals across silos, combining customer behavior, operational telemetry, market trends, and external data streams to produce multidimensional perspectives that inform strategy. In doing so, agents help organizations move from reactive analysis to proactive foresight, enabling faster, more adaptive responses to changing conditions. The impact of these insights extends beyond operational efficiency:

- In strategic planning, agents can simulate future scenarios, evaluate trade-offs, and recommend optimal paths as constraints evolve.
- In customer engagement, they can personalize experiences by predicting needs and preferences before they're expressed.
- In risk management, agents can flag emerging threats and model mitigation strategies with precision and speed. These capabilities reshape how organizations think, plan, and act.

However, the rise of agent-generated insights also introduces new governance challenges. Organizations must ensure that these insights are interpretable, auditable, and aligned with business objectives. Human oversight remains critical, not to replicate the agent's analysis, but to validate its relevance, ethical implications, and strategic fit. As agents take on more advisory roles, the boundary between machine-generated intelligence and human judgment becomes more fluid and more consequential. In the future, business systems will be defined not just by their ability to execute, but by their capacity to learn, adapt, and advise. Agent-generated insights will be central to this evolution, enabling enterprises to operate with greater agility, precision, and foresight.

*The organizations that thrive will be those that treat agents not as tools, but as partners in intelligence; integrated, accountable, and aligned with human purpose.*

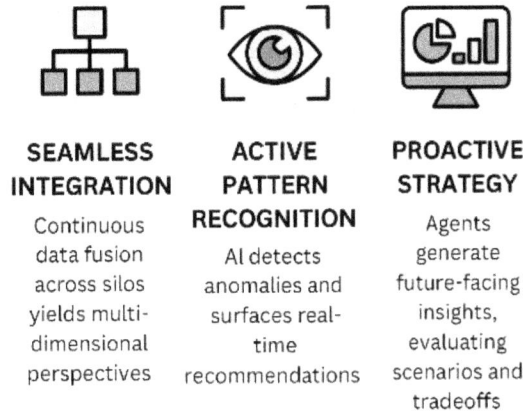

**SEAMLESS INTEGRATION**

Continuous data fusion across silos yields multidimensional perspectives

**ACTIVE PATTERN RECOGNITION**

AI detects anomalies and surfaces real-time recommendations

**PROACTIVE STRATEGY**

Agents generate future-facing insights, evaluating scenarios and tradeoffs

Figure 60: Agent-Generated Insights and Their Impact on Future Business Systems.

Figure 60 illustrates the evolving role of agentic AI as a source of strategic insight within enterprise systems. The first pillar, seamless integration, highlights how agents synthesize data across silos, by merging operational telemetry, customer signals, and external market indicators into unified, multidimensional perspectives. This continuous fusion enables agents to surface insights that are broader in scope and more contextually relevant than those from traditional analytics pipelines. The second and third pillars, active pattern recognition and proactive strategy, underscore the agent's capacity to detect anomalies, recommend actions, and simulate future scenarios in real time. These capabilities shift the enterprise from reactive analysis to anticipatory decision-making, where agents not only inform strategy but actively shape it. As organizations embrace agent-generated insights, they move toward an intelligence model that is adaptive, collaborative, and deeply embedded in the rhythms of business.

## 12.5 Business Use Case: Agentic AI in Enterprise Supply Chain Optimization

A global manufacturing firm deploys agentic AI to optimize its end-to-end supply chain operations from raw material sourcing to final product delivery. The system includes autonomous agents embedded across procurement, logistics, inventory, and demand forecasting functions.

To ensure reliability and control, the firm implements a three-layered architecture:

- **Agent monitoring tools** provide real-time visibility into agent behavior, flagging anomalies such as over-ordering, delayed shipments, or misaligned inventory thresholds.
- **Governance technologies** enforce operational boundaries, ensuring agents adhere to procurement policies, vendor compliance rules, and ethical sourcing standards.
- **Safety detection platforms** simulate edge-case disruptions such as geopolitical shocks or supplier bankruptcies and embed runtime safeguards to prevent cascading failures.

Each agent is designed with integrity in mind: objectives are clearly defined, autonomy is bounded, and decision logic includes embedded fairness constraints. Agents are cryptographically identifiable and traceable, allowing the firm to audit decisions and attribute actions to specific agent instances. Human-centered governance protocols ensure that sensitive decisions, such as supplier exclusion or rerouting high-value goods, trigger escalation workflows and remain transparent to stakeholders.

As the system matures, agents begin generating insights that reshape strategic planning. By integrating data across silos of supplier performance, transportation telemetry, and market demand signals, agents surface patterns that inform long-term sourcing strategies and inventory positioning. They detect emerging risks, recommend mitigation paths, and simulate trade-offs between cost, speed, and resilience. These insights influence board-level decisions on supplier diversification, regional investment, and sustainability commitments.

The firm's adoption of composable agent architectures allows it to scale and adapt the system across regions and product lines. Domain-specific agents specialize in local logistics, customs compliance, and regional market dynamics. AgentOps platforms provide centralized oversight, enabling the enterprise to manage agent lifecycles, enforce policies, and monitor performance across its global footprint.

**Outcome**: A supply chain that is not only faster and more efficient but also more transparent, resilient, and ethically governed. Agentic AI becomes a strategic partner. It is one that learns, adapts, and advises. It helps the firm navigate complexity with intelligence and integrity.

Figure 61 illustrates the sequential logic of agentic AI deployment within a modern enterprise supply chain. It begins with monitoring, where agents provide real-time visibility into logistics, procurement, and inventory flows, surfacing anomalies and enabling early intervention. Governance technologies then establish operational boundaries, ensuring agents comply with sourcing policies, ethical standards, and contractual obligations. Safety mechanisms follow, simulating disruptions and embedding safeguards that prevent cascading failures across the system.

MONITORING     GOVERNANCE     SAFETY     INSIGHTS

Figure 61: Agentic AI Optimizes an Enterprise Supply Chain.

The final stage is insight generation: from automation to intelligence. Agents synthesize data across silos, detect emerging patterns, and model future scenarios that inform executive decision-making. The result is a supply chain that is not only efficient and resilient, but also adaptive and ethically governed. This use case demonstrates how agentic AI can evolve from a tactical tool into a strategic partner, one that learns, advises, and aligns with enterprise values at every level of operation.

## 12.6 Key Takeaways

- **Agentic system failures** can range from benign misalignments to catastrophic outcomes; resilience requires layered safeguards.
- **Agent monitoring tools** provide real-time visibility, behavioral logging, and human-in-the-loop controls to detect anomalies early.
- **Governance technologies** enforce ethical and operational boundaries through policies, permissions, and explainability modules.
- **Safety detection platforms** proactively identify and neutralize harmful behaviors via simulations, red-teaming, and runtime safeguards.
- **Agent integrity** depends on clarity of purpose, cryptographic identity, and human-centered governance to ensure ethical deployment.
- **Composable agent architectures** and **domain-specific ecosystems** enable scalable, context-aware agent networks.

- **AgentOps platforms** support lifecycle management, observability, and compliance, turning agents into operational entities.
- **Agent-generated insights** shift AI from automation to strategic collaboration, enabling proactive, multidimensional decision-making.
- A supply chain use case illustrates how monitoring, governance, safety, and insight converge to create adaptive, ethically governed systems.

## 12.7 Discussion Questions / Exercises

### Conceptual Reflection

1. Why is it insufficient to rely on traditional debugging methods in agentic AI systems?
2. How do governance technologies differ from safety detection platforms in their role and timing?
3. What does "agent integrity" mean in the context of enterprise AI and why is it foundational?

### Applied Analysis

4. Analyze a real-world failure (e.g., algorithmic bias, automation error) through the lens of monitoring, governance, and safety. What safeguards were missing?
5. Compare composable agent architectures with monolithic agent design. What trade-offs emerge in terms of scalability and control?
6. Evaluate the ethical implications of agent-generated insights in high-stakes domains like healthcare or finance.

### Hands-On Exercise

7. Design a three-layered defense architecture for a hypothetical agentic system in HR or marketing. Include monitoring, governance, and safety components.
8. Draft a governance policy for an agent responsible for customer data handling. Include permissions, escalation paths, and audit requirements.
9. Create a scenario where agent-generated insights influence executive decision-making. Map the data sources, agent roles, and oversight checkpoints.

# CHAPTER 13

# The Agents Evolved
# While We Were Writing

## 13.1 The Acceleration Effect

It's a remarkable moment when you realize that *even as you're writing a book about AI*, the landscape beneath your feet is moving. In the span of just a few months, the AI Agent ecosystem has made significant strides. Major innovations that were merely ideas at the start of this book have become reality by its conclusion. For example, during the final editing of *AI Agents at Work*, both Microsoft and Glean released groundbreaking new platforms for building AI agents: Microsoft 365 Copilot's custom Copilot Agents and Glean's no-code Agent Builder. These announcements underscore a core theme of this chapter: the pace of change in AI agents is blistering, and it's *only accelerating*.

To set the tone, consider this scenario: In early 2024, many companies were dabbling with GPT-powered chatbots and pilot projects. By late 2024 and into 2025, those pilots evolved into full-fledged enterprise agent platforms, available to thousands of organizations. Figure 62 illustrates this rapid progression, with a timeline of key launches: from early experiments to Microsoft's Copilot Agents and Glean's Agent Builder. It's as if we were writing about a moving train, and by the chapter's end, the train turned into a rocket.

Let's briefly recap the book's core themes and then dive into the new Copilot Agents from Microsoft and Glean's Agent Builder, examining what they are and why they matter. We'll use a common IT

Helpdesk scenario to compare how each platform enables agent creation and deployment in a practical context. Finally, we'll conclude with a forward-looking discussion on what this rapid evolution means for enterprises, for those building these agents, and for all of us as users. If one thing is clear, it's that the train isn't slowing down. So, let's jump aboard and see where it's headed.

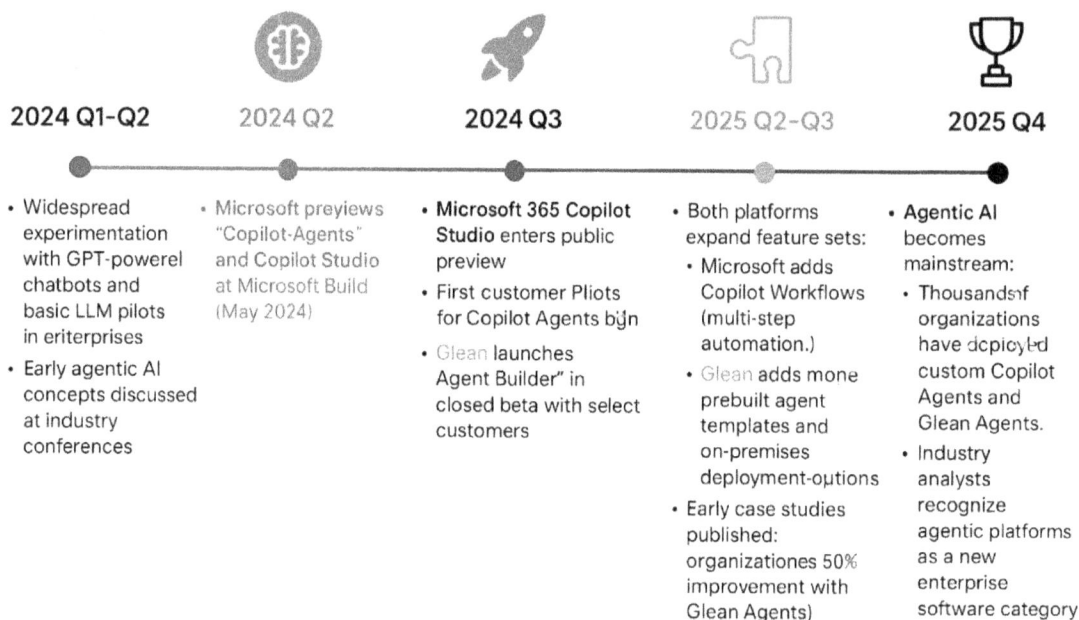

| 2024 Q1-Q2 | 2024 Q2 | 2024 Q3 | 2025 Q2-Q3 | 2025 Q4 |
|---|---|---|---|---|
| • Widespread experimentation with GPT-powerel chatbots and basic LLM pilots in eriterprises<br>• Early agentic AI concepts discussed at industry conferences | • Microsoft preyiews "Copilot-Agents" and Copilot Studio at Microsoft Build (May 2024) | • **Microsoft 365 Copilot Studio** enters public preview<br>• First customer Pliots for Copilot Agents bÿn<br>• Glean launches Agent Builder" in closed beta with select customers | • Both platforms expand feature sets:<br>• Microsoft adds Copilot Workflows (multi-step automation.)<br>• Glean adds mone prebuilt agent templates and on-premises deployment-options<br>• Early case studies published: organizationes 50% improvement with Glean Agents) | • **Agentic AI** becomes mainstream:<br>• Thousandsnf organizations have dcpicyłd custom Copilot Agents and Glean Agents.<br>• Industry analysts recognize agentic platforms as a new enterprise software category |

Figure 62: Timeline of AI Agent Evolution, 2024–2025. Key milestones include Microsoft's Copilot Agents preview in 2024 and GA in 2025, and Glean's Agent Builder launch in early 2025. This visual underscores how quickly new capabilities emerged during the writing of this book.

## 13.2 Recap of Core Themes

Before exploring these recent developments, it's worth pausing to reflect on the journey this book has taken us on. Throughout the chapters, we've traced the evolution of AI agents in the workplace. From rudimentary chatbots to sophisticated workflow assistants. Themes include:

- **From Automation to Collaboration:** AI has moved from automating simple, repetitive tasks to collaborating with humans on complex ones. The most effective agents act as copilots, not autopilots. They augment human effort rather than replace it.

- **The Importance of Grounding in Data:** An AI agent is only as useful as the knowledge it can draw on. Successful enterprise agents are deeply integrated with company data, making them far more accurate and contextually relevant.

- **No-Code Empowerment versus Professional Development:** The democratization of AI development means that power users and domain experts can now create their own agents. This "citizen developer" movement is reaching new heights with the latest platforms.

- **Governance, Trust, and Ethics:** With great power comes great responsibility. We explored the need for governance, privacy, and responsible AI guidelines, especially as agents become more autonomous.

- **The Evolving Definition of "Agent":** The term "agent" now spans a spectrum from reactive Q&A bots to proactive, multi-step workflow orchestrators. In this chapter, "agent" means a software AI entity that can perceive, decide, and act in a work context, often in response to natural language instructions.

In summary, the book's core lessons of human-centric design, data grounding, ease of creation, and strong governance, *remain vital in this fast-moving landscape.* As new tools lower the barrier to creating agents everywhere, these principles matter more than ever.

## 13.3 Copilot Agents and Glean's Agent Builder

Within a single year, two significant offerings have emerged that enable organizations to create and deploy AI agents more easily:

- **Microsoft 365 Copilot Studio – Custom Copilot Agents**, which brings agent-building into the Microsoft 365 ecosystem.

- **Glean's AI Agent Platform – Agent Builder**, from a rising Work AI platform company, focused on integrating knowledge across all enterprise tools.

Both aim to enable enterprise users to build powerful AI agents without requiring deep coding skills, but they approach this task from slightly different angles and strengths.

### 13.3.1 Microsoft 365 Copilot and Copilot Studio: Agents for Everyone

Microsoft introduced the term "Copilot" in 2023 for AI assistants in Office apps. By 2024, they expanded this with Microsoft 365 Copilot Studio, letting users build custom Copilot agents without coding. Organizations can define an agent's knowledge, response style, and actions through a no-code interface.

For example, setting up an internal IT Support Copilot involves naming the agent, linking it to systems such as ServiceNow or SharePoint, and assigning skills, including answering questions and creating tickets. Most configurations are handled through simple forms and checkboxes, making setup accessible even to non-technical users.

Once approved, these agents integrate seamlessly with Microsoft Teams, Outlook, and Office.com, enabling users to receive assistance via chat. Agents leverage Microsoft-hosted LLMs to solve issues by drawing from connected knowledge bases and can escalate unresolved problems by automatically creating support tickets.

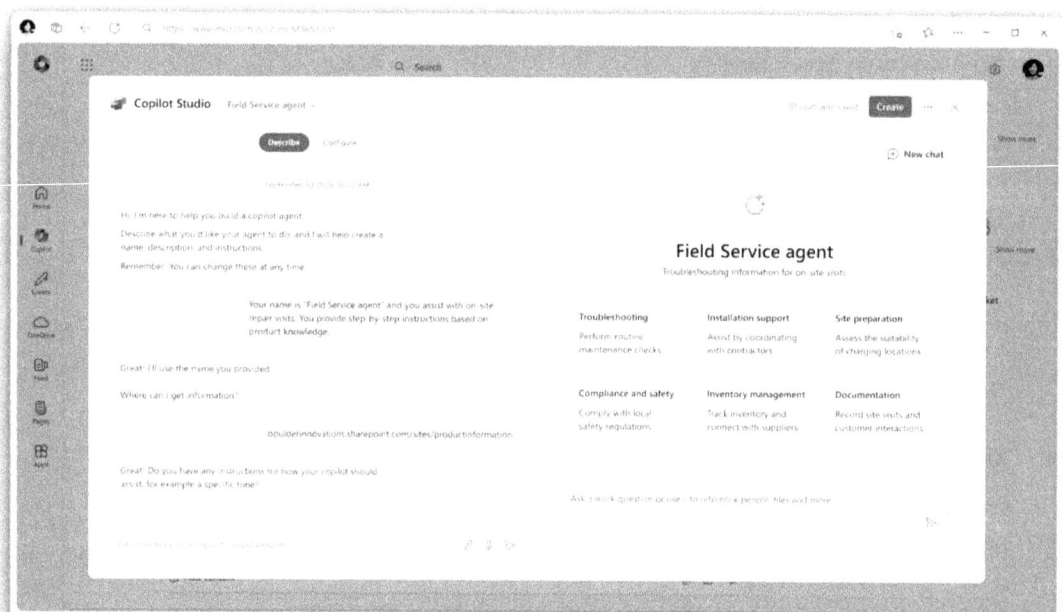

Figure 63: Screenshot of Microsoft Copilot Studio's Agent Builder. The example shows an "IT Helpdesk Agent" being configured with ServiceNow KB and ticketing integration.

The standout feature is the ease of deployment and integration within Microsoft 365's secure environment. Every interaction is logged for compliance purposes, and access controls mirror existing company policies, ensuring that sensitive data is protected. Admin tools allow granular permissions, usage monitoring, and content filtering. Overall, Copilot Agents offer scalable, governed AI assistance directly within familiar productivity tools, lowering barriers for enterprise adoption while addressing security and trust concerns.

## 13.3.2 Glean's Agent Builder: Embracing the Bottom-Up Creator

Glean, a Silicon Valley startup, began with an AI-powered enterprise search tool that connected to numerous workplace apps, enabling employees to find information across multiple platforms. In late 2025, it launched the Glean Agent Builder ("Glean CoPilot"), which enables users, even without programming skills, to create custom AI agents that can take action, not just retrieve data, via a user-friendly visual workflow interface. Unlike Microsoft's tightly integrated approach, Glean's platform is app-agnostic, supporting broad orchestration and allowing for flexible workflows across various tools.

With Glean, users design agent processes visually, adding steps like asking questions, searching databases, summarizing results, triggering emails, or integrating APIs. The platform's natural language input turns high-level instructions into actionable workflows. Glean's strength lies in its wide array of built-in connectors, making agents capable of using information from multiple systems and performing more complex, cross-silo tasks. Agents are testable within safe sandboxes before deployment.

Glean offers governance features, including model flexibility (users can switch between language models or utilize on-premises solutions), customizable hosting options, and admin controls for publishing agents. However, this flexibility requires careful configuration and oversight to avoid unintended behavior, as agents act using assigned service credentials rather than individual user identities.

In summary, Microsoft delivers a highly integrated and managed agent ecosystem mainly within its own platform, supporting common scenarios with strong administrative control. In contrast, Glean offers greater flexibility and innovation potential through cross-system integration and user-driven workflows, suitable for organizations willing to manage added complexity and responsibility.

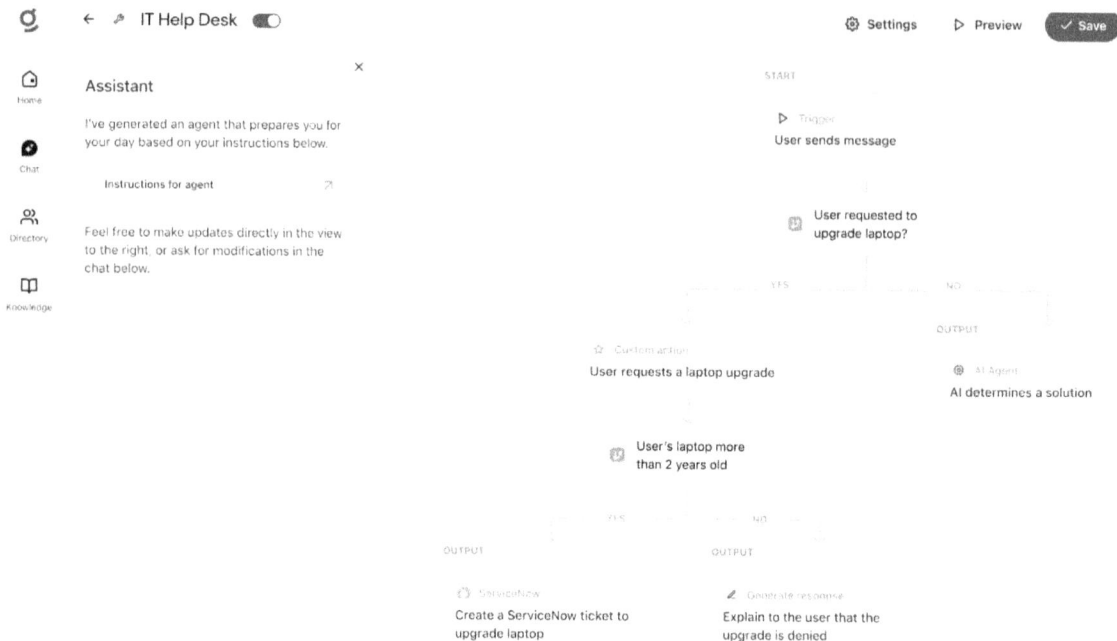

Figure 64: Screenshot of Glean's Agent Builder Workflow Editor.

Figure 64: Screenshot of Glean's Agent Builder Workflow Editor. The example illustrates an "IT Support Agent" with steps for handling user queries, knowledge search, answer generation, and ticket creation.

## 13.4 Comparative Analysis: Copilot versus Glean for an IT Helpdesk Agent

To crystallize these differences, let's revisit our IT Helpdesk support agent scenario and compare the side-by-side architectural implementation of Microsoft Copilot versus Glean's Agent Builder. Table 8 provides a breakdown using key architectural and operational lenses that have been recurring themes in this book (orchestration, integration, memory/context handling, action capability, and governance). This comparison exemplifies a broader point: enterprise AI agents are being adopted into mainstream use through two complementary routes, embedding into existing workflows (top-down integration) and open orchestration platforms (bottom-up innovation).

| Aspect | Microsoft Copilot Agent (IT Helpdesk) | Glean Agent (IT Helpdesk) |
|---|---|---|
| Orchestration & Workflow | High-level, template-driven; workflow is mostly implicit and simple to set up, but less customizable. | Explicit, visual workflow; highly customizable with branching and logic, but requires more setup. |
| Data Integration & Knowledge | Tight integration with the Microsoft ecosystem (e.g., ServiceNow, SharePoint); easy setup; focused sources. | Broad integration across many apps (Google, Slack, Confluence, etc.); richer answers if sources are connected. |
| Memory & Context | Uses Teams chat/session context; remembers within a session; long-term learning is not built in. | Accesses all indexed data; stateless unless designed otherwise; can retrieve historical info. |
| User Experience | Seamlessly embedded in M365 apps (Teams, Outlook); conversational; personalized; no context-switching. | Accessed via Glean UI, Slack, Teams, or web; can be embedded; user may switch interfaces if not integrated. |
| Action & Extensibility | Built-in skills (e.g., create ticket, send email); extensible via Power Automate/Logic Apps; mostly reactive. | Highly extensible via APIs/scripts; supports proactive and scheduled actions; more manual setup for new actions. |
| Governance & Compliance | Centralized, enterprise-grade controls; all data stays within the tenant; strong admin oversight. | Respects source permissions; flexible model/data hosting; admin oversight required for safe use. |

Table 8: An IT Support Agent: Microsoft 365 Copilot versus Glean Agent Builder.

Many organizations will leverage both approaches. You might use Microsoft's Copilot Agents for common tasks where you want quick deployment and guaranteed compatibility (for instance, a sales proposal assistant that pulls data from Dynamics 365 and SharePoint can be up in no time if you're a Microsoft shop). Simultaneously, you might employ a platform like Glean for more unique or advanced scenarios (maybe your HR team wants an onboarding agent that interacts with Workday, ServiceNow, and your custom training portal, a mix that a generic platform doesn't neatly cover but Glean can because it lets you integrate all three). The emergence of these platforms also underscores the trend of "AI for everyone." Chapter 5 discussed how conversational AI platforms were evolving, and here in these examples, we see the evolution specifically oriented towards agentic behavior. It's not just about chatbots answering questions; it's about agents performing tasks and multi-step workflows. Microsoft and Glean are early exemplars, but they're not alone. Others, such as ServiceNow (with its Now Assist and upcoming AI Agent Studio features), and open-source frameworks (like Dust or LangChain's agent hubs), are all contributing to an ecosystem where creating a specialized AI agent could become as commonplace as creating a spreadsheet macro. To illustrate how these workflows unfold in practice, see Figure 65 for an example conversation with Microsoft's IT Helpdesk Copilot Agent.

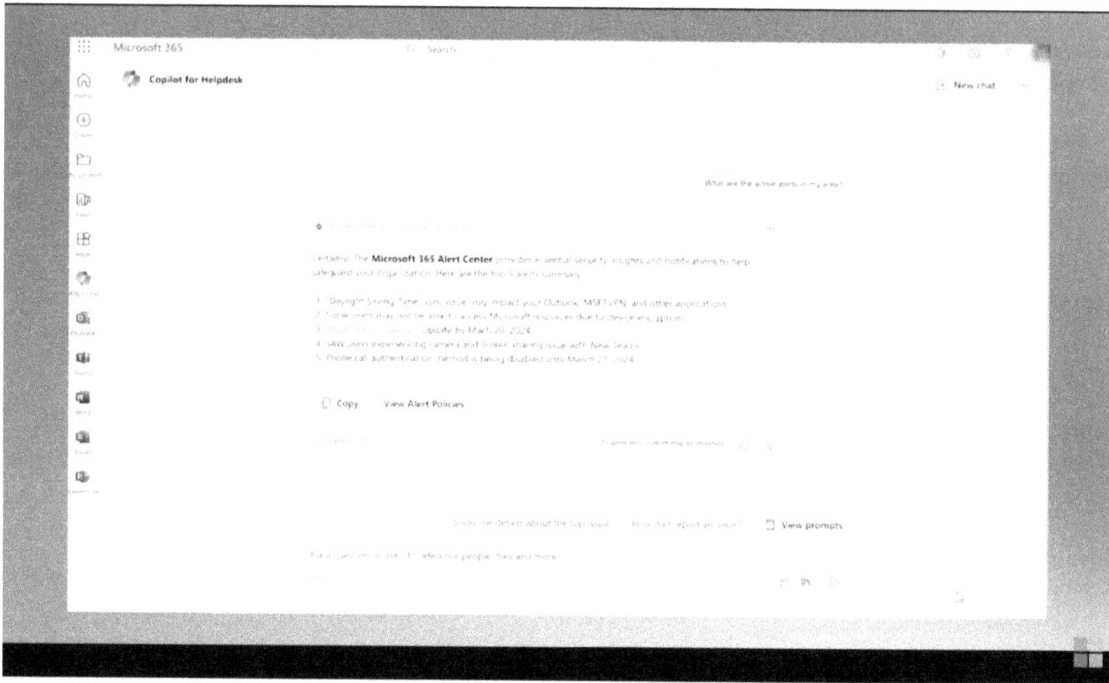

Figure 65: Conversation with Microsoft's IT Helpdesk Copilot Agent (Example).

## 13.5 When to Use Which

- **Speed versus Flexibility:** Microsoft offers speed and familiarity; Glean offers flexibility and breadth.
- **Adoption:** Both integrate into common work hubs; adoption follows where work already happens.
- **Vendor Strategy:** Microsoft is a paid add-on for M365; Glean is a separate platform.
- **AI Advancement:** Both are rapidly evolving, with new features and templates emerging.

Organizations may use both: Copilot Agents for common use cases and Glean for complex or cross-cutting agents.

## 13.6 Racing into the Future of Work with AI Agents

- The rapid succession of Microsoft's Copilot Agents and Glean's Agent Builder launches during the writing of this book is a testament to how quickly this field is evolving.
- **For Enterprises:** AI agents are becoming ubiquitous. Early adopters are seeing dramatic ROI involving productivity boosts, cost savings, and new capabilities.
- **For Builders:** No-code agent builders empower "citizen developers." New skills for prompt engineering, data integration, and workflow design are becoming essential.
- **For Employees:** Specialized AI agents will become as common as email. Proficiency in collaborating with AI will be a standard part of digital literacy.
- **Governance:** "Shadow AI" is a real risk. Enterprises must update governance policies, centralize agent inventories, and provide responsible AI training.
- **The Road Ahead:** Expect smarter autonomy, better context-awareness, and tighter human-AI collaboration. The most effective organizations will blend human judgment with AI augmentation.

## 13.7 Final Thoughts

*The story of AI agents is not a one-time revolution but an ongoing journey.*

By the time this book is in your hands, new features or even new products will likely have appeared. Staying informed and adaptable is key. You need to cultivate a culture of learning around AI. You should share successes, learn from failures, and stay aware of external trends.

Our journey began by setting the stage with a focus on *Data for AI*, establishing the foundation essential for intelligent systems. Now, with *AI Agents at Work*, we are just getting started as the real transformation is beginning to unfold. Today's pioneers are writing the future of work. With the knowledge you've gained and the momentum of technology at your back, you are well-equipped to navigate and shape what comes next. The pace of innovation, as you've seen throughout this book, is relentless, and the breakthroughs occurring are a testament to how quickly the field is evolving.

In our upcoming works, we plan to dive deeper into the following frontiers:

- **Agentic AI in the Wild:** Real-world case studies of organizations that have moved beyond pilots to production-scale, multi-agent ecosystems. What worked? What failed? And what surprised even the experts?

- **AgentOps and the New Operating Model:** Practical frameworks for managing fleets of agents, including advanced governance, cost attribution, and continuous improvement. These will be drawn on lessons from DevOps, MLOps, and the emerging discipline of AgentOps.

- **Human-Agent Collaboration:** Exploring the evolving relationship between humans and AI agents, including new roles, skills, and organizational structures. How do we design workflows where agents and people truly co-create value?

- **Ethics, Regulation, and Societal Impact:** As agents become more autonomous and influential, what new ethical dilemmas and regulatory challenges arise? How do we ensure fairness, transparency, and accountability at scale?

- **The Next Generation of Agentic Platforms:** A technical deep dive into the architectures, protocols, and standards that will define the agentic AI landscape of the late 2020s. Including open agent frameworks, composable agent ecosystems, and the convergence of LLMs, RPA, and IoT.

We invite you to join this ongoing exploration. Share your stories, challenges, and aspirations. The agentic AI community is growing rapidly, and the most valuable insights will come from those on the front lines. Whether you are deploying your first agent or managing a thousand, your experiences will shape the next chapters of this field. Future works will include hands-on guides, new case studies, and frameworks for scaling agentic AI responsibly and effectively. If you'd like to be notified about upcoming publications, workshops, or research collaborations, please contact us (Kinshuk and Scott). We are working on a channel for communication. In the meantime, please contact us on LinkedIn.

# References

Accenture. (2025). *AI Orchestration and Workflow Automation Survey*. Accenture Research.

Accenture. (2025). *FinOps for AI and Agentic Automation: Balancing Performance and Cost*. Accenture Research.

Apache Airflow Foundation. (2024). Airflow Documentation. Version 2.8.

Automation Anywhere. (2025, March). *Case Study: Petrobras Unearths $120 Million in Savings in Three Weeks. Automation Anywhere Inc*. https://www.automationanywhere.com

Business Insider. (2025). *AI Transforms Last-Mile Delivery*.

Cureus. (2024). *Clinical Impact of Artificial Intelligence-Based Triage Systems in Emergency Departments: A Systematic Review*.

DARPA OFFSET Program. *Official Publications and Research Papers*. Retrieved from https://arxiv.org.

DARPA. (2016–2025). *Explainable Artificial Intelligence (XAI) program* (program page and industry-day materials). Defense Advanced Research Projects Agency. Retrieved October 11, 2025.

DARPA. (2025, February). *Explainable AI (XAI): Industry day presentation* (D. Gunning). Defense Advanced Research Projects Agency.

Deloitte. (2022). *Global RPA Survey*. Deloitte Insights.

Deloitte. (2024). *The AI Enterprise Resilience Report 2024*. Deloitte Insights.

Deloitte. (2025). *AI Enterprise Report 2025*. Deloitte Insights.

Deloitte. *AI in Financial Services: Compliance and Fraud Detection with Multi-Agent Systems*. 2025. Deloitte Insights.

Deloitte. *Where Is the Value of AI in Multi-Agent Systems?* 2025. Deloitte Insights.

European Union (EU). (2016, May 4). *Regulation (EU) 2016/679 (General Data Protection Regulation GDPR)* (Official Journal). EUR-Lex.

EY. (2025, April 9). *EY announces large-scale integration of leading-edge AI technology into global assurance technology platform* (news release). Ernst and Young.

EY. (n.d.). *EY Blockchain Analyzer: Reconciler* (product page). Ernst and Young.

FinOps Foundation. (2024). *AI and Machine Learning Cost Optimization Guide*. finops.org.

Gartner. (2023). *Market Guide for Robotic Process Automation Software*. Gartner Research.

Gartner. (2025). *AI Governance Forecast 2025*. Gartner Research.

Gartner. (2025). *Enterprise AI Forecast and Adoption Trends 2025*. Gartner Research.

Gartner. (2025). *Forecast Analysis: Multi-Agent Systems and Orchestration Platforms*. Gartner Research.

Gibion. (2024). *Case Study: H&M AI Deployment*.

Google Research. (2024, April 19). *Improving Gboard language models via private federated analytics*. Google.

Google Research. (2025, July 24). *Synthetic and federated: Privacy-preserving domain adaptation with LLMs for mobile applications*. Google.

Google. (n.d.). *Federated learning* (overview site). Federated Learning.

HHS: U.S. Department of Health and Human Services. (2024, December 30). *Summary of the HIPAA Security Rule*. U.S. Department of Health and Human Services.

HHS: U.S. Department of Health and Human Services. (2024, September 27). *HIPAA Privacy Rule*. U.S. Department of Health and Human Services.

HHS: U.S. Department of Health and Human Services. (2025, March 14). *Summary of the HIPAA Privacy Rule*. U.S. Department of Health and Human Services.

IBM. (2023). *Cost of a Data Breach Report*. IBM Security and Ponemon Institute.

IEEE Standards Association. (2022, April 19). *IEEE 7002-2022: IEEE Standard for Data Privacy Process* (overview page). IEEE.

IEEE Standards Association. (2022, March 4). *IEEE 7001-2021: IEEE Standard for Transparency of Autonomous Systems* (overview page). IEEE.

IEEE Standards Association. (n.d.). *Autonomous and Intelligent Systems (AIS) standards: 7000-series overview* (initiative page). IEEE.

IEEE. (2023). IEEE 7007–7009 Series: Ontological Standards for AI System Trustworthiness. IEEE Standards Association.

Klover AI. JPMorgan *AI Strategy: Chasing AI Dominance*. LangGraph Consortium. (2025).

Latenode. *AI Multi-Agent Systems: Understanding the Power of Collaborative Intelligence*. 2024.

MarkTechPost. (2025). *OpenAI Swarm and the Future of Collaborative Agents*.

McKinsey and Company. (2023). *State of AI in Retail Operations*.

Microsoft Azure Architecture Center. (2025). *Designing Idempotent Workflows for Cloud Applications*. Microsoft Docs.

Microsoft Azure. (2025). FinOps for AI Workloads Overview. Microsoft Docs.

Microsoft. (2024). *Administering and Governing Agents in Copilot Studio*. Microsoft Adoption Library.

MIT Sloan Management Review. (2024). *AI Agents in Supply Chain and Retail Inventory Management*.

NAND Research (McDowell, S.). (2024, February 18). *Quick take: Tanium's Autonomous Endpoint Management (AEM)*. NAND Research.

NAND Research (McDowell, S.). (2024, November 26). *Research note: Tanium's new AEM and cloud workload solutions*. NAND Research.

Netflix Engineering. (2023). *Circuit Breakers and Bulkhead Patterns in Distributed Systems*. Netflix Tech Blog.

NHS Digital. (2023). *AI Triage Pilots in Emergency Care*. National Health Service (UK).

NIST. (2023). *AI Risk Management Framework (AI RMF 1.0)*. National Institute of Standards and Technology.

OECD. (2019). *Recommendation of the Council on Artificial Intelligence (OECD AI Principles)*. Organisation for Economic Co-operation and Development.

OECD. (2019–present). *AI principles* (topic hub). Organisation for Economic Co-operation and Development.

Ongaro, D., and Ousterhout, J. (2014). *In search of an understandable consensus algorithm (Raft)*. Proceedings of the USENIX Annual Technical Conference.

PwC. (2025). *AI Agent Survey: Operational Adoption and Governance Trends*. PwC Research.

PwC. (2025). *AI Governance and Compliance in Distributed Systems*. PwC Research.

Quinn, M. (2024, Nov 19). *Tanium launches Autonomous Endpoint Management Platform*. Help Net Security.

Raza, A., Tran, K. P., Koehl, L., and Li, S. (2022). *Designing ECG monitoring healthcare system with federated transfer learning and explainable AI*. Knowledge-Based Systems, *236*, 107763. (Preprint: arXiv:2105.12497).

ServiceNow. (2024). *Agent Performance Framework and Workflow Quality Controls*. Knowledge 2024 Conference Proceedings.

State of California Department of Justice. (2024, March 13). *California Consumer Privacy Act (CCPA): Overview and resources*. Office of the Attorney General.

State of California Department of Justice. (2025, March 15). *California Consumer Privacy Act regulations: Final regulation text (PDF)*. Office of the Attorney General.

SuperAGI. (2025). *AI in Cybersecurity Case Study*.

Tabassi, E., et al. (2023). *Artificial Intelligence Risk Management Framework (AI RMF 1.0)*. National Institute of Standards and Technology.

Tanium. (2024, February 20). *Tanium reduced software vulnerability by 97% according to new study* (blog/summary).

Tanium. (2024, May 1). *Total Economic Impact study reveals Tanium XEM platform delivered 97% reduction in software vulnerability and more than 200% ROI for interviewed organizations* (press release). Tanium Inc.

Tanium. (2025). *Autonomous Endpoint Management (AEM) Solution Brief*. Tanium Inc.

Tanium. (n.d.). *Federal agency improves security posture with Tanium* (case study). Tanium Inc.

Tanium. (n.d.). *Government agency replaces BigFix with Tanium* (PDF case study). Tanium Inc.

Tanium. (n.d.). *The University of Manchester strengthens cybersecurity with Tanium* (case study). Tanium Inc.

TechRadar Pro. (2025). *The Rise of Agentic Orchestration Frameworks*.

TechRadar Pro. *How Enterprises Can Transition Their Knowledge and Systems for Agentic AI*. 2025.

TechRadar Pro. *RAG is Dead: Why Enterprises Are Shifting to Agent-Based AI Architectures*. 2025.

TechRadar Pro. *Smarter Networks in the Agentic AI Revolution*. 2025.

Wall Street Journal. *AI Agents Are Learning How to Collaborate. Companies Need to Work With Them*. 2025.

Wired (Greenberg, A.). (2020, October 7). *How Google's Android keyboard keeps "Smart Replies" private*. Wired.

# Index